To Da[...]

of yo[...]

with love for Robert.

A SMALL WAR
IN THE BALKANS

Michael McConville

A SMALL WAR IN THE BALKANS

*British Military Involvement in
Wartime Yugoslavia, 1941–1945*

MACMILLAN
LONDON

First published 1986 by
MACMILLAN LONDON LIMITED
4 Little Essex Street London WC2R 3LF
and Basingstoke

Associated companies in Auckland, Delhi, Dublin, Gaborone,
Hamburg, Harare, Hong Kong, Johannesburg, Kuala Lumpur,
Lagos, Manzini, Melbourne, Mexico City, Nairobi, New York,
Singapore and Tokyo

British Library Cataloguing in Publication Data

McConville, Michael
    A small war in the Balkans: British military involvement in
    wartime Yugoslavia, 1941–1945.
    1. World War, 1941–1945 —— Campaigns ——
    Yugoslavia   2. Great Britain —— Armed Forces
    —— History —— World War, 1939–1945
    I. Title
    940.54'21   D766.6

    ISBN 0-333-38675-2

Filmset in Linotron Times by
Columns of Reading
Printed and bound in Great Britain by
The Garden City Press Limited Letchworth, Hertfordshire SG6 1JS

Photographs reproduced by permission of the
Imperial War Museum, London.

Contents

List of Illustrations

Acknowledgements

In July 1973, the History Department of the School of Slavonic and East European Studies, University of London, convened a conference to re-examine British wartime attitudes towards the resistance movements in Yugoslavia and in Greece. Participants who contributed to the Yugoslav part of the discussion included Sir William Deakin, Sir Fitzroy Maclean, Mr Basil Davidson, Mr Stephen Clissold and Sir John Henniker-Major, all of whom had served with the British Military Mission to Marshal Tito's Partisans and two of whom, Deakin and Maclean, had successively commanded it; Sir Alexander Glen, who had been from 1943 until 1945 the Personal Representative to Yugoslavia of the Commander-in-Chief, Mediterranean; Colonel S.W. Bailey, who had commanded the British Military Mission to General Draža Mihailović's Chetniks; Mr George Taylor, Mr Bickham Sweet-Escott and Professor G.H.N. Seton-Watson, who had been senior members of the staff of Special Operations Executive in Cairo or London or both, and who had been concerned with the monitoring and analysis of developing events in wartime Yugoslavia and with the recommending and implementation of policy; Miss Elizabeth Barker, from 1942 until 1945 the Head of the Balkan Region of the Political Warfare Executive; Professor Phyllis Auty, first of the BBC Yugoslav Section, later of the Middle East Intelligence Centre; and Major-General Sir Colin Gubbins, the Director of Operations and Training of SOE from 1940 until 1943, and its Head from then until the end of the war.

The papers submitted to this conference, and a record of the discussions that followed them, were later edited by

Acknowledgements

Professor Auty and Mr Richard Clogg, and in 1975 were published by Macmillan under the title *British Policy Towards Wartime Resistance in Yugoslavia and Greece*. The compilation provided a rich vein of authoritative information which I tapped extensively for the early part of this book.

Also, for the years 1941–3 I have relied heavily upon *The Embattled Mountain* by Sir William Deakin, the first British officer to parachute to Marshal Tito's headquarters, and upon *Eastern Approaches* by Sir Fitzroy Maclean. If compression has generated any distortion, the responsibility is entirely mine.

For the post-1943 period, the seventeen months during which British commandos, gunners and special forces fought alongside the Partisans in the Dalmatian islands and in Montenegro, the motor torpedo boats and motor gunboats of the Royal Navy ruled the waves of the Yugoslav Adriatic coast, and the Allied air forces supplied the Partisans with massive logistic and tactical support, the prime sources have been contemporary reports and assessments now lodged in the Public Record Office at Kew and in the Naval Historical Branch of the Ministry of Defence. Chief among them were the war diaries of No. 2 Commando, No. 40 Royal Marine Commando, No. 43 Royal Marine Commando, the Raiding Support Regiment, the 2nd Battalion of the Highland Light Infantry, and 111 Field Regiment, Royal Artillery; and action reports of commanding officers from the Royal Navy Coastal Forces. I would like to record my warm gratitude for the kindliness and exemplary efficiency shown by the staff of the Public Record Office and of the Naval Historical Branch.

A number of the participants in these wartime events kindly agreed to be interviewed and to put their recollections on tape. They are Mr Bill Ash, Dr Ralph Bazeley, Colonel J.M.T.F. Churchill, Major-General T.B.L. Churchill, Mr Ernest Cox, Mr George Frost, Mr Hugh Fuller, Mr J.C.D. Hudspith, Mr Walter Iredale, Mr Ron Jeffs, Major-General R.B. Loudoun, Mr Norris Peak, Mr Reg Skinner, Mr Jack Stevens, Mr Harry Thirkell, Mr Frank Vautrey, Bishop James Wakeling and members of the London Branch of the Royal Navy Coastal Forces Association.

All were very helpful. Three, because of their particular experience and detailed knowledge, were exceptionally so. These were Major-General T.B.L. Churchill, who commanded the Commando Brigade on the island of Vis; his brother, Colonel J.M.T.F. Churchill, the Commanding Officer of No. 2 Commando until he was wounded and captured in the Brač battle; and Major-General R.B. Loudoun, the only assault troop commander of 43 Commando in the Brač battle to survive the action. His recorded interview aside, Bob Loudoun, my troop commander in wartime Yugoslavia (I joined No. 43 Commando as a replacement after the Brač battle) and a friend ever since, has filled in many gaps, and has revived many recollections, in a series of casual conversations over a glass or two of this and that from the time of the conception of this book.

Sir Alf Blake, Mr Clifford James and Mr John Wisdom were kind enough to answer my telephoned enquiries. Mrs Davidson, widow of the late Private Douglas Davidson of No. 2 Commando, generously lent me his lecture notes. Captain Nigel Clogstoun-Willmott gave me a helpful steer to sources. Mr E.D. Roberts chanced to hear of the existence of the typescript, asked Macmillan for a copy, and volunteered some informed and useful comments. Colonel Pat Turner generously allowed me to plunder his personal collection of photographs. The staff of the Imperial War Museum were helpfulness itself over the selection of others of the illustrations.

For the description of the part played by the Allied air forces in these operations I have drawn upon Volume 3 of *Royal Air Force 1939–1945: The Fight is Won*, the official history by Hilary St George Saunders. The contribution of the Long Range Desert Group derives from *Providence Their Guide*, written by their commanding officer, now Major-General David Lloyd Owen.

I am grateful too to James Hale, Peter James, Brenda Stephenson, Juliet Brightmore and Nada Watt for their invaluable help with the text and illustrations.

My thanks to them all.

Michael McConville
Dublin, 1986

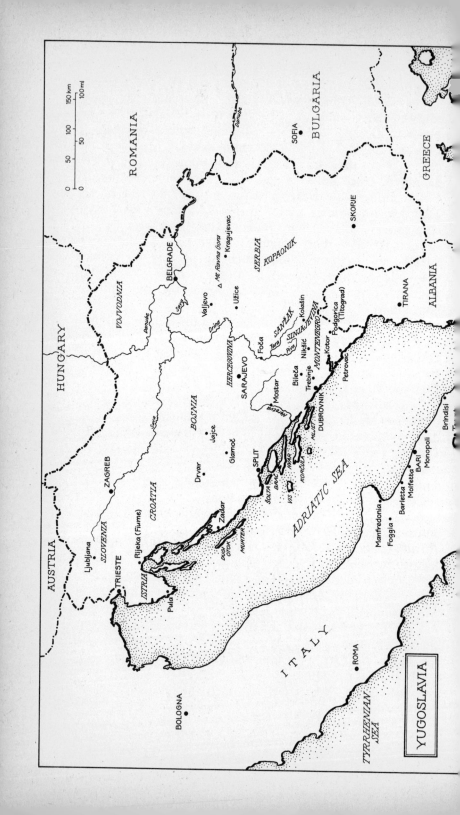

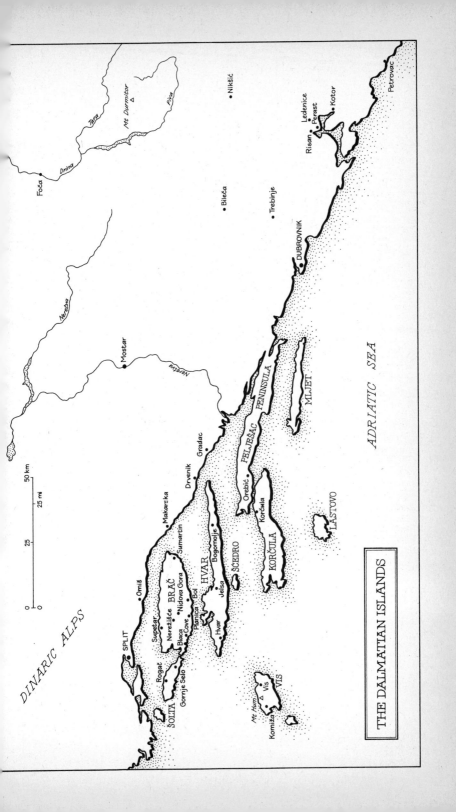

THE DALMATIAN ISLANDS

'One general aspect of our operations in the Balkans . . . has always seemed strange to me – that is, why it took so long for General Headquarters in the Middle East to realise that they had on their hands in their own theatre a major war in which they were really taking no interest at all.'

Major-General Sir Colin Gubbins, wartime Head of Special Operations Executive, speaking in 1973

Prologue

In August 1941, the Royal Navy radio monitoring station at Portishead heard the first of a sporadic series of weak signals from a set transmitting in the Balkans. The senders claimed to be operating with Colonel Draža Mihailović, who had been Chief of the Operations Division of the Yugoslav General Staff at the time of the German invasion of his country during the previous April. At first there was a sensible scepticism about the provenance of the transmissions. By the end of the month their authenticity was established beyond doubt. They gave confirmation to earlier reports and rumours, assembled, collated and assessed by British intelligence officers in Istanbul, of a Yugoslav guerrilla rising against the Germans. Mihailović was on Ravna Gora, in the mountains of western Serbia twenty miles north of Čačak. His followers were former soldiers of the Royal Yugoslav Army who either had never laid down their arms or had very soon taken them up again after the débâcle of the previous spring.

In a year during which British fortunes had not prospered, the news from Ravna Gora was a pleasing nugget of encouragement. With the exceptions of Sweden, Switzerland and the Iberian peninsula, the whole of continental Europe was under the politico-military control of Nazi Germany and its subordinate client allies. A spectacular British success over the Italian army in Egypt and Libya at the beginning of the year had been followed by a succession of disasters. The intervention in North Africa of German panzer divisions led by General Rommel had led to the loss of most of the territory taken from the Italians. A British and Commonwealth force, sent to help

1

the Greeks for reasons that were politically praiseworthy but militarily suicidal, had been thrown out of Greece by the Germans at the cost of much blood and material. Crete had fallen to a protracted airborne assault with further heavy inroads on lives and equipment, and with major damage to the Royal Navy. The tonnage of shipping sunk by U-boats in the Atlantic was being inexorably increased. In June, Germany's attack upon its earlier passive partner in international brigandage, the Soviet Union, had at last furnished Britain, who had for a year been fighting on its own, with an ally of immense potential, but the early phases of Operation Barbarossa were less than inspiring. The familiarly sinister German blitzkrieg formula of sophisticated interaction between armour and airpower had so far worked as devastatingly as ever. Huge expanses of western Russia and the Ukraine had been overrun, Moscow seemed at imminent risk, and soldiers of the Red Army had been slaughtered or taken captive by the hundreds of thousands.

Word of the birth of an obscure resistance movement on a remote Balkan massif could hardly be said to offset this catalogue of cumulative gloom. But it offered a small sliver of light. Small sparks sometimes cause big fires. Special Operations Executive, the organisation enjoined by Winston Churchill to 'set Europe ablaze' by promoting guerrilla opposition to German occupiers, had little fuel to spare to nourish this particular spark, and even fewer resources available to deliver whatever fuel it had. But it was clearly a spark that should be looked at and studied with care.

On 20 September 1941, a submarine from the Mediterranean Fleet arrived off the Gulf of Kotor on the Adriatic coast of Montenegro, which in the distribution of territorial plunder following the Yugoslav defeat had been allocated to the Italians. From the submarine two officers of the Royal Yugoslav Air Force, a Yugoslav wireless operator and Captain D.T. Hudson of SOE were ferried ashore to a beach near Petrovac. Hudson, a South African mining engineer, had in civilian life worked at the Trepča mines in Serbia. He was fluent in Serbo-Croat, was of a robust physique and of an adventurous disposition, and had for some time before the German invasion been in the clandestine employ of a precursor of SOE known as Section D, part of the Secret Intelligence Service. For Section D he had undertaken some sabotage of Axis ships moored in Dalmatian ports.

Hudson's instructions were to contact, investigate and report on all resistance elements regardless of their nationality, religion or political belief. The manner in which he set about his task had to be left to his own resourcefulness, and to luck. There had been so little information available to him before his departure from Malta that he had never heard the name Mihailović. He would shortly both hear the name and meet its owner. Shortly, too, he would hear the name Tito and meet its owner – the first British soldier to do either.

One of the handicaps attendant upon Hudson's mission was that he had no wireless set of his own. He had his personal cyphers, but for the sending of messages he had to rely upon the sets held and operated by his hosts. One was possessed by the two air force officers. Another, when he reached it, was the set whose signals had earlier been picked up by Portishead. He had otherwise to rely on any set that he might come across. Within a short time of his arrival Hudson was reporting that he had found himself among some unexpected complexities. He had become the unpopular and unsuccessful mediator in a murderously conducted civil war between two incompatible bodies of resisters, the Royalist Chetniks of Draža Mihailović and the Communist Partisans led by Tito.

Hudson, the first British soldier to enter occupied Yugoslavia, for eighteen months embodied in himself the entire strength of the British armed forces there. He was not brought out until March 1944, two-and-a-half years after his landing at Petrovac. The *last* British operational soldiers to leave wartime Yugoslavia were a patrol of the Long Range Desert Group, commanded by Captain John Olivey, who drove across the frontier from Istria to Italy after the German surrender in May 1945.

The circumstances of the LRDG departure were in some ways as militarily unconventional as the situation with which Hudson was faced upon his arrival. Olivey's patrol was the only active one of his unit not to have been put under arrest by the Yugoslav allies alongside whom they had been fighting for the past year or more. The tone of the divorce proceedings that brought to an end what had been a highly profitable alliance to both parties was encapsulated in a signal sent a few days earlier by another LRDG patrol leader, confronted with the alternatives of evacuation by sea or an indeterminate stretch of detention in the country in whose interests he had been risking his neck. 'I would prefer to be picked up by the Navy,' wirelessed this embittered officer, 'rather than be shanghaied by these garlic-eating bandits.'

If the story of the British military involvement in wartime Yugoslavia had an unpromising beginning and a grotesque ending, it also had a middle of solid achievement. This book is about the contribution, expressed in terms of blood, men and material, made by the Royal Navy and Royal Marines, the army and the Royal Air Force to the defeat of the Germans in Yugoslavia. It was a rather more elaborate entanglement than is sometimes realised.

PART ONE

The British Missions

ONE

Yugoslavia and the Axis Invasion

Yugoslavia as a political entity came into being in 1918 as a product of the Peace Conference that followed the First World War. The country's first title – evocative and Zendaesque – was the Kingdom of the Serbs, Croats and Slovenes. Brevity and accuracy were well served when in 1929 it became Yugoslavia, the Land of the South Slavs. The ancestors of the South Slavs had been at the forward edge of the fifth- and sixth-century Slav migrations from the expanses between the Vistula and the Dnieper. By 1919 the descendants of these migrants still had in common their Slavdom, sometimes heavily diluted by other racial strains, and a language that held wide regional variations and two different written scripts. The spoken version of any one region was more or less comprehensible to inhabitants of most of the others, give or take a lacing of confusion brought about by eccentricities in diction and receptiveness.

The new state covered an area of 99,181 square miles, roughly the same size as Britain, of which about nine-tenths was a wild and beautiful complex of barren mountains interspersed with narrow, intricate river valleys. Those nine-tenths were natural guerrilla country, inhabited by natural hereditary guerrillas. The other tenth, the Pannonian Plain in the north, a deep stretch of flatlands on a section of the Dalmatian coast, and a few extensive river valleys in the hinterland, carried fertile soil and the bulk of the urban population.

There were 12 million inhabitants in the birth year of the new nation. Of these, half – Croats, Slovenes and Bosnians – had until then been subjects of the Austro-Hungarian

Dual Monarchy, and as such had been at war with most of
the other half – Serbs and Montenegrins who had been
allies of Britain, France and Imperial Russia.* The Serbs,
who during the war had lost 1½ million dead from a
population of 5 million, who had been on the winning side,
and whose king was the new head of state, were not
unnaturally disposed to look upon themselves as the
dominant partner in the infant body politic. The Croats saw
matters differently. The concept of a South Slav state had
originated in Croatia during the nineteenth century, but the
Croatian leaders considered that the ideal had not been
realised. What they wanted was a semi-autonomous
Croatian state within a Yugoslav federal framework. What
the Serbs wanted was a centralised, unified Yugoslavia
governed from Belgrade. It was an unrepaired breach that
bedevilled the Kingdom throughout the twenty-two years
of its *de facto* existence and the following four years, the
Second World War years, of its nominal existence. It was
central to the savagery that was a characteristic of the
settlement of internecine differences between 1941 and
1945.

Even if the continuing Croatian–Serbian dispute had
never started there would still have been formidable
difficulties over welding the components of the new nation
into a united whole. Individual pieces of the structure had
had their affairs ordered for them in differing ways. Serbia
and Montenegro, after centuries of Turkish rule, had been
independent for the previous six years. Slovenia and
Dalmatia had been run by the Austrian half of the Dual
Monarchy. Croatia, Slavonia and the Vojvodina had been
the responsibility of the Hungarian half. Bosnia and
Hercegovina had had a joint Austro-Hungarian administration. Until 1912 Macedonia had been the property of the
Turks, and had since been governed by the Serbs.
Boundary adjustments with Austria and Hungary had led

*A young Croat conscript, Josip Broz, had been one of the Austrian
soldiers. In 1941, when – now known as Tito – he was organising the
Communist rising in western Serbia, his staff found it advisable to tell
him tactfully that although they were deeply interested in his reminiscences of his bygone battles against Serbs in territory through which they
were currently passing, it might be helpful to recruiting if he glossed over
this part of his personal history.

to the acquisition of nearly 400 square miles with a non-Slav population. There were other non-Slav minorities: Germans, Hungarians and Romanians in Croatia and the Vojvodina, Albanians in south Serbia, and Italians along the Dalmatian littoral.

The diversity of former political systems was complemented by religious and cultural divisiveness. The Croats and Slovenes were Catholics. The Serbs and Macedonians were Eastern Orthodox. The Bosnians were mostly Moslem. Spread among the Christian areas were other Moslems, descendants of converts to Islam at the time of the Ottoman Empire. The Croats and Slovenes had down the centuries absorbed and contributed to Western European literature, music, painting, sculpture, philosophy and science. They tended to a sophisticated disdain of Serbs, Montenegrins and Macedonians, whose historical preoccupations with resisting Turks had been admirable and heroic, but had nonetheless left them with insufficient time and opportunity to nourish and savour the finer things in life.

A further disability with which the new state had to contend arose from simple peasant parochialism. The notion of consolidating all the South Slavs into a single nation was romantically attractive to the intellectuals who conceived it, and had a more practical appeal, patriotic or self-serving, to the politicians who would control it – even if the question of how it was to be controlled generated acrimonious controversy from the start. To the largely illiterate majority who lived in isolated rural holdings and hamlets, on bleak and inaccessible highlands, the national design was only sketchily comprehensible. Their horizons were invincibly local. Real life for them had to do with hard toil on infertile patches of land, herding sheep and goats on over-grazed mountain pastures, and the violent settlement of recent or inherited grudges against neighbouring communities and individuals. Blood feuds, particularly in Montenegro, were traditional and still in fashion. Entrenched peasant attitudes were to be another contributory cause of the slaughter of one-tenth of all resident Yugoslavs between 1941 and 1945.

External threats to the new regime were, in its early days at least, less of a problem than were internal strains. A

Balkan country with land frontiers with Italy, Austria, Hungary, Romania, Bulgaria, Greece and Albania would be imprudent not to look to its defences, but for the time being none of the neighbours was ostentatiously troublesome. One of them, Austria, became potentially so in 1938 when the Anschluss took it into the Third Reich and Yugoslavia found itself with a German army across one of its borders. Another, Italy, developed an unwelcome tactical interest in the wilder reaches of extremist Croatian nationalism, and after Mussolini's accession to power sheltered and nurtured exiled dissidents. In the Soviet Union, separated from Yugoslavia by a wide belt of intervening territory, plans to subvert the new, cobbled-together nation were slowly maturing. Involved in some of the early planning was young Josip Broz. He had been wounded and captured while fighting in his Austrian unit against the Tsarist army, and then released from his prisoner-of-war camp in the confusion of the Russian Revolution. He had witnessed some of the significant events of that Revolution, and had been impressed. His succession of aliases began with Walter, progressed through Engineer Slavko Babić, Engineer Kostanjić and Tomanek, and was to end lastingly as Tito.

The history of the inter-war years in Yugoslavia is a mess of good intentions, abandoned opportunities, myopic sectional chauvinism and unscrupulous politicking, the whole leavened by a measure of brutality and not infrequently embellished by the sound of gunfire. Most of the happenings were of solely domestic interest. Some had a direct, some an indirect, influence upon the ambience in which a sizeable number of British troops, mostly puzzled, were to find themselves operating in the early 1940s.

Elections were held in November 1920. A centralist constitution, framed to Serb specifications, was approved by the Regent, shortly to become King Alexander, on 1 January 1921. The Croats had largely themselves to blame for this setback. They staged a histrionic walkout from the negotiations, and thereby left their opponents with a free run of the votes. A portent lay in the election of fifty-eight Communist deputies to the legislature.

In 1922 a Communist assassinated the Minister of the Interior. The Party was banned, went underground, and from thereon was harassed and extensively penetrated by the security police.

The Croats maintained a boycott of the Assembly until 1928. By then, Radić, the Croat Peasant Party leader, had become convinced of the boycott's futility and led his colleagues back to Belgrade. A trigger-happy Montenegrin Deputy took exception to him and shot him and two other Croats in the Assembly building. Radić died of wounds. The other two were killed instantly.

King Alexander suspended the constitution and substituted a personal, dictatorial rule. There was press censorship and restriction of the rights to associate or assemble. The security police, who were no more fastidious in their methods than any other contemporary Balkan security police, became busier. Most of those working in Croatia were Serbs.

The King restored constitutional rule in 1931. It did little good. The Serb politicians split into bickering factions, the Croats stayed resentful. Around this time Ante Pavelić, the leader of the Ustashi, an extreme Croat Fascist organisation, left Croatia for abroad, a few steps ahead of the security police.

In October 1934, King Alexander went on a state visit to France. The Ustashi murdered him with a bomb in Marseilles.

The heir to the throne, King Peter, was a boy of eleven. His uncle Paul was appointed Regent. Prince Paul was by inclination an Anglophile. He had spent more time out of Yugoslavia than in it, and his personal tastes were cultural rather than political. But he was a dutiful man who applied himself conscientiously to his new task. Both internationally and domestically his problems began to assume a menacing quality beyond anything that his assassinated brother had had to deal with. In Italy Mussolini was rattling his sabre with assiduity. Hitler was in power in Germany and was not reticent about his intentions of expanding the boundaries of the Reich. Disaffection and disillusionment with Yugoslavia were spreading in Croatia, where a conviction was growing among a large minority that the best hope for the Croatian

future would be the establishment of an entirely independent Croatian state, sustained by Fascist ideals and
supported by German force. And in both Serbia and
Croatia the Communists, reinvigorated and reorganised
from Zagreb by Engineer Babić, Kostanjić, Tomanek or
whatever alias Tito was then using, were once more making
ground. This time there was a subtlety of approach that
they had not shown earlier. Their once leaky security had
improved immeasurably. Traitors, police informers and the
ideologically suspect among them were being eliminated
mercilessly. The Party had been notably successful in the
recruitment of new members at the University of Belgrade.

As the thirties rolled by, and Europe slid relentlessly
towards another war, Prince Paul concluded that his duty
to safeguard his nephew's subjects must take clear precedence over his personal Anglophilism and his detestation of
Nazi Germany and all that it stood for. As he saw it, only
Yugoslav neutrality could meet that objective.

By the summer of 1940, Nazi Germany had already, by
means of a shifting combination of direct action, threats
and diplomacy, reoccupied the Rhineland, united itself
with Austria and taken over Czecho-Slovakia; and by
straightforward force of arms had conquered in succession
western Poland, Denmark, Norway, Holland, Belgium and
France. The British were the only opponents left in the
fight. The performance of the RAF in the Battle of Britain,
and the threat from the Royal Navy, diminished by
casualties but powerful enough to deter the planners of an
essentially land and air military apparatus from risking an
amphibious expedition across the English Channel and the
North Sea, had by the autumn preserved the island from
invasion. But in Eastern Europe the victory looked to be
more of a respite than a salvation. And even if the British
could hold on it was clear that they had nothing in their
armoury to spare for any friends who might join them.
German and Italian diplomacy was prompt in pointing the
lesson. With France out of the war, and Italy now in it on
Germany's side, the Axis provided the only market for the
export of Yugoslav foodstuffs and raw materials. Prince
Paul and his ministers took the hint.

As matters then stood, Yugoslavia had a fair chance of being left to its neutrality. Two developments reduced the comfort. Mussolini, in a vain attempt to demonstrate that he too could overrun somebody else's country, invaded Greece in October without telling the Germans of his intentions. The Greeks fought back strongly, and the campaign bogged down. The RAF sent some squadrons to help the Greeks, and thereby caused concern to the Germans, who were planning an unrelated project, the invasion of Russia. RAF airfields within range of Romanian oil wells would add an unforeseen danger when the Russian operation began. The airfields could only be eliminated if the Germans took a hand in clearing up the mess that the Italians had got themselves into in Greece. A German attack on Greece through Bulgaria was quickly put on to the drawing board.

Operation Barbarossa, the German invasion of the Soviet Union, was of infinitely greater importance to Hitler than the Greek imbroglio. Barbarossa required a secure southern flank. Hungary and Romania were already German satellites. Only Yugoslavia was a potential threat, and not it seemed an unusually dangerous one. It was in the German interest to neutralise it by bullying diplomatic pressure rather than by a diversion of some of the force preparing for Barbarossa. The pressure was applied with persistence and skill. After negotiations during which he was left in no doubt about what would happen to his country if he failed to put his signature to the Tripartite Pact, Prince Paul duly signed in Vienna on 24 March 1941. Still philosophically anti-German and pro-British, he calculated that he had taken the only course open to him to preserve Yugoslavia from destruction. His estimate was that he had saved between 200,000 and 300,000 Yugoslav lives. In return for his undertaking to stay benignly neutral he had been given German guarantees, for what German guarantees of the day were worth, that there would be no demands for Axis troops to pass through Yugoslavia and no insistence upon Yugoslav military help against Germany's enemies. Unless, of course, Yugoslavia chose to volunteer it.

Hitler was unreservedly pleased with his pact. Prince Paul and his ministers were pleased too, but with the

13

qualified pleasure of people who have chosen the less undesirable of two pernicious alternatives. The immediate outcome in Belgrade was a surprise to both sets of signatories. There was a *coup d'état* on 27 March led by senior air force officers. Prince Paul was deposed, his ministers were sacked, the young King Peter assumed the throne, and General Simović, until then the Air Minister, took over as Prime Minister. *'Bolje rat nego pakt!'* chanted enthusiastic crowds in the streets – 'Better war than the pact!' War came to them on 6 April.

Among Hitler's plentiful recorded comments in reaction to the *coup* was the statement that he 'would burn out for good this festering sore in the Balkans'. He set about the cauterisation with the maximum of brutality and with total efficiency. German aircraft, estimated by a Yugoslav air force officer who was at the receiving end to be of a strength of 400 bombers and 200 fighters, attacked Belgrade in a shuttle that lasted for two days. There were 10,000 civilian dead, the first of the notional 200,000 to 300,000 that Prince Paul had hoped to have saved, and of the actual 1½ million Yugoslavs who were destined to be killed in the next four years. The same air force officer puts the overall number of Axis aircraft in use during the brief campaign as 2000. The defenders had a total of about 360, of which the first-line hotchpotch of British Blenheims, Italian Savoias and German Dorniers and Messerschmitts was obsolescent, and the second-line job-lot of biplanes was obsolete. Between sixty and eighty Yugoslav aircraft were destroyed during the first day, two-thirds of them on the ground, the latter process being greatly helped by Captain Vladimir Kren of the Zagreb Air Base, who defected to the opposition shortly before fighting broke out and identified for them the locations of concealed Yugoslav airfields.

The Yugoslav army, deployed well forward near the Austrian, Hungarian and Bulgarian frontiers, was destroyed by an onslaught of panzers and motorised infantry. The speed of the breakthrough surprised the Yugoslav General Staff. The Croatian formations to the west disintegrated with particular rapidity, and many of their members, following the example of Captain Kren, went over to the enemy.

On 13 April, one week after the assault was launched, Simović sent emissaries to ask for an armistice. The emissaries returned from the parley for further instructions, but the Germans simply substituted for them another set of senior officers who were by now in their hands, and these surrendered unconditionally on 17 April. Hostilities ceased on the 18th. (Greece, also invaded by German forces on 6 April, was overrun by the beginning of May.) On the 19th and 20th the survivors of the Yugoslav government and some air force and naval officers flew to Cairo, the Allied base nearest to the Balkans, and headquarters of the Allied Commander-in-Chief, Middle East. And that, it seemed to the more optimistic of the Germans, was the Yugoslav nuisance disposed of.

Although the arrival by submarine off the Gulf of Kotor of Captain Hudson five months after this fiasco represented in a solitary manner the advanced guard of British military intervention in Yugoslavia, some *sub rosa* operations against the Germans and Italians had before the invasion been run from Belgrade by SOE and its predecessor, Section D. These illicit shenanigans had had to be conducted with unusual secrecy. Their originators found it necessary to conceal their identities not only from their Axis opponents, as was natural, and from the neutral Yugoslav host government, as was also natural, but from the British Minister in Belgrade and his Legation staff as well. The Minister, a professional diplomat who professionally implemented his instructions from the Foreign Office, followed an entirely defensible policy. This was founded upon the consideration that a neutral Yugoslavia which – aside from the provision of some agricultural products and raw materials – did not help Germany much was in the circumstances of the times more of an asset to Britain than would be a belligerent Yugoslavia which would require military help beyond the then resources of the British to provide. Anything that might provoke German action against Yugoslavia was thus to be avoided.

SOE in London, which throughout the war was to be in

almost permanent disagreement with the Foreign Office over policy towards Yugoslavia, took a different, and again logically defensible, view of the matter. It seemed to them that it would be possible to perform a certain amount of sabotage against Axis interests without risking damage to Yugoslav neutrality, provided that the programme was conducted with a suitable discretion in an untraceable manner. SOE went ahead. Piquancy was added to the enterprise by the fact that some of the sabotage team were on the Minister's own staff, in the guise of service attachés, an assistant information officer and the like. Other recruits to the organisation came from the British expatriate commercial and industrial community, of whom two were later to have roles as guerrilla liaison officers and to have a strong influence on a major shift in British policy that affected the future of Yugoslavia.

These two were S.W. Bailey and D.T. Hudson (he of the submarine landing in Montenegro), both employees of the Trepča mines in Serbia. The mines were owned by the Selection Trust Group, a London-based conglomerate the chairman of which was Chester Beatty. Beatty was an American-born millionaire who had made his fortune as a mining engineer and prospector in Canada, received a British knighthood, and ultimately retired to the Republic of Ireland, with which he endowed a notable gallery and museum of oriental art. He was a dedicated supporter of SOE, and on occasion personally funded some of its activities when official financial backing was scarce.

The pre-invasion cloak-and-dagger period did not last for long. Not surprisingly, given the constraints within which its operators worked, it achieved very little and nothing of decisive significance. Some Slovene railwaymen were persuaded to put sand in the axle-boxes of trains carrying strategic war materials to Germany. An attempt to make contact with an Austrian underground movement was frustrated. So was an elaborate, and potentially profitable, plan to block the Danube against the passage of oil barges from the Romanian oilfields to Germany. Some Italian merchant ships were sabotaged when tied up in a Dalmatian port. One operative claimed to have killed a German agent whom he met in the dining-car of a train, and to have thrown the body out of the lavatory window. A

16

lamentably insecure German official had his brief-case stolen from a night club. Some transiently useful propaganda and counter-propaganda were disseminated. Encouragement, moral and financial, was given to the Agrarian Party in Belgrade, who opposed all things German, and further encouragement, unaccompanied by a subsidy, to serving officers who did likewise. The Agrarian Party backed the *coup* of late March, but SOE were under no illusions that their own intervention was a major influence in stimulating the revolt. It was a self-generated outburst of spontaneous revulsion at the expedient abandonment of a hallowed national, primarily Serbian, custom of hitting back hard in the teeth of threats and to hell with the consequences.

The fact that the consequences were calamitous negated almost everything that Section D and SOE had so far done. Most of their team left the capital in the road convoy of Allied diplomatic staff which wound its way along the narrow Balkan roads to the Montenegrin fjord that appears recurrently in this account, the Gulf of Kotor. From there, arrangements had been made for them to be picked up either by RAF flying-boat or by a Royal Navy submarine. Elements of the Italian invasion force were there before the diplomats, but were pleasingly correct in their observance of international diplomatic niceties. HMS *Regent* surfaced in the Gulf. A submarine officer came ashore to discuss embarkation procedures with the Italians. In turn, two Italian officers obligingly boarded *Regent* as pledges against any attempted skulduggery upon the naval officer. The negotiations were in smooth flow when three German Stukas, uninvited by the Italians, appeared in the sky and put in a brisk dive-bombing attack on the submarine. *Regent* closed her hatches, submerged and departed for Malta, leaving the diplomats, real and spurious, on the shore, and taking the disconsolate Italian hostages as passengers.

Thus, on a note of bathos, ended temporarily the preface to a much more substantial British military involvement. The satisfying postscript to the preface was that the scrupulously *protocolaire* Italians soon repatriated by air all the diplomats, real or otherwise, in accordance with accepted civilised practice. Some of the otherwise lived to fight another day.

TWO

Pavelić, Mihailović, Tito

To German strategists the reduction of Yugoslavia was an essential, but minor, necessity. Their minds were concentrated upon the operation that would determine the future of Europe, by extension of the world, and of their own dominant role in it: the destruction of the Soviet Union. The priority which they gave to Yugoslavia was apparent in the dispositions that they made for its management. Yugoslavia needed to be kept quiet, and its road and railway communications to Greece kept open. In pursuance of these objectives the country was carved up in a way that put the minimum strain upon German manpower. The hangers-on were given a liberal share of the booty.

Essential strategic bits of it, much of Serbia (which became a new state under the quisling General Nedić), parts of Slovenia, and the eastern Vojvodina (which was put in the hands of the resident German minority) were retained as a direct German responsibility. The Italians in an assortment of constitutional guises became the rulers of Montenegro, about half of Dalmatia, Kosovo and western Macedonia. They were also given the segment of Slovenia not wanted by the Germans. The Bulgarians got most of Macedonia. Hungary took over the west Vojvodina and a little piece of Croatia.

In all these areas of devolved administration an appalling number of lives was lost during the next few years. But it was in the remaining component, under the scheme for the allocation of spoils and power, that death and fear were laid comprehensively upon the people on a scale unrivalled in the rest of the country. The Independent State of Croatia, expanded to take in Bosnia and that part of

Dalmatia not pre-empted by the Italians, was set up under the control of Ante Pavelić and his Ustashi, the killers of King Alexander in Marseilles in 1934, and the fanatical enthusiasts for the restoration of Croatia to what in their clouded perceptions they assumed it once had been. They thought that Croatia had in the past been populated exclusively by Croats. It no longer was. The logically simple remedy was to kill the non-Croatian inhabitants.

Of these, 1½ million were Serbs who had for one reason or another down the generations come to live in Croatia. The state's eastern boundary was now delineated by the River Drina. 'Across the Drina or into the Drina,' was the formula prescribed for these undesirables by Pavelić. It was a notably figurative formula. Its reality was massacre, from which escape was a matter of exceptional luck or of a speedy religious conversion from Orthodoxy to Catholicism, the latter option (with rare exceptions) not open to Jews or Gypsies. Pavelić was as ostentatiously devout in his Catholicism as he was unforgivingly direct in the implementation of his political cleansing programme. He built a private chapel in his official residence in Zagreb, and there he went daily to Mass with his wife and children. Early in his rule he had an audience with the Pope. He was prepared to tolerate non-Catholic Croats provided that their Croat ethnicity was beyond argument. Indeed, the Bosnian Moslems – Croats who had embraced Islam under Turkish rule – were among his more dedicated exterminators.

In March the status of Pavelić had been that of a terrorist conspirator living in exile in Italy with a following of a not very large gang of lethally romantic ideologues and less reflective thugs. No early realisation of the dreams of any of them had been in prospect. Pavelić was suddenly elevated to the dictatorship of his homeland as a consequence of the Belgrade *coup* and of the German response to it. He took up his new duties as *Poglavnik* or Leader in early May. By the end of the month he had organised his Ustashi Force, fashioned largely from those trained Croats of the disbanded Royal Yugoslav Army who had failed to fight the invaders in April. Pavelić's plans for racial purification were ready. Their implementation began in June, to reach a peak of intensity in July and August.

The eradication process ranged from the murder of entire families, communities and village populations to the razing of such symbols of the Serb presence as the Orthodox cathedral in Banja Luka after the killing of its elderly bishop. In Glina, one wounded man, left for dead, was the only survivor of 160 Serbs who were herded into the Orthodox church, taunted, beaten, forced to watch the desecration of the altar and the ikons, and then collectively butchered, most with knives, a few by guns.

Milovan Djilas, on his way by train in July to Montenegro to raise the Communist revolt, met a small group of Serbian refugees from Croatia at a railway station near Bileča.

> They were fleeing from the Ustashi terror. A fair, robust peasant in his thirties, with bruised cheekbones and curly hair matted with dried blood, told us how the Ustashi had surrounded his village and driven everyone – men and women, young and old – to a rocky ravine, then struck them down with clubs. . . . 'They were killing every Serb in sight. . . . Like cattle – a blow on the head, then down the ditch.'

The peasant, clubbed in the face, worked his bonds free and ran to some brush-covered boulders. He was one of the luckier ones.*

Glina and the story told to Djilas were representative examples, not isolated or exceptional horrors. Estimates of the number of Serbs killed in the pogrom are no more than estimates. Six hundred thousand men, women and children was the figure quoted by General Nedić, the Serb leader; 900,000 is another estimate. The slaughter inevitably generated a ferocious reaction among those who escaped, or were bereaved by it. Mihailović's Chetniks and Tito's Partisans, who were early at one another's throats, had at least one bond in common. Both fought the Ustashi, who for the rest of the war remained a gruesome constant in a politically tangled jungle. To that extent Pavelić, in his horrible way, was something of a bonus to future British policy-makers trying to determine who was doing what, and

*Milovan Djilas, *Wartime* (London: Martin Secker & Warburg, 1977).

who should be supported, in Yugoslavia. There was no ambiguity about the Ustashi. They were a brutish enemy, the checkered red and white of their colours nailed firmly beneath the swastika on the German mast.

Of the other two leaders whose decisions in wartime shaped the long-term future of Yugoslavia, one – Tito – knew precisely what he wanted to do and, allowing for some tactical flexibility within the defined limits laid down by his Marxist–Leninist creed, knew how he wanted to do it. The other, Mihailović, knew what he would have liked to have done, but throughout was haunted by uncertainties, hesitations and scruples of a kind that left the confidently dogma-sustained Tito untroubled. Tito looked upon the loss of lives, Partisan or civilian, as a regrettably necessary sacrifice in the cause of dislodging the Germans and establishing a Yugoslav Marxist state. Mihailović, a Serb first and a Yugoslav some way behind, wanted a restored Serbian-dominated monarchy. He considered that restoration would be made possible only by a landing by the Allies, and that the guerrilla function was to stay in being until the time came to co-operate with the landers. With some exceptions, interim operations would be militarily useless, and would provoke hideous German reprisals upon civilians, to widespread sorrow and no conceivable gain. In this assessment he was influenced strongly by a First World War precedent.

Draža Mihailović was forty-eight years of age in 1941. He was an able regular soldier who had scaled the promotion ladder steadily, and had served twice as a military attaché, once in Prague and once in Sofia. In 1940, when he was stationed in Slovenia, he had irritated his superiors by tactlessly expressed criticism, sadly proved to be justified, of their defensive preparations. The friction stimulated by these strictures did not stop his posting to Belgrade as Chief of the Operations Division of the General Staff. The British Military Attaché there described him as having an excellent professional reputation.

During the disastrous ten days of the German campaign Mihailović personally witnessed the collapse and defection of Croatian troops, and drew his own conclusions.

Immediately after the surrender he took practical measures to demonstrate his unwillingness to accept defeat. He assembled a small nucleus, twenty-six strong, of Serbian officers, NCOs and gendarmes, and marched them through the mountains of Bosnia to the mountains of western Serbia. On 11 May 1941, when Pavelić was still refining his plans for genocide in Croatia, and Tito, the Comintern agent, was doing nothing to discommode the German occupiers because they were partners in the Nazi–Soviet Pact, Mihailović reached Ravna Gora and set up his headquarters. His *cheta*, the armed band from which the name Chetnik derived, attracted many like-minded reinforcements. His wireless operators made contact with the British through Portishead; and British propaganda spread word of the emergence of a gallant and effective national Yugoslav resistance movement, fierce in its opposition to Nazism. To a very considerable extent the propaganda was creating an illusion.

Had Draža Mihailović operated in a less disordered country with a more homogeneous population he might well have emerged from the war as a national hero with an international reputation as a wise guerrilla leader of rare quality. He was the first to raise the banner of resistance. He was a patriot and an experienced soldier. He carried out in the early days sufficient local operations to let it be known what he was about. His overriding policy, of holding back and conserving his forces until they could fight decisively in co-operation with an Allied landing (that he was sure would sooner or later be mounted) by properly armed and supported troops, made military sense. It had the same rationale as the policy of the French, Dutch and Norwegian resistance movements, and indeed it accorded with the early preference of the Yugoslav government-in-exile and the Allied High Command.

There was sound reason for his fears about German reprisals against civilians. He was bitterly familiar with an episode of 1917 during the previous war. The British, French and Serbian commanders in Salonika had sent in Kosta Pečanac to the Toplica area of central Serbia to organise a popular rising against the German and Bulgarian

occupying armies. Pečanac, in possibly the pioneer enterprise of its kind, was delivered behind the lines by
aeroplane. A resourceful and attractive leader, he soon
developed a large following. Their forays were extensive
and destructive, carried out in isolation, unsupported in
any way by the Allied command that had promoted them.
A string of tactical successes was followed by a devastating
defeat. The defeat in turn was followed by the retributive
massacre of 35,000 men, women and children. Mihailović
had no reason to believe that a new generation of
Germans, especially Nazi Germans, would be any less
ruthless. In October 1941 he was shown to be right.

In the middle of that month a German column, on its
way back to its base town of Kragujevac after a fight with
Partisans, was ambushed by more Partisans. The Germans
lost a dozen killed and about thirty wounded. On the
morning of 21 October the Germans established blocks at
all exits from the town and rounded up all males. Initially
the townspeople assumed that a more than usually large
selection of forced labour was to be made. The total
muster was about 7000 strong. But they were split into
batches of forty, and machine-gunned. Among the dead
were the headmaster and staff of the secondary school, all
the pupils of the three senior classes, everyone who had
been in the law-court from the magistrate to the accused
and including the lawyers, gaolers and witnesses, and the
sort of people to be found going about their business on any
day in any moderately large town anywhere – doctors, taxi-
drivers, barmen, priests, shop assistants, newspaper-sellers.
Some were reprieved for reasons of convenience, not from
pity. Six hundred or so were preserved as hostages, to be
killed in groups should there be further attacks upon the
occupying forces. Several hundred more were let loose to
spread word of what they had seen. Eye-witnesses were
more effective propagandists than were the drafters of
proclamations that threatened the deaths of one hundred
civilians in retaliation for every German soldier killed.

The Kragujevac slaughter was both a dreadful confirmation of what Mihailović had forecast and the final
determinant in his developing belief that if he were to save
his people from near extinction he must first safeguard
them from the consequences of Partisan actions, before

returning his attentions to a realistic programme of anti-German resistance. Partisan provocations, in his assessment, were of a criminal irresponsibility. The Partisan leaders had been impervious to his advocacy. They would have to be taught their lesson forcefully. In the first week in November he turned his Chetniks on them.

When, two years later in 1943, the British had at last acquired sufficient information to provide a reasonably clear picture of what was happening in Yugoslavia, and had studied the picture in a reappraisal of policy towards the rival resistance organisations, some misunderstandings developed from the use by Mihailović of the term Chetnik. There was a natural assumption among some that Mihailović, the top Chetnik, controlled and was responsible for everything done by Chetniks. This was inaccurate.

Chetniks had been celebrated in Serbian deed, history and legend for 150 years. They had originated in the volunteer banding together of peasants who took up their weapons, left their lands and gathered together in the woods and hills to harass oppressive Turkish rulers and similar objectionable interlopers. Chetniks had had a significant guerrilla influence upon the nineteenth-century Serbian revolts, the Balkan wars of 1912 and 1913, and the fighting against the Germans and the Bulgarians in the First World War. After the establishment of Yugoslavia in 1918 the Chetnik tradition provided the base upon which a loosely knit Serbian national organisation was built, a freemasonry prepared when necessary to defend with violence Serbian honour and interests. A far from precise parallel would be with the Orange Order in Ireland towards the end of the eighteenth century. There was a supreme leader in Belgrade, and local branches were spread about the country. Regular army officers held many of the more important positions. The Serbian-dominated central government used the institution from time to time to coerce inconvenient dissidents in the non-Serb provinces. Various Croats, Slovenes, Bosnians and Albanians had sound reasons for fearing and disliking it.

Mihailović's Chetniks, in drawing their inspiration from bygone Chetnik feats of valour and defiance, were fully entitled to the use of the name, but they had no monopoly of it. There were other Chetniks. Some, the 'legalised' Chetniks, still led by Kosta Pečanac, put themselves at the disposal of the puppet government of General Nedić, and, since they were implacably anti-Communist, were recognised formally by the Germans as allies. Some actually helped to form a joint German–Yugoslav SS division. Others were essentially private-enterprise operators who had combined together in the spirit of the old times, reacting spontaneously to local pressures, rather than to any nationally applied policy. There were subordinate commanders of Mihailović who did not necessarily obey those of his orders with which they disagreed, and who acted unpredictably on a scale between independence and conformity.

There were Chetnik initiatives of which Mihailović was unaware, others which were pursued contrary to his orders, and others still for which he could have no responsibility and which were anathema to him. Inevitably his name became associated with all of them.

At the time of the German invasion in April 1941, Josip Broz, later Tito, was living in Zagreb, the ancient capital of Croatia. He was a well-dressed, sturdy man in his late forties, and he was known to those who met him casually as Engineer Tomanek, a Czech. To those few who knew him more intimately he was the Secretary General of the Yugoslav Communist Party. The Party line came straight from the Comintern in Moscow and Tito was its Yugoslav mouthpiece. In the autumn of 1940, at a clandestine meeting held in Zagreb of Party leaders from all over the country, the Party's attitude to the war between Nazi Germany and its only antagonist still in the field, Britain and its Commonwealth and Empire, had been enshrined in a resolution drafted and proposed by Tito and endorsed by all those present. The agents of rival imperialist powers were seeking to drag Yugoslavia into a capitalist war. The Yugoslav Communist Party was resolutely opposed to all attempts to draw the nation into this bloody conflict.

This piece of loyalist conformity to the dictates of one of the partners to the Nazi–Soviet Pact of 1939 had been preceded by a speech from the Secretary General which contained passages not entirely consistent with the tone of the formal resolution. Party cells, for example, were to be formed among the armed forces. The cells must be prepared for the education of the fighting masses, ready to band together if need be all who wished to take up arms against the Nazi Fascists. Some of the most successful Partisan commanders were shortly to make their presence felt as a result of a nicely struck pragmatic balance between doctrinal orthodoxy and a realistic weighing of international probabilities.

Until the Belgrade *coup* of 27 March the Yugoslav Communists had continued to favour neutrality. As a disciplined Party they had no option. The *coup* would clearly stimulate an immediate German attack, which, in the entirely accurate Tito analysis, would be followed by an almost equally immediate Yugoslav defeat. The defeat in its turn would give the Party opportunities of an exploitable quality that had not before presented themselves during its short history. The fragile mutual opportunism that held the Nazi–Soviet Pact together could not last indefinitely. When it cracked there would be a call from the Comintern for a Communist-led rising in Yugoslavia. The Secretary General put his contingency planning in hand.

He asked for, and was given, Comintern help in the recovery from internment and the inconspicuous return to Yugoslavia of a select group of Yugoslav Communists with fighting experience in the Spanish Civil War. He was in Belgrade within a few hours of the *coup* and presiding at a meeting of the Party's provincial committee for Serbia. The *coup*, he told them, was of major importance in that the Axis powers had been slapped in the face. But its leadership was without exception reactionary, and Communists must not be misled by it. He listed in a directive the steps that were to be taken.

Everything must be done to destroy the monarchy. The Party would assist all elements, regardless of their ideology and character, who were bent on this purpose. Those assisted would include separatist movements. The Ustashi were among those mentioned.

Party members called up to the army would have three tasks. The first was to undermine its powers of resistance by creating confusion. Defeat could then be attributed to the incompetence of the officer corps. The second was to collect and hide weapons and equipment thrown away in the panic. The third was to identify non-Communist officers and men of potential use to the Party should the Soviet Union come into the war.

The victorious Germans and Italians would set up quisling separatist regimes in the various provinces. Preliminary arrangements were to be made for the infiltration of these for intelligence and other purposes.

In issuing these instructions Tito, as was his custom, was looking several moves ahead. The nature of his prophetic vision would not have enchanted the Chief of the Operations Division of the General Staff, Colonel Draža Mihailović, had he known of it either at the time of its conception or some months later in western Serbia, when he was briefly engaged in negotiations with Tito aimed at the co-ordination of a joint resistance to the common German enemy.

Germany invaded Russia on 22 June, forty-five days after the Yugoslav surrender. During that period the Communist Party went ahead with its provisional preparations for a revolt, but in terms of deeds was inactive. Its underground organisation remained almost completely intact. On the first evening following the German attack on Russia an emergency meeting of the Party Central Committee was held in Belgrade and a proclamation of revolt was distributed secretly to all Party sub-organisations throughout the country. Proletarians were urged to rally round their vanguard, the Communist Party of Yugoslavia. They could not, they were told, stand idly by while the precious blood of the heroic people of Soviet Russia was shed. They were to mobilise all their strength to prevent their country from being turned into a base to supply the Fascist hordes who had unleashed their fury on the Soviet Union, 'our dear socialist Fatherland, our hope, the beacon to which the eyes of working folk throughout the world are turned in longing. . . .'

If this rather florid call to arms might seem superficially to have not a great deal to do with the mobilisation of

practically expressed resentment against the German viola-
tion of Yugoslav national territory, it in fact hit the note
that a large number of people had been listening for. To
these, the old Yugoslavia had become a frustrated dream,
an elaborate, untidy mess maladministered by squabbling,
venal politicians. It had demonstrated its final touch of
futility by provoking an invasion against which its preparations had been pitiful, losing the campaign in ten days, and
compounding the damage by leaving the people to face the
consequences while its self-appointed leaders ran away to
safety in somebody else's country.

This new declaration of intent by the Communists
restored a hope that had been abandoned. Sympathetic
admiration for the lone British fight against the Germans
had been widespread, but there had been no prospect of a
single-handed British victory and no prospect either of a
useful British intervention in Yugoslavia. Now that the
Russians were in the war, there was a reasonable chance
that it might in the long run be won. There was also a
powerful psychological factor, reflected in the wording of
the manifesto, a traditional, emotional fellow-feeling for
Russia particularly strong among the peasants of Serbia,
and stronger still in Montenegro. The previous activities of
an outlawed Party had by necessity been clandestine, but
its propaganda had been effective and its influence
growing. And who better to organise and direct a resistance
movement than a Party that by its nature had been doing
just that, if on a small scale, for twenty years?

Tito, undetected by the German and quisling Serb
security apparatus, stayed in Belgrade until the end of
August, studying his problems, making his arrangements,
issuing instructions. In a return to the Comintern sent on
15 August he reported the Party strength at 11,879 full
members, 14,873 youth members, and 200,000 sym-
pathisers. They made up too small a total to carry a
successful rising unaided. There would have to be a
Popular Front, led by the Party, and open to all patriots
regardless of race, creed or political affiliation.

Towards the end of the month Tito went personally to
war, by train and motor-car. An Orthodox priest accompanied him to add credence at railway checkpoints to his
carefully contrived appearance of respectability, and to his

convincing identity and travel papers. He got off the train at Požega, lunched with the priest, and took the car that was waiting for him to the headquarters of the Partisan detachment at Valjevo, in western Serbia. The detachment, along with numbers of other Partisan detachments in the area, had already been active against both intrusive German soldiers and Serbian gendarmes who had remained at their posts. About thirty miles in a straight line to the south of Valjevo was Ravna Gora, where Draža Mihailović had been at his post at his Chetnik headquarters for the past three months.

THREE

The First Mission

Hudson's landing was, in the jargon of his new trade, blind. No advance arrangements were made, or could have been made, for his reception. The submarine that brought him to Montenegro was committed primarily to the sinking of Axis shipping in the Adriatic. To her captain the delivery of Funnies upon hostile coasts was an incidental chore that had to be fitted in between other, more pressing tasks. The time of arrival could not be forecast. Even if it could have been the Royal Navy would not have passed it to the representatives of an untested guerrilla group whose communications might be compromised, whose security was possibly unreliable, and who could well be subject to treachery and betrayal. Hudson and his three Yugoslav companions* disembarked on 20 September into an immediate future that carried only two known certainties. The Italians were in occupation of Montenegro, and a Chetnik headquarters was on Ravna Gora in Serbia, 140 miles away as the crow flew (and the crow would cross some intimidatingly rough mountain country on its journey). The

---

*The subsequent doings of these three are neatly illustrative of the torn loyalties, and the harrowing decisions, that faced resisters in wartime Yugoslavia. The two air force officers, Ostojić and Lalatović, stayed with the Chetniks to the end. In 1943, during heavy fighting around the Neretva river against the Partisans by a combined German and Chetnik force, Ostojić was one of the Chetnik commanders who ordered that all Partisan prisoners should be executed 'after a brief interrogation'. Dragičević, the wireless operator, remained for a while with the Chetniks, changed his allegiance to the Partisans and married a Montenegrin girl. Both he and his wife were killed during the German attack on Tito's headquarters at Drvar in Bosnia in May 1944.

job in hand was to get from Petrovac to Ravna Gora by the best means that could be improvised.

Some well-organised help almost immediately supplemented the improvisation. An anti-Italian and anti-collaborationist rising, an event of which the British had known nothing, orchestrated by a body of which they had known nothing either, had been in transitorily successful progress for some weeks. Communist Partisans had much support from the peasants, and controlled most of the villages, including those around Petrovac. The landing party was soon confronted and welcomed. Horses were provided for the carriage of the heavy radio equipment, and in a series of night cross-country marches through the mountains, with sleep by day in the shelter of woods, the group was escorted to Partisan Montenegrin headquarters at Radovce. The journey took five nights. At Radovce were two leaders who were to become outstandingly famous in the Partisan movement, and who after the war was over were not to benefit for long from their contribution to military victory and to the founding of the Marxist state.

Milovan Djilas, a subtle thinker, skilled propagandist, poetic writer and incisive man of violent action, had been the Party's Youth organiser before he raised the Montenegrin rebellion. He was shortly to leave Montenegro to rejoin the Partisan main headquarters, and throughout the war he was to remain at Tito's side. He became number three in the Party hierarchy, and was subsequently a Vice-President of Yugoslavia. In 1954 he was imprisoned after publishing trenchant criticisms of what he saw as a materialistic drift among the Party leadership in betrayal of its original idealism. He has been in and out of gaol ever since, more out than in, but forbidden to leave the country when out. The restriction has not inhibited him from publishing in the West some remarkable books about his philosophy and experiences.

Arso Jovanović, with Djilas at Radovce, was a former Royalist junior officer who cut his guerrilla teeth in the Montenegrin rising, established a formidable reputation for military effectiveness, and soon became Chief of Staff of the Partisan army. His was the credit for nearly all their successes. In 1948, when Tito broke with Stalin, Jovanović's preference was for Stalin. He was, it was officially put out, 'killed by Yugoslav frontier guards' while trying to escape to Romania to join the Russians.

Even had they been able to foresee their personal futures it seems unlikely that Djilas or Jovanović would have been deterred from doing what they were doing in Montenegro in 1941. The Communist revolution to which each was committed demanded sacrifices. They were ruthlessly indiscriminate in imposing sacrifice upon others, and fearless in their willingness to sacrifice themselves. It was an approach to life that two-and-a-half years later was to surprise, discomfit and not infrequently outrage a body of British troops to whom politics was more a matter for tolerant cynicism than for homicidal or suicidal fanaticism. Hudson, the experienced former resident of Serbia, had less reason for surprise and no latitude for either discomfiture or outrage. His job was to encourage as many Yugoslavs as possible to fight Germans.

Djilas has given an account of Hudson's first meeting with Partisans.* Djilas himself was scrupulously courteous, but mistrustful of a representative of 'British imperialism' who worked for an intelligence service with a reputation for devious ingenuity for which Djilas had a flatteringly exaggerated respect. Since, however, Britain was now an ally of the Soviet Union, it behoved Djilas to be as co-operative as possible with this otherwise suspect emissary. In any case, as Djilas soon found, Hudson was not nearly as tricky as was feared. He made no attempt to conceal either his familiarity with Serbo-Croat or his intention of making his way to Mihailović. He said unequivocally that his role was to signal to British intelligence about the enemy. He asked about the chances of recovering a radio hidden by him in Montenegro before the April collapse. At Partisan request he applied his engineering background to a

---

*Hudson doubtless wirelessed his version to SOE in Cairo, but a copy no longer exists. When the Afrika Korps reached Alamein in the summer of 1942, British staffs in Cairo were ordered to burn their records in case there was a German breakthrough. All Hudson's earlier signals, copies of the replies, and papers about his mission went up in smoke before SOE was evacuated to Jerusalem. The lack of these records caused British planners much subsequent confusion about Yugoslav internal developments. The Djilas account is in his book *Wartime*.

survey of the plain at Radovce to see if it could be turned into an airstrip. It could, he advised, with some extension work.

He stayed at Radovce for five days. Djilas's impression of him was that he was 'restrained, even cold – just as we imagined Englishmen to be. . . . Very sparing in humour, he was more like a civil servant than an adventurer.' It is not a description that tallies closely with those from Hudson's friends, who recall an athletic extrovert given on occasion to knocking out people in bars with whom he was in disagreement, but it says something for the self-disciplined restraint of a man instructed to investigate and recommend, not empowered to commit. If he left few memories of warmth, he certainly generated a respect that is evident in later passages in Djilas's book about his war.

Arso Jovanović and a Partisan escort went with Hudson and the two air force officers on the next leg of their travels. As before, there were horses for the radio, and as before there was a hard, slogging march through the mountains, forests and valleys. Hudson briefly met Tito at his new headquarters in Užice, a small west Serbian town from which the German garrison had recently withdrawn in the face of Partisan attacks. Tito was outspoken about Mihailović's failure to combine in active operations against Germans.

Jovanović remained with Tito. Hudson and his two air force envoys from the Royalist government-in-exile tramped on to Ravna Gora. They completed their march in mid-October, nearly a month after being rowed ashore from the submarine at Petrovac. It did not take long in the company of Mihailović for Hudson to appreciate that there was an almost irreconcilable schism between the two resistance movements, one the embodiment of a romantic devotion to a proud, ramshackle monarchy, the other to him an entirely unexpected vigorous local manifestation of an international revolutionary conspiracy. The breach's long-term political resolution was in any case nothing to do with him. An immediate compromise was what he needed, a tactical, temporary burying of differences that would unite Chetniks, Partisans and the distant British war machine of which he was the sole representative present, against the only enemy who really counted. He did his best, energetically.

*

In August, almost immediately after Tito's arrival in the area from Belgrade, Mihailović had met him at Struganik. Their talks were inconclusive, but not unfriendly. The differences of approach were identified and defined. Tito wanted early co-operative armed action against the Germans. Mihailović was against premature adventures that he thought would prejudice ultimate victory.

So Tito went ahead without Mihailović. The revolt scored many initial successes, and spread fast. A number of Chetnik leaders joined it in defiance of Mihailović's orders, and they had exhilarating successes too. They kept their independence of command, but operated jointly with the Partisans, while their commander stayed angrily and aloofly inactive on Ravna Gora. There was a surge of recruits to both Partisans and Chetniks. There were also some defections. A few Chetnik bands, one led by a bellicose Orthodox priest, transferred *en masse* to a body that demonstrably hit the enemy where it hurt instead of sitting about advancing theories on how it might best be done.

During this preliminary period the Germans were off-balance, surprised by and unprepared for what was happening to them. Tito, who genuinely wanted a united resistance as a part of his Popular Front concept, continued to urge Mihailović to join in. Mihailović preserved his inhibitions, but authorised some limited Chetnik operations.

Mihailović's reservations were strengthened by the tidings brought to him by Ostojić and Lalatović, Hudson's travelling companions. The message they delivered, and possibly embellished, from the government-in-exile was that Mihailović's renown as a guerrilla leader had become a matter of international legend, and that he could rely upon wholehearted British backing. British radio propaganda was already persistent in stressing these two points, and the current Russian anxiety to placate their only allies – the British – found one of its expressions in identical radio propaganda praising Mihailović. Not surprisingly, he began to wonder why he, the legitimate resident representative of his country's lawful government, was having to trim his military policy to conform with that of an emergent brigand who a few months ago had been high on the Wanted List of the Royalist security police. But the brigand, manifestly powerful, and for the time being at least militarily triumphant, could not be ignored.

Mihailović sent to him to ask for his detailed views on how Chetnik–Partisan co-operation could be formalised. Tito's reply listed twelve requirements. Some made plain common sense. Joint operations, joint equipment and supply, joint sharing of war booty, joint local commands, joint commissions to adjust differences. The rest, largely proposals for the administration of liberated areas, were politically unacceptable. Tito wanted national liberation committees to replace the traditional organs of local government, regarded by him as discredited, regarded by Mihailović as one of the things that he was fighting to preserve.

Tito agreed to meet Mihailović on Ravna Gora to discuss the twelve-point letter and the other unresolved differences. It was the last time they met. Hudson was excluded from the talks. Tito wanted him in, in the hope that if the negotiations broke down, as seemed likely, Hudson would report to the British that the blame lay with Mihailović. Mihailović wanted no foreigner present at an internal disagreement over purely Yugoslav domestic matters.

There was accord on some minor points, none on anything of substance. While the talking continued, the latent friction between some of the Chetniks and some of the Partisans with whom they had been collaborating had already led to fighting between the two, over such bones of contention as who should stay in occupation of objectives taken in joint ventures, and who had let down whom in abortive attacks. The carefree days of attacks on lightly manned, unorganised German positions were in any case coming to an end. The Germans put in a major offensive against both groups of quarrelling rebels. Then, in late October, came the ghastly massacre at Kragujevac, the turning by Mihailović of all Chetniks upon all Partisans, and three weeks of ferocious in-fighting. Towards the end of November attempts were made, with Hudson prominent in them, to patch up a truce. They were of little relevance. The German sweep retook the towns earlier occupied by Partisans or Chetniks, cleared the valleys and drove away

or dispersed both parties. Hudson, the tireless inter-
mediary, was with Tito when the assault was really pressed
home.

The small town of Užice, the Partisan stronghold where
Hudson had first met Tito during the previous month, was
attacked by German infantry supported by armoured cars,
artillery and aircraft. In conjunction with the action against
the town, another force of infantry, with further armoured
cars on the sparse roads, was sent to intercept the escape
routes through the mountains to the south-west. The
Partisans withdrew from the town, Tito and Hudson
together in a limousine being among the last to leave. They
stopped at a gorge to watch demolitions being prepared
and Tito sent off the car to take a message to his troops
further ahead in the retreat. They and their small escort
came under almost immediate attack from low-flying
aircraft, and they passed some time sheltering behind a
stone wall amid a growing disturbance by bombs and
machine-gunning. When they heard the sound of orders
shouted in German among the infantry follow-up they
decided that, bombs or not, it was time to go. They
scrambled down a hillside to a stream, followed a ravine
and rejoined the main body at two o'clock in the morning,
a reunion that brought much relief to a worried Partisan
staff.
  Hudson stayed with the Partisans while they extricated
themselves from the German attempt at interception and
evaded the follow-up, at the cost of extensive casualties and
the loss of equipment. They reached the mountains of the
Sandžak, where much Partisan reorganisation, rethinking
and replanning took place. A few Serbian units were sent
back again to stir things up once more in Serbia. Hudson,
who as usual was open about his intention to rejoin
Mihailović, went with them, with Tito's blessing.
  Hudson's Serbian escort took him safely to the edge of
Chetnik territory, and he continued alone. But by the time
he reached Ravna Gora again Mihailović had vanished. In
accordance with good guerrilla tactics his followers had
melted away in dispersal in the face of an elaborately
supported attack by a superior conventional force. The

good guerrilla tactics had been unmatched by good guerrilla manners. Mihailović had left no word of his whereabouts to his only link with the outside world, his Allied liaison officer.

Hudson, out of touch with both Chetniks and Partisans, isolated among inhospitable Balkan mountains with viciously aggressive Germans in the towns and valleys and a developing depth of snow on the heights, spent a miserable, lonely winter. He kept out the cold by dressing in skins, and he assuaged his hunger by scavenging for roots in abandoned farms. Peasants helped him, but he was sparing of the exploitation of their generosity. The penalty for them if they were detected would be death for themselves and their families, probably preceded by torture.

He was also out of touch with his base in Cairo. He had hidden his wireless, but the batteries were flat. When his silence had been prolonged beyond the point at which any reasonable hypothesis could account for it, SOE posted him as missing, believed killed.

FOUR

The Atherton Fiasco

Hudson's signals ceased in late November 1941. Mihailović went off the air during the same month. It seemed probable to SOE Cairo that the Germans in Serbia had dispersed and chased away both Mihailović's and Tito's followers, and that if Hudson were still alive, which was uncertain, he was with one or the other. Hudson's fate aside, there was an urgent need to find out what was happening in Yugoslavia. It was decided to send in three missions blind, to discover what they could. These were code-named Henna, Hydra and Disclaim. The first two went by submarine, the third by parachute. Henna was exclusively a Royal Yugoslav enterprise. Hydra and Disclaim were mixed British and Yugoslav.

Henna and Hydra were the first to go. They embarked at Alexandria in HMS *Thorn* in mid-January 1942. *Thorn* set a course for the Adriatic, and on 27 January landed the Henna party on the Dalmatian island of Šolta, about ten miles from the port of Split. It was a two-man team of Slovenes, Lieutenant Rapotec and Sergeant Shinko. They had a wireless and were well supplied with Italian lire. It was a long time before they were heard from again.

Thorn took Hydra Mission much farther south, to Petrovac in Montenegro, where Hudson had begun his adventures. Hydra was commanded by Major Terence Atherton, in civilian life a journalist who had worked for ten years in Belgrade, and whose wife was a Bosnian Moslem. His radio operator was an Irish sergeant named O'Donovan. The third member of Hydra was Captain Nedeljković of the Royal Yugoslav Air Force. As with Hudson's party, Atherton and Nedeljković had separate instructions from separate sources. Atherton's orders came from SOE Cairo. Nedeljković's were from the Royal Yugoslav government, transmitted through their military staff in Egypt.

Atherton's brief was to get in touch with the Communist bands reported in October by Hudson as being active around Podgorica (now called Titograd) near the Albanian border; to gather what word he could about Hudson and Mihailović; to signal back information about the relationship between the Chetniks and the Partisans; and to identify Partisan leaders and the location of their headquarters. He was to make arrangements to supply the Partisans by sea. He was to stay in Montenegro.

Again as with Hudson, Hydra Mission was soon in the company of the Lovćen Partisans. Their welcome was distant. The Hudson precedent had not been reassuring. Hudson's two Royal Yugoslav Air Force companions were now with Chetnik bands, fighting ferociously against the Partisans. Atherton had brought yet another Royal Yugoslav Air Force officer with him. The Hydra party were treated with reserve, and were marched across country to the headquarters, in a small village near Nikšić, of Ivan Milutinović, Djilas's successor as the senior Communist in Montenegro. There Atherton offered to provide Milutinović with automatic weapons, boots, uniforms and so on, and pressed for a meeting with Tito. Milutinović passed this news in a message carried by courier to Tito, then at Foča in Bosnia, adding that he would hold the Hydra party until he had found out what they were really up to. As the days went by Milutinović's suspicions developed further. Atherton, 'a very sly character', claimed to be unable to raise Cairo on his wireless, had accepted Partisan signals for despatch but had not said whether or not there had been replies, and gave no explanation of why his set would not work. Nedeljković seemed 'very suspicious and scared'.

It is of course quite possible that Atherton's set was genuinely out of order. But Partisan sensitivities, always sharp, were particularly so at the moment. Tito, through a radio transmitter secreted in a cellar in Zagreb, was negotiating with the Russians for the despatch to the Partisans of a Soviet military mission. The Russians had little prospect in practical terms of sending one. They had been forced so far back by the German army that they were almost out of flying range of Yugoslavia. Tito nonetheless was still hoping. The report of Atherton's unexpected arrival had complicated the issue. It became more complicated still on the night of 5 February, when Disclaim Mission were parachuted by an aircraft based on Malta to Romanija Mountain in eastern Bosnia.

The leader of Disclaim was Major Cavan Elliott. With him were a British radio operator, Sergeant Robert Chapman, and two Royal Yugoslav soldiers, Lieutenant Crnjanski and Sergeant Miljković. Within two days of their drop they were captured by Ustashi, taken to Sarajevo and interrogated. A report of what they told their questioners was passed immediately to the Partisans by a Ustashi colonel, a Partisan agent who later became a Partisan officer. The two Yugoslavs claimed to have been flown from Benghazi. 'The British officer states that he has nothing to say.' The prisoners were taken to Belgrade by the Germans.

By coincidence, Elliott's group had parachuted close to a landing strip that had been prepared, in provisional agreement with Moscow, for the arrival of the Soviet military mission should the request for one materialise. Tito was left wondering whether, without his knowledge, arrangements had been made to send a joint British–Soviet mission. There was much speculative and cautious correspondence between various Partisan headquarters.* Tito now had further reports about the Henna Slovene party. It had made its way successfully from Šolta to the mainland. Tito decided to refer 'the whole question' of these three unsolicited liaison parties to the Comintern in Moscow. He asked what to do.

He also told Milutinović to send the Atherton Mission to the Partisan Supreme Staff at Foča. Milutinović showed such reluctance, and became so critical of the Atherton team, that Tito began to wonder if there were a genuine danger that Milutinović might dispose of the problem by disposing of Hydra Mission. A message from Tito, 'Inform the comrades that they will answer with their heads that

---

*The correspondence is quoted extensively in F.W.D. Deakin, *The Embattled Mountain* (Oxford: Oxford University Press, 1971).

this mission arrives here in one piece,' put an end to any chance of that. But it must be remembered that all these exchanges were by means of written messages carried over long distances through mountainous country by couriers travelling on foot in conditions of civil war. There were long delays between despatch and response.

Atherton reached Tito at Foča on 20 March. The Partisan staff prepared a dossier of evidence of Mihailović's collaboration with Axis units. Its persuasiveness was underlined by the coincidence that at the time of Atherton's arrival the Chetniks had mounted an anti-Partisan offensive. Tito reported to Moscow that Atherton agreed that a new Yugoslav government of 'democratic elements' should be formed. A few days later Tito was writing of squabbling among the British party, carried to the point where Atherton and Nedeljković ate separately and 'do not go about together'. And then, on the night of 15 April, after Atherton had dined with Vlatko Velebit, a senior member of the Partisan Supreme Staff, the Atherton mission disappeared. They left their wireless behind. They took with them General Novaković, an ambitious and unstable Royal Yugoslav Army regular officer.

Novaković, possibly patriotic, certainly confused and confusing, had earlier escaped from a military hospital, and had negotiated successively and unsuccessfully with Mihailović, with Kosta Pećanac, the leader of the official Chetniks openly in collaboration with the Germans, and with the clandestine Communist committee in Belgrade. All, for varying reasons, mistrusted him. He had then set up a private resistance movement of his own, that from time to time operated in conjunction with local Partisan units. This unilateralism added to the complexities of an already complex situation. Eventually Tito had ordered that Novaković and his private army should be disarmed and brought to his headquarters. Now Novaković had fled. Atherton may have had sound reasons to run off with this curious travelling companion. Whatever they were, they did nothing to diminish Tito's suspicions of Atherton himself and of Atherton's employers.

Atherton's disappearance has never been satisfactorily accounted for. It has been hinted that he might have scented a chance to gather material for a really sensational newspaper story, and that he allowed this consideration to override the responsibilities with which he had been charged. Whatever were his motives, he left behind him a cloud of confusion, Partisan suspicion of British intentions and a reputation for inexplicable deviousness. He remained a source of contention after his death.

While Atherton was still at Foča, Tito had sent a confidential letter to the Party leadership in Croatia. Atherton cannot have inspired its sentiments entirely by himself, though he seems to have provided good cause for the reinforcement of existing doubts. One paragraph gives the flavour of the letter:

> We have proof that British policy aims at sabotaging and compromising the struggle for national liberation so that when the situation is favourable and Italy leaves Hitler and comes within their grasp, the British will land troops in Dalmatia and elsewhere and appear as 'liberators' to save the country from chaos. To this end about ten [*sic*] so-called military missions have already arrived and are doing their dirty work in different parts of Yugoslavia. One such mission has arrived at our headquarters, another has landed in Dalmatia, and others are in different parts of the country, exactly where we do not know.

The letter went on to blame British assistance for recent Chetnik successes against the Partisans in Montenegro. Its contents were to be shown only to 'leading persons in the Army and Party'. Publicly, the alliance between the Soviet Union, Britain and the United States was to continue to be stressed, and the last two were to be depicted as the allies of the Partisans. 'But their agents and pawns inside our country must be opposed.' (The United States had been brought into the war by the Japanese attack on Pearl Harbor in December 1941.)

In the event, after Atherton had vanished neither Tito nor any other Partisan leader was to see a properly briefed and accredited British agent for more than a year, although from time to time escaped British prisoners-of-war or baled-out aircrew on the run found their way into Partisan hands. During this interlude of no physical British presence and no form of communication whatsoever, Tito concluded that the British authorities held him to be responsible for the murder of Atherton. There is no room for doubt that Atherton and O'Donovan *were* murdered. There is equally no doubt that when Atherton's disappearance from Foča was discovered the Partisan Supreme Staff mounted a pursuit led by the head of their Security Section, and sent out search-parties to beat likely escape routes by the River Drina, the assumption being that Atherton and 'that old skunk of a general', Novaković, were heading for Mihailović's headquarters. Tito interpreted Atherton's defection in suspect company as conclusive evidence of a convoluted British plot to devote its support and supply exclusively to the Chetniks. All Partisan pursuers and searchers reported failure.

On 10 May, twenty-five days after the Atherton group's departure from Foča, Nedeljković, travelling alone, made his way to a Chetnik *odred* (or group) commanded by Major Ostojić, who had been one of the two Royal Yugoslav companions of Hudson at his submarine landing of October 1941. Ostojić reported to Mihailović. Mihailović signalled to the government-in-exile in London that he had heard for the first time that another British mission was in Yugoslavia. Atherton, from 'somewhere in Bosnia', sent a letter through the Chetnik courier system to Mihailović to say that he was trying to reach him. Hudson, who had regained contact with the Chetniks and was now back with Mihailović, went to question Nedeljković at Ostojić's headquarters. Only Nedeljković's account of this interview survives. (Hudson's signalled report was one of the casualties of the big SOE bonfire of papers in Cairo in 1942.) The Nedeljković version was that Atherton and O'Donovan had parted from him and were making towards Serbia.

By 20 June there was still no sign of Atherton and O'Donovan. General Novaković had written to Mihailović in self-abasing words, undertaking not to rock the boat again. Hudson had for some time been urging that a formal investigation was essential. So had the Royal Yugoslav government in London. Mihailović convened it, in the shape of a former gendarmerie officer. Its findings, transmitted in summary and commented upon by Hudson to Cairo, were that the 'escape' from the Partisans at Foča had been engineered by General Novaković in collaboration with Spasoje Dakić, a Bosnian Chetnik leader. For a week the group hid in a cave near a small village by the River Drina. There was quarrelling in the cave between Novaković and Nedeljković on the one hand and Atherton on the other. On 22 April Atherton and O'Donovan, accompanied by Dakić, left. Some time later Dakić, wearing Atherton's boots and bearing Atherton's binoculars, arrived at Mihailović's headquarters. No bodies were ever found. Nor was the mission's fund of 2000 gold sovereigns and 1,000,000 lire. To Hudson it seemed probable that Dakić had killed Atherton and O'Donovan for the money. Never again was a British mission sent in carrying such large sums.

Dakić, reported Hudson, paid only nominal allegiance to Mihailović. He was one of the quasi-independent Chetnik operators over whom Mihailović had little or no control, but for whose actions he was later to be held responsible. In this case, concerning the deaths of Atherton and O'Donovan, Hudson believed that Mihailović knew at least something of what had happened. Whether he did or not, Mihailović made the most of an opportunity to use the incident as an instrument of anti-Partisan propaganda. As early as 27 May, over three weeks before the formal enquiry, and at a time when there had been no overt suggestion that Atherton was dead, Mihailović had told the London Yugoslavs that Atherton and O'Donovan had been murdered by Partisans. Mihailović had declared 'open warfare' against Tito's forces.

The story was spread assiduously both within and outside Yugoslavia. The two Slovenes of Henna Mission, Rapotec and Shinko, who had been landed on Šolta in January, picked it up on their extensive travels. Rapotec got out to Istanbul, using a forged Italian passport, at the beginning of July. He passed on the story to British intelligence officers. In London, the Yugoslav Prime Minister, quoting 'a report from Madrid', told the Foreign Office that Atherton had been killed by Partisans who had taken the money meant for Mihailović. In February of the following year, 1943, the *New York Times* printed a story from their London correspondent about the killing by Partisans of

British officers, including Atherton. Moscow sent the relevant part of the text to Tito. His rebuttal was broadcast on Radio Free Yugoslavia, the resistance propaganda station situated at Kuibyschev deep in the Soviet Union. Atherton, O'Donovan and Nedeljković had, he said, come to Partisan headquarters. 'They left as freely as they came, although playing an obscure role.' Partisan obligations to the Allies induced them to keep silent about Atherton's activities. There might be an opportunity for explanation after the war.

Much later, when further British officers were parachuted to Yugoslavia both to Mihailović and to Tito, attempts were made to discover once and for all what had really become of Atherton and O'Donovan. By the nature of the times, and given the interests of those questioned, the enquiries could only be partial and superficial. But such evidence as there was suggested that the two had indeed been murdered for gain by Dakić.

Of the Yugoslavs closely associated with Hydra Mission, General Novaković was captured and shot by Partisans of the 5th Montenegrin Brigade in late 1943; Dakić was killed in 1946 in a sweep against surviving Chetniks by what was by then the army of the Socialist Federal Republic of Yugoslavia; and Nedeljković vanished from Mihailović's headquarters, shortly after he had arrived there, as surreptitiously as he had departed from Tito's a few weeks earlier. There was a suggestion that the Germans might have taken him later. If so, they left no more trace of him than he did of himself.*

Of the three missions sent to Yugoslavia in early 1942, the two British-led ones had ended in disaster. Cavan Elliott's Disclaim team had been rounded up before they had the chance to achieve anything. Atherton with Hydra Mission might have had deviously constructive intentions, but if he had it will never be known what they were. His legacy to both Tito and Mihailović was one of enhanced suspicion of British machinations. The Slovene Henna party got one of

---

*An absorbing account of the Atherton episode appears in Deakin's *The Embattled Mountain*.

its members out, the one debriefed by SOE representatives in Istanbul. But Rapotec's prime loyalties were to the Royal Yugoslav government. It had to be assumed that his report was at least in part selective.

Hudson, once again the sole British armed presence in Yugoslavia, remained with Mihailović. He still had his own codes. He had no wireless of his own. He was dependent upon Mihailović for the use of his. Although Hudson was in no sense under duress his movements were circumscribed physically by the need to stay largely within areas under Chetnik control. SOE Cairo were no closer than they had been at the start of the year to assembling an informed and comprehensive picture, details supplied by a spread of dispassionate observers, of what was happening in the largest country in the Balkans.

One communications disability was lifted in late August 1942. A British officer with two wireless operators, and extra sets, parachuted successfully to the Bosnia-Montenegro border and joined Hudson. Hudson now had his own secure link with Cairo. Mihailović, whose own codes were thought (rightly) to have been compromised and read by the Germans, was now in regular touch with his exiled government in London. The British officer who had dropped in with the signallers and their equipment was Captain Charles Robertson. He was a Yugoslav by nationality and a ship's wireless operator by peacetime profession. His reports supplemented those of Hudson. The joint burden of both was that Mihailović, as a matter of policy, was not engaged in serious operations against either the Germans or the Italians; that Montenegrin Chetniks under Mihailović's control had entered into accommodations with the Italians under which the Chetniks would keep their parts of Montenegro peaceful in exchange for a supply of Italian food, clothing, weapons and ammunition; and that Mihailović's top military priority was the elimination of the Communist Partisans, not the harassment of Italians and Germans.

SOE Cairo wanted to know more about all this, from a source other than Hudson, who might be right, but who also might be misinformed, over-tired by his experiences of the past year, or compromised. Some credence was given to the last possibility by Hudson's failure to include in his signals his security check, an unobtrusive use of an agreed word or phrase that would indicate that he was not being coerced. Colonel S.W. Bailey was the man chosen to supersede Hudson. There were delays between his selection and his despatch. He first had to be parachute-trained. The training was followed by a recurrence of malaria. Then there was an acute shortage of suitable aircraft. Bailey was not dropped to Mihailović until Christmas Day, 1942.

He landed on Sinjajevina Mountain in Montenegro, about ten miles to the north of Kolašin. Like Hudson, Bailey had worked before the war at the Trepča mines. He spoke fluent Serbo-Croat, had taken an experienced interest in Yugoslav political developments, and before the German invasion had been a leading figure in the small Section D and SOE group in Belgrade. He had been with SOE ever since. His instructions were to evaluate the military usefulness of the Chetniks, to urge Mihailović to be more active, immediately, and to suggest means by which the Chetniks and the Partisans could be induced to co-operate in joint action against the Germans and the Italians. Bailey brought with him letters of introduction to Mihailović from Anthony Eden, the British Foreign Secretary, and from the Commander-in-Chief, Middle East. Both letters were emphatic about the need for Mihailović to begin at once to make the utmost contribution to the common war effort.

FIVE

Evaluating the Chetniks

On the day after his parachute drop, 26 December 1942, Bailey reported formally to Mihailović's Chetnik headquarters, in a small house on a low hill above the hamlet of Gornje Lipovo. Bailey's first impressions of Mihailović were of a medium-sized introvert with a melancholy expression. He was flanked by staff officers, in a little room crowded by junior officers, batmen, bodyguards and miscellaneous hangers-on. They were not, as Bailey was later to discover to his irritation, mustered specially for the occasion, but a regular feature of the Mihailović style of command. Neither at that first meeting, nor subsequently, was Bailey able to talk to Mihailović in private. It was a serious handicap to the leader of a military mission with a negotiating and bluff-calling brief of a high delicacy. The nearest that Mihailović would ever come to privacy, when Bailey pressed for it, was to reduce the number of his supporters to one: Lalatović, one of the two air force officers who had landed by submarine with Hudson in 1941. To these meetings with a limited cast Bailey always brought Hudson with him, to balance the teams.

A few of the Chetniks present wore items of military uniform, but the wear and tear of nearly two years of guerrilla life had caused their extensive replacement by homespun peasant coats and breeches, with rank badges still worn on the shoulders. All were long-haired and luxuriantly bearded. They had taken an oath not to shave or to cut their hair until the shame of their defeat in 1941 had been expunged by the liberation of their country. The headquarters was made up solely of staff officers, signallers and a small guard unit. Mihailović had no fighting troops under his direct command. Through his wireless sets he kept in touch with his outlying subordinate commanders in Serbia, Montenegro and Hercegovina, transmitting his orders and receiving their intelligence reports. Many of the transmitted orders were to do with military trivia, routine promotions, postings and so on, an administrative obsession with irrelevancies that Bailey soon diagnosed as Mihailović's greatest practical weakness. In the light of later knowledge, Bailey concluded that in fact there might have been some advantage in the crowding of the air waves with this hotchpotch of trifles. The Germans had broken Mihailović's codes and were listening in. The probability was that they were either baffled or became too bored to unscramble more than a fraction of the traffic.

The preliminary courtesies completed, Bailey wasted no time before beginning his task of assessing the military value of the Chetniks. He made it one of his first jobs to clear up the doubts that had developed in some British minds, notably in the Foreign Office, about the accuracy of Hudson's earlier reporting, and the related suspicion that Hudson might have been captured by the Germans and could have been signalling under duress. Hudson's account of Mihailović's attitudes did not accord with notions held in Whitehall and in Cairo, and fostered for international public consumption by the BBC, of a single-minded guerrilla leader, his constitutional status embellished by his recent appointment as Minister for War in the Royal Yugoslav government, who was at the head of a homogeneous resistance movement fighting hard against the German and Italian occupiers.

Hudson's version of what was really happening was summarised in a signal of his sent on 15 November 1942:

> Mihailović has . . . agreed to adopt the policy of collaboration with the Italians pursued by the Montenegrin Chetniks. . . . Mihailović remains opposed to undertaking sabotage against the Italians. He insists that they will collapse shortly, when he expects to secure their arms and equipment, with which he plans to defend Montenegro against the Germans. . . . In Serbia, Mihailović's Chetniks . . . are little more than symbols of

resistance. . . . When the general is satisfied that victory
is certain, blood will not be spared, but until then I
consider him perfectly capable of coming to any
understanding with either Italians or Germans. . . . I do
not know whether Mihailović has an agreement with the
Axis involving his inactivity in Serbia and their anti-
Communist drive in north-west Bosnia. . . .

Bailey confirmed that all this was true, that doubts about
the authorship of Hudson's telegrams were unfounded, and
that Hudson had an excellent grasp of all aspects of the
situation. This message from Bailey, and later ones in
which he said that the feud between the Partisans and the
Yugoslav army (i.e. the Chetniks) was so deep and bitter
that there was no hope of bringing them together on the
same territory, led to further consideration in Whitehall and
Cairo about the value of Mihailović to the Allied war effort.
The arguments evolved slowly, and were blurred by a
complexity of military, political and moral components.
Since it was clear from the most reliable of all possible
sources, the Germans' and Italians' own wireless traffic,
that the Partisans were fighting hard and holding down
large numbers of Axis troops, and it was equally clear from
Bailey's reports that the Chetniks were not, did it not make
military sense to transfer support from Mihailović to Tito?
Or, alternatively, to supply both, but to warn Mihailović
that, unless he became more active, support would be
withdrawn from him? Could political factors be omitted
from the equation? The Partisans were Communists. A
post-war Communist Yugoslavia would not be in British
interests. Should Britain really prejudice those long-term
interests for the sake of a short-term military advantage?
And what about the obligations, moral as well as formal, of
the British government to the government of an ally, the
Kingdom of Yugoslavia?
While these questions were being asked, answered or
begged, Bailey continued to observe, discuss with Hudson,
evaluate, report and recommend. Mihailović, he signalled,
had become so used to blind, unquestioning British
support, even if it was more to do with commendatory
propaganda than with material supply, that he thought the
purpose of the British Military Mission to be no more than a

conduit for demands for supply drops, all requests to be honoured promptly. He was deceitful about his true priorities, chief of which was the elimination of the Partisans. The time had come to treat him firmly. 'He must be made to realise that we can make or break him. In return for former we demand frank and sincere co-operation.' Not surprisingly, relations between Mihailović and Bailey were soon less than cordial.

The making or breaking of Mihailović was a phrase that over-simplified the options into polarities, doubtless used by Bailey in the interests of economising upon words in coded signals. What Bailey wanted to do, and what SOE in Cairo wanted Bailey to do, was to substitute a bending for the breaking alternative, to provide attractive inducements to make Mihailović amenable, and to threaten realistically to discontinue them unless he entered into serious action against the Germans and Italians. The only inducement likely to be persuasive was the delivery of elaborate supplies by air, on a regular basis. From the moment of Bailey's arrival, Mihailović had assumed that it would be immediately available. It was not. What was dropped, from the only two RAF aircraft which could be spared in a period of ten weeks from competing priorities elsewhere, was strong on elaboration and idiosyncratic to the point of idiocy. Whoever controlled the loading in North Africa was either half-witted or malevolent.

Bailey's only effective bargaining counter was subverted farcically by the arrival from the sky of, among a few more useful aids to warfare, 30 million Italian East African Occupation lire, overprinted with the word 'Ethiopia'; several hundred boxes of tropical anti-snake-bite serum; 500 left-footed boots; and another load of boots, correctly paired, but all of them size six. Bailey ignored instructions from Cairo to count the useless bank notes, and to furnish a receipt, countersigned by Hudson and Robertson. He dumped the tropical snake-bite remedy in the Montenegrin snow. The left-footed boots were an insoluble problem, but the size-six pairs, provided for some of the largest people with some of the largest feet in Europe, were put to good use in a distribution to children, a handsome gesture purportedly illustrative of thoughtful British humanitarianism. There were further difficulties over items of more direct military value. In one drop a consignment of grenades was packed in a separate canister from the fuse and detonator sets that had to be inserted to make the grenades live. It was a sensible division, designed to prevent an accidental explosion when the canisters hit the ground. It would have been more sensible still had Cairo sent advance warning of how the packing had been done. The two canisters became the centre of violent contention between two Chetnik commanders, who resolved their disagreement by taking one each. One went away with 600 unfused, and unexplodable, grenades. The other took 600 detonator sets with nothing to put them into.

The paucity of the airdrops, and the lunatic oddity of some of their content, enraged Mihailović to the point of a public denunciation of his British allies. His disappointment at the failure to supply him on the scale that he had assumed would follow naturally upon Bailey's arrival was compounded by two other severe irritants. He now knew that his comparative passivity, and his tolerance of the accommodations made by his Montenegrin commanders with the Italians, had been described in detail first by Hudson, and then by Bailey, to Cairo and London. A dilution of British support for the Chetniks seemed to him to be foreshadowed in recent BBC broadcasts. Hitherto, all guerrilla activity in Yugoslavia, whatever its provenance, had been credited by the BBC to Mihailović's forces. Now the broadcasters had taken to the praise of the fighting achievements of his deadliest enemies, the Partisans. Mihailović's temper broke at a christening ceremony at the end of February.

The christened was the child of the mayor of Gornje Lipovo. It was only fair to admit, wrote Bailey years afterwards, 'that by the time Mihailović lost control of himself a good deal of plum brandy had been consumed by all present except the baby'. Mihailović was bitterly critical of Allied policy towards his country and his movement. His own military priorities, he said, started with the need to liquidate his internal enemies in the order Partisans first, and then in succession the Croats, the Moslems and the Ustashi. Nothing that the Allies could do or threaten would turn him from his objective of exterminating the Partisans, or change his attitude to the Italians, his sole source of supply. He needed no further contact with the Western democracies.

Bailey reported this harangue, delivered by a man who was a minister in the Royal Yugoslav government as well as its Commander-in-Chief in the field, to London, where it provoked a considerable stir. The report arrived at a time when evidence of the effectiveness of Partisan operations against the Germans had accumulated to a degre that made it almost inevitable that the British policy of exclusive support to Mihailović would be changed to one of at least shared support for both the Chetniks and the Partisans. The matter went to the top. Churchill told the Yugoslav Prime Minister in London that he trusted that Mihailović would be instructed to take a line more in accord with the agreed approach of the Yugoslav and British governments. Unless he changed his policies towards the Italians, and to his compatriots who were actively resisting the enemy, the British government might cease to favour him to the exclusion of other resistance leaders. The phraseology was stylishly diplomatic. The message was unambiguous. It was passed by the Royalists to Mihailović, whose reply gave little satisfaction. He had always looked upon the Germans and the Italians as his principal enemies, he said. Before he could engage them properly it was necessary for him to dispose of all those standing in the way.

Some of those standing in his way at that time ceased to stand. They strode towards him. A major Partisan force moved down southwards, crossed the Neretva river and entered into Montenegro and Hercegovina. Mihailović disappeared from his headquarters and went off to co-ordinate a Chetnik battle against them. From early March onwards, Bailey and his staff, recently augmented by the parachuting in of Major Kenneth Greenlees, all still at Gornje Lipovo, heard the sound, coming from the north-west, of protracted, heavy gunfire. Mihailović's absence, the constant movement of Chetnik troops and the reason for the gunfire were not explained to Bailey. It was not too hard for him to guess.

Before the christening incident had soured almost irreme-diably the personal relationship between Mihailović and

Bailey, the two had agreed that nine additional British parties would be dropped to an assortment of Chetnik headquarters in different parts of Serbia. Despite the gathering scepticism in London and Cairo about Mihailović's seriousness as an opponent of common enemies, these sub-missions began to arrive in April. Each had a wireless link direct with Cairo, not routed through Bailey. Each was briefed to evaluate the effectiveness of the Chetnik organisation to which it was attached, and was equipped for the sabotage of communications and mining machinery.

The individual wireless links had been decided upon as a matter of operational convenience, but they provided an unplanned advantage to the weighers-in-the-balance in Cairo of the overall usefulness of the Chetnik effort. There were now ten independent reporting stations, each uninfluenced in its assessments by any of the others or by Bailey. The reports were uneven, but pointed almost unanimously in one direction. There were exceptional local Chetnik commanders who acted aggressively on their own initiatives against the Germans, the Italians and the satellite occupiers. The Chetnik movement as a whole was largely quiescent, or evasive about its intentions, or downright misleading. The picture in Serbia was remarkably similar to that in Montenegro painted by Hudson and Bailey.

The first of the new missions to go in, led by Captain Morgan, was to Poreč, in Macedonia. It was a blind drop, made against Bailey's advice. The advice had been wise. Morgan's party were soon prisoners of the occupying Bulgarian army. Three days later, on 18 April, a team commanded by Major Erik Greenwood landed in north-east Serbia, near Homolje. Greenwood was strengthened just over a month later by two additional officers, Captain Jasper Rootham and Lieutenant Hargreaves, a New Zealander. The group's aim, to be achieved it was hoped with Chetnik assistance, was to interfere with German shipping on the Danube and to see what could be done about sabotaging the huge copper mine at Bor. It was six months before the Danube enterprise came to partial fruition in an entirely British operation led by Greenwood. He caused considerable disruption, of a limited duration, to river traffic. The Bor mines, strongly guarded by White Russian soldiers enlisted in the German army, stayed untouched. The defences were too formidable for Greenwood's party to take on unaided with any hope of success. The Chetnik commander declined to provide the aid.

At much the same time in October that the frustrated Greenwood was eyeing the Bor mines, and feeling hard done by because of lukewarm Chetnik co-operation, a local Chetnik leader of a different cast was helping Captain Archie Jack's team to sever the railway line between Sarajevo and Belgrade by demolishing the bridge at Višegrad, about twenty-five miles to the west of Užice. Jack and his explosives specialists attended to the blow. The Chetniks supplied the necessary protection while the charges were laid. The resultant bang dropped the bridge into a river-bed in one of the largest bridge destructions in the Balkans during the Second World War (*the* largest, in the estimation of its perpetrator, Jack). It was an example of what could be accomplished, given the will. The example was rarely copied.

An area in which it was conspicuously not copied was Kopaonik, in the mountain borderlands between western Serbia and Montenegro. Major Neil Selby dropped there in late May, to take command of a party that had gone in a month earlier with Captain Wade and Lieutenant More. The resident Chetnik leader, a man named Keserović, was consistently obstructive. Selby passed three months in trying unavailingly to persuade Keserović to support him in demolitions of vulnerable stretches of the railway line running along the valley of the River Morava, and met a similar stonewall when he and his officers attempted a backdoor wooing of some of Keserović's junior commanders. Selby lost patience in late August. He decided to go over to the Partisans, who were doing some real fighting and whose nearest formation was not too far away on Jastrebac Mountain. Before his unilateral transfer of his services, he asked for instructions from Cairo. The Chetniks, he signalled, were more pro-Fascist than pro-Allies. Selby himself was prepared to go deeper into enemy-occupied territory with one wireless set and one man, 'if you so direct', and do more in one week than he had done in months on Kopaonik. He did not await the directions that he had asked for. He went. He was picked up by Serb quislings in a village called Kulina, and delivered to the Germans. In the gaol in Belgrade he was interrogated regularly by the Gestapo. He escaped from his cell, killed two SS men, and was himself killed when he reached the prison courtyard.

Another mission to come to grief dropped in mid-April. Its objective was to limit, at best to stop, the production of the Allatini chrome mines. Captain John Sehmer was the leader. A back-up party led by Captain Hawksworth parachuted in later. Five of the party were ambushed and captured by Bulgarians, who then shot them. Sehmer himself was not present at this ambush. He lived to fight again, and died in the following year in Mauthausen concentration camp, after capture in Slovakia in August 1944.

SIX

Backing the Partisans

Until shortly after Bailey was dropped to Mihailović on Christmas Day, 1942, SOE in Cairo knew very little about the activities of the Partisans in Yugoslavia. Hudson's early signals had referred to his meetings with Communist-led guerrillas, but Hudson had been off the air for months on end and such messages as he had managed to send when he rejoined Mihailović had necessarily been concerned largely with the affairs of the Chetniks. The Royal Yugoslav government-in-exile in London had encouraged the view that the only effective resistance movement in Yugoslavia was the one sponsored by them and led by Mihailović. Reports in the neutral press and on Radio Free Yugoslavia made it plain that a great deal of fighting went on in areas, Croatia and Slovenia, where Mihailović neither had, nor claimed to have, any influence. There was no information available to SOE to establish whether this harassment of the Germans and Italians was centrally directed or was the product of individual spontaneous local initiatives.

Hard evidence that the Partisans were a formidable fighting force had in fact been in British hands for months, but it had not been shown to SOE either in London or in Cairo. The knowledge that German wireless codes had been broken was a secret shared by a rigorously restricted small number of senior politicians, officials, service commanders and intelligence officers, plus the staff necessary to collate and distribute the material. Protection of the source was vital to the successful prosecution of the war. If the secret were blown, inadvertently or by the taking of specific action that could only have been taken with the help of information gleaned from German signals traffic, German codes would be changed, cypher machines replaced and a priceless well of intelligence about enemy intentions, movements and strengths would run dry. SOE was not on the distribution list for Yugoslav intercepts.

But the Foreign Office and General Headquarters, Middle East, were. Both did nothing in 1942 to foster relations with the Partisans. The Foreign Office were still hoping to promote, with Soviet help, a reconciliation between the Chetniks and the Partisans that would lead to a united resistance movement. The Partisans were known to be fighting much harder than were the Chetniks, but Mihailović was thought to be biding his time until the situation became favourable for an all-out onslaught upon the Germans and Italians. In any case, for most of 1942 there was no possibility of giving worthwhile help to any Balkan guerrilla force. It could only come from the Middle East, where Rommel had concentrated the minds of British commanders upon the saving of the desert army from destruction. All resources were needed to keep Rommel out. Nothing could be spared for distant Balkan adventures of no immediate strategic significance to pressing events in the desert. This last, naturally enough, was also the view of GHQ Middle East.

A chance posting enabled SOE in Cairo to become privy to the intercepts, and so to assemble an impressively accurate picture of the extent of Partisan activity. The SOE Cairo organisation was part civilian, part military. At the beginning of 1943 its civilian head was Lord Glenconner. His recently appointed military Chief of Staff was Colonel C.M. Keble. Keble, in his previous job at GHQ, had been cleared for access to the intercepts. His name was not deleted from the list after his transfer and he continued as a recipient. He saw no reason to point out that he was no longer eligible. All descriptions of Keble are scattered about with words like ambitious, devious, unscrupulous, unlovable, forceful and efficient. His almost insane personal ambition brought him to professional grief a few months later, but in the interim he became the progenitor of a decisive change in British policy towards Yugoslavia. He put his money on the Partisan horse, and he did it very skilfully.

Keble, without bothering about the propriety or, bearing

in mind the Official Secrets Act, the legality of disclosing the existence of the intercept harvest to anyone not on the closely controlled authorised list, took the two officers in the SOE Yugoslav Section in Cairo into his confidence. These were Major Basil Davidson, the Head of the Section, and his assistant, Captain Bill Deakin. From the signals, mostly *Sicherheitsdienst* (SD, the SS Security Service) messages sent within Yugoslavia, the two were able to plot on a map a developing mosaic of which German units were in action, where, when and against whom. The where was predominantly in Slovenia, Croatia and parts of Bosnia. The when was fairly frequently. The opposing whom was Partisan.

From the map and the intercepts Keble, helped by Davidson and Deakin, prepared a paper that summarised recent and current Partisan operations. It ended with the recommendation that since the probability was that the war would move to the northern shore of the Mediterranean within a few months (Rommel had been defeated at Alamein in the previous October, and the Afrika Korps were on the run), it was high time to get in touch with these so far uncontacted guerrillas who were causing so much trouble to the Germans. Their political colouring was militarily irrelevant. What mattered was to sustain the Partisan effort, which was attracting the attentions of a large number of enemy divisions which would otherwise be available against the British and the Americans. The first step should be for SOE to parachute in a mission, or missions, to see what could be arranged.

In the normal course of events this submission would have been fed into the decision-making machinery through Glenconner, and would have become the subject of much minuting and debate between the service chiefs, the Foreign Office and the London headquarters of SOE. Keble decided to short-circuit the formal processes by delivering it directly to the Prime Minister, due in Cairo at the end of January. Full colonels do not have personal access to prime ministers. By a happy coincidence Captain Bill Deakin had. In civilian life, Deakin was an academic historian. He had worked as a research assistant for Winston Churchill when the latter was writing his *Life of Marlborough*. What more natural than that Deakin should ask to be allowed to pay his respects to his old boss? The old boss assented, and later summoned Keble, who brought his paper with him. Keble's advocacy was convincing. Churchill, on his return to London, minuted that he agreed with the memorandum 'in general terms'. The Foreign Office liked it too. There were subsequent hesitations, changings of feet, and reservations when the scheme came up for discussion with SOE London and among the Chiefs of Staff, and it was a further two months before the policy of supporting both Chetniks and Partisans was adopted formally. But the prime ministerial endorsement and the approval of the Foreign Office were sufficient to allow Keble to start planning for the first parties to be dropped blind to locations deduced from the intercepts to be currently in Partisan control.

Planning became reality in May 1943. The first to go were a party of Communist Croats who had emigrated to Canada before the war, and who had been recruited to SOE by Bailey, now liaising with the Partisans' arch-enemy, Mihailović. The Croats were valuable both for linguistic reasons and because they knew their way around the area in which they were dropped. The precision of the intelligence garnered from the intercepts was demonstrated at once. Within a few days of their landing the Canadian Croats were signalling to Cairo from the main headquarters of the Partisan Croatian Command. A second exploratory group parachuted to eastern Bosnia was not heard from for some time. A third, led by Captain William Jones, a highly decorated, one-eyed Canadian veteran of the First World War, who was accompanied by Captain Anthony Hunter, dropped to the same area as the Croats. On 17 May the mission relayed to Cairo an invitation from the Partisan central headquarters in Montenegro: 'We regard co-operation with the Allies as logical. Let them send a liaison officer to our staff. He could parachute at once . . . near Durmitor.' The man selected by SOE for the task was Captain Bill Deakin.

Deakin's team consisted of Captain Bill Stuart, a Canadian who was the mission's Intelligence Officer; two signal sergeants, Wroughton and Rose;* an interpreter, another of the Canadian Croats named Starčević; and Sergeant Campbell of the Royal Marines, who combined bodyguarding with cypher-clerking. Code-named 'Typical', the mission was divided in two, the parts working jointly. Deakin and Stuart shared the leadership – Deakin represented SOE, Stuart the Military Intelligence Branch of General Headquarters in Cairo. Both were under the orders of GHQ.

Deakin at the time spoke little Serbo-Croat, which was why Starčević was brought along. Stuart was fluent in the language. He had in the past served in the Canadian Department of Immigration, where his job had been the screening of Yugoslavs applying to settle in Canada. Until the invasion of Yugoslavia in 1941 he had been attached to the British Consulate-General in Zagreb. Afterwards he had helped Bailey in the recruitment of the Canadian Communist Croats. There was one good reason, ignored by both Keble and Deakin, why Deakin should not have been on the mission at all. Deakin was in on the intercept secret. Such men were forbidden to place themselves within range of possible capture, in order to avoid interrogation by the Gestapo using its grisly techniques.

The mission was assembled and equipped in great haste. Further messages from the Partisan central headquarters, and passed through the mission in Croatia, made it clear that extensive fighting was in progress around the suggested

---

*It was a long time before 'Rose' disclosed to Deakin that his true name was Peretz Rosenberg, that he was a German Jew, and that he had been a pioneer settler in the 1930s on a Jewish commune in Palestine, then a territory mandated to Britain by the League of Nations. The Cairo branch of the Jewish Agency, whose longer-term objectives included the ending of the British Mandate and the establishment of the State of Israel, instructed Rosenberg, a gifted radio specialist, to volunteer for the British army. One of the tasks given to him by the Agency was to discover what he could about the fate of the Jews in Yugoslavia. He took a parachute course and found his way to Deakin's mission. After the war he became the senior signals organiser of the Hagana, the Jewish underground organisation dedicated to the eviction of the British from Palestine by force of arms. Deakin held Rosenberg in continued high admiration – 'Wroughton and "Rose" between them made possible the survival of our mission' – and visited him in Israel in the 1960s. They 'continued where we had left off'.

dropping zone. Eight German divisions were trying to clean up Montenegro and Hercegovina. 'Send quickly representatives and explosives . . . ,' was the last pressing message. A last-minute ruling from London forbade the taking of explosives. They would have to await Typical Mission's preliminary report on what the Partisans were up to. Deakin and Stuart argued that they could hardly arrive in the middle of someone else's battle without bearing some sort of gifts, and suggested medical supplies as both humanitarian and uncontroversial. This was agreed, only to be rescinded at the last minute, to Deakin's and Stuart's fury. The medical stores were unloaded from the aircraft waiting on Derna airstrip in Libya. A brief officers' mutiny, abetted by the RAF Station Commander, ensued. Stores and huts were plundered for boots, clothing, webbing equipment and so on, anything that might be remotely useful to hard-pressed guerrillas who had been out of touch with the outside world for two years. This booty was packed into canisters and put aboard.

On 24 May, a week after the initial Partisan invitation, there came a pressing signal from Montenegro. The Partisans would make reception arrangements on Mount Durmitor on the next night. The Germans were trying to advance with strong forces. If the weather were bad the Partisans would wait for one more night. The British must be no later.

The weather was bad. The aircraft, crewed by young New Zealanders, ran into an electrical storm that forced it off course. It returned to Derna. At three o'clock on the following morning, the pilot throttled back over identification fires laid out in the pattern of a St Andrew's cross. It was a very dark night. Aside from the fires, the only illumination came from a pervasive flashing of gunfire. The green light over the exit hatch came on, and Typical Mission jumped into the middle of one of the biggest battles of the Partisan war.

A strong wind blew the parachutes away from the signal fires below. The fires disappeared, and in total darkness each member of the party floated down to hit the unseen ground. Remarkably, nobody was injured in this landing, literally blind, on some of the wildest and rockiest country in Montenegro. Whistle signals brought them all together. Deakin flashed a torch at the aircraft. It came in for a second run and dropped the supplies containers, before winking a good-luck message and flying back to North Africa. Contact with the Partisans was established a little while later, in a manner that illustrated two Partisan characteristics with which many British soldiers were to become familiar during the next eighteen months: the uninhibited warmth of a human embrace, regardless of the sex of the embraced; and an equally uninhibited indifference to the conventions observed in the British armed forces over the discharge of firearms. Deakin, who had ordered his party to stay together while he went searching, bumped into somebody in the dark. The somebody cried out in Serbian, Deakin identified himself as a British officer, and was promptly hugged with enthusiasm. The hugger next fired off his rifle, thereby alarming the rest of Typical Mission, who ran up fearing that their joint leader was no more.

It was by now becoming lighter. More Partisans arrived, youths and young men dressed in a variety of civilian clothes and frayed items of grey uniforms, armed with a miscellany of weapons. They gave excited greetings, asked a barrage of questions, collected the stores from the containers and escorted the party away over a wide plateau. A three-hour march, over the plateau, through a burnt-out village, beside the Black Lake with Mount Durmitor looming behind it, past a single file of small ponies carrying wounded, brought them to a glade in a beechwood. Sitting in a rough circle on tree stumps in the clearing was a party of uniformed men, all armed. These stood up as Deakin's team approached. One, 'slim and neat in a grey uniform with no badges of rank . . . wearing an army side-cap and black riding boots', detached himself and came forward. He was clearly the leader. Deakin halted his party. They all saluted. It was the first direct British contact with Tito since the fiasco of the Atherton mission.

*

That night there started a forced march, savagely harried, that lasted for the best part of two months.* It was an epic achievement, a successful struggle for survival, expensively bought with lives and suffering. The price was exacted by a German command which aimed to squeeze Tito and the main body of his National Liberation Army into the jagged mountains and precipitous valleys of a rough triangle bounded by the Tara and Piva rivers and the convoluted mountain feature of which Mount Durmitor, at 7000 feet, was the highest peak. Once the ring was closed, the German objective was destruction. Not destruction as interpreted in the operational orders of most Western armies, a killing of some enemies, the wounding of others and the persuasion of most to surrender, but total annihilation. A captured German order, taken in the fighting during the early days of the march, prescribed exactly what the German commander, General Lüters, had in mind: 'After the successful and complete closing of the ring, the Communists will attempt a partial breakout through the front. Order: No man capable of bearing arms must leave the circle alive. Women to be searched in case they are men in disguise.'

Over 100,000 men were under German command in this essay in extermination. The 50,000 strong German element included the SS Mountain Division Prinz Eugen, the 1st Alpine Division and the Brandenburg Division. There were 40,000 Italians plus Ustashi, Chetniks and Bulgarians. There was a powerful backing of aircraft, armour to hold the ring, and artillery. The operation was code-named *Schwarz*. It did not accomplish its stated aim, but it did get a long way towards it. The long Partisan columns of ragged, hungry, weary men and women, bombed and machine-gunned from the air, mortared, shelled and machine-gunned from the ground, plodded up wooded mountainsides, slithered down the reverse slopes, forded or bridged swollen streams, climbed again. Progress was slowed to a devoted adherence to one of Tito's central tenets of Partisan warfare: the wounded and sick must not be abandoned. They grew in number daily, and were

*It is vividly and movingly described in Deakin's *The Embattled Mountain*.

escorted along, the worst cases carried in litters or held on to mules and horses, the rest helping each other, hobbling on sticks, dragging themselves up and down the ridges, through the quickly flowing waters of upland streams. Body lice, almost the badge of Partisan life, added to the casualties. There was an outbreak of typhus. For both sick and wounded there were from the start no drugs, and soon, for some, no bandages.

Typical Mission travelled close by Tito's headquarters group. The signallers, Rose and Wroughton, managed to send occasional brief messages to Cairo, reporting that the mission was still with the Partisans, under heavy pressure. There was no possibility of Deakin and Stuart being able to prepare, let alone transmit, considered assessments of the competence and strength of the Partisan movement. They were caught up in a communal striving towards extricating themselves from the Axis ring. By the second week in June, the last of the Partisan rations were given to the shock troops who in a self-sacrificial series of assaults had been clearing a way at the head of the columns. The mission was down to one tin of sardines. They shared the nettle soup of Tito's headquarters staff.

Among the trees on the hills looking down on the Sutjeska river, the headquarters and the mission with it became the dawn target of a mixed flying circus of Stukas, Dorniers, Henschels and miscellaneous light aircraft. The bombers bombed in geometrical patterns. Their machine-gunners machine-gunned from low level. The light aircraft threw grenades over the side. Tito and Deakin were hit by fragments of the same bomb, Tito in the shoulder, Deakin in the leg. Several of the Partisan escort battalion were killed. Deakin, one of whose boots had been blown off, limped over to talk to Stuart. Stuart was lying dead behind a tree. Rose, his wireless operator, had been saved by a pack of cards that he kept in his breast pocket. A bomb splinter was lodged in it. For the rest of the day, movement from the hill was impossible. A rock overhang gave some shelter from ceaseless air attacks, and an improvised barrier of stones diminished the effect of Spandau and rifle fire from German infantry in a position on a slope across the valley, on the other side of the Sutjeska river.

At nightfall the dead, Stuart among more than a hundred

of them, were buried. The Partisan advance guard crossed the valley, overran the German infantry posts in the dark, and moved on. The main body trudged after them, Deakin now astride an emaciated horse. They passed the German dead, stripped by their killers of clothes, boots, equipment and weapons in a standard exploitation of the Partisan chief source of supply, and came suddenly upon German soldiers grouped around a campfire in a little clearing in the woods. The Partisan leading scout silently knifed the sentry. The rest of the Partisan group with which Deakin now found himself, numbering about thirty, slipped through the trees on the edge of the clearing. Ahead, shock troops, in a series of murderously expensive attacks, had cracked a thin gap in the German ring. Bridles on the horses were muffled, everybody moved with noiseless care in a long single file between two German strongpoints, and the party was clear.

So were a great many other parties, of fighting troops, walking wounded and sick, and Tito and his staff, to a total of about 10,000 men and women. Left behind was the Partisan 3rd Division, with the role of doing what they could to protect the immovable casualties. These were split up into small groups and hidden in caves, clearings, isolated cottages – anywhere that gave a chance of avoiding detection. Few did avoid it. The depleted 3rd Division could not shield them all, and soon lost most of its effectives in ferocious diversionary assaults. The Germans were thorough and merciless. One by one the hospitals were located, and their patients and the Partisan girls tending them butchered. So were civilians who had helped, or who were suspected of having helped, the Partisans. When it was all over the German command ordered a body count of the enemy dead. In the fighting leading up to the encirclement, during the encirclement, and during the breakout, and also including the post-operational massacres, 5697 Partisans were killed. In addition 2537 civilians were shot, and fifty villages were burned. Not all prisoners were shot. The 1st Alpine Division, for example, took 498 and killed 411 of them.

There was still a long way for Tito, his 10,000 Partisans and the British Military Mission to march, but it was a journey largely unimpeded by enemies. Tito steered his columns towards central Bosnia, where he intended to set up a Free Territory in the richly forested mountains and valleys. Food was no longer a problem. There was plenty of it to be had from the farmlands which they crossed. The lack of medical stores remained a grave handicap. The mission was now able to send more than terse signals to say that it was still in being, but heavy fighting continued.

Deakin had been given a list of essential medical stores by the Partisan chief doctor in early June. An airdrop would have been impossible in the battle conditions of the time, but in July he indented to Cairo for the first sortie of what was to become a crowded programme of British air supply to the Partisans. Three drops in five days brought in enough drugs and dressings to enable the doctors and nurses to ease the sufferings of patients so bereft of elementary needs that bandages were being washed again and again until they disintegrated, and were stripped from the dying for use on those for whom there was hope. (Later, in August, when the new base in Bosnia was established, a British surgeon, Major Ian MacKenzie of the Royal Army Medical Corps, arrived by parachute to work with the Partisan doctors. Later still, after Partisan control of some areas had become, sometimes temporarily, sufficiently complete for airstrips to be levelled, incoming RAF supply Dakotas took back with them lifts of wounded for treatment in hospitals in Italy, Malta and Egypt. Similar cargoes went by sea from the Dalmatian island of Vis. Medical care was arguably the finest British service to wartime Yugoslavia.)

More than medical supplies were delivered by air. The path of the march took it across some of the railway lines that carried German military and economic traffic to and from the central hub of Sarajevo. The Partisan Supreme Staff had on its strength a demolitions specialist named Smirnov, an enthusiast of White Russian origin. Deakin signalled for plastic explosive. Smirnov and his sappers blew fifty-seven holes and destroyed twelve bridges on the railway layout in July alone. Also in July, Deakin's team was strengthened by the arrival of two more officers, Lieutenants Thompson and Mackay, and an additional wireless operator, Sergeant Crozier.

In general, Deakin got more or less what he had asked for in his airdrops, but he was not altogether spared from the vagaries that had bedevilled Bailey's dealings with Mihailović. Deakin too was sent a load of left-footed boots. Immense quantities of Atabrin, a prophylactic against malaria, were delivered to a part of Bosnia where malaria was unheard of. But Tito and his staff were clearly impressed by most of what they were getting, and by the potential for expansion of what was to them a novel method of replenishment.

Deakin himself had every reason to be impressed by what he had seen of the Partisans. The intercepts that he had studied in Cairo had shown without ambivalence that large numbers of Yugoslavs in different places were fighting sufficiently hard to require the undivided attentions of at least twelve German divisions, and an uncounted total of less effective Italian and satellite divisions. What had not been evident from the intercepts was that this Yugoslav resistance was effected by an organised, disciplined, powerfully motivated movement, centrally directed by a leader whose quality Deakin had been able to observe during the extreme and persistent pressures of a lengthy, pitilessly fought battle. It had been a quality of a very high order. When the heat of the extrication fight had abated, Deakin had more opportunity, through long conversations conducted in German, to build up a character sketch of Tito. Deakin preceded each of these talks with a small but rigid formality. Even if Tito were a few yards away, at a halt on a hillside or by a stream, Deakin would never simply wander over and start chatting. He always sent one of his Partisan escort to seek an appointment, in an extension of diplomatic practice to the field that both parties found to be convenient and proper.

The picture assembled by Deakin was of a calm, quietly authoritative man, tightly self-controlled, quick in decision, unruffled in adversity, fastidious about his personal appearance even in the rough-and-ready circumstances of guerrilla war. When the official business to do with military co-operation had been disposed of, Tito enjoyed relaxed talk. Deakin had expected to find himself dealing with an inflexible Communist zealot. There could be no doubt that Tito was zealous in his Communism, but he was open-minded in discussion and had a deep interest in all manner of subjects, a well-developed sense of humour and a pleasing wit. If it was British policy to bet on alternative Yugoslav resistance leaders, Tito was the man to back.

By August the long migration was reaching its end. There was a two-week pause on the plateau of Petrovo Polje, and then a final move, in so far as any Partisan move could be described as final, to Jajce, once the mediaeval capital of Bosnia. In this more settled ambience Deakin and his staff were able to piece together a sketch of the overall Partisan strength and organisation. They concluded that about 75,000 men were under arms in regular military formations, mostly led by former officers and NCOs of the Royal Yugoslav Army. The ideological purity of these divisions was preserved by the attachment of political commissars to units and sub-units. The commissars ensured that leadership stayed firmly in Communist hands, although perhaps only about a quarter of the soldiers were Party members. In addition to this main force there was a mass of locally raised bands and detachments under Partisan control, or conforming to Partisan principles where circumstances made detailed control an impossibility. Unlike the Chetniks, whose ethos was Serbian, the Partisan movement was a pan-Yugoslav body embracing all Yugoslav nationalities and determined to keep the state intact, albeit under different management.

Deakin wirelessed his recommendations to Cairo. They were unsentimental, concerned solely with the practical advantages, defined in terms of saved British blood and endeavour, of giving the maximum help to Tito and his Partisans. Deakin felt that the purpose of his own exploratory instructions had by now been satisfied. What was wanted was an officer of the rank of brigadier who should command a high-level mission, and through whom all communications to and from sub-missions should be channelled in the interests of enforcing a centralised control. The last recommendation was a product of experience. By now, in late August, there were ten British missions with Partisan units in Bosnia, Croatia and Slovenia, each in communication with Cairo, and none knowing much about what the others were doing. It was essential that the new brigadier, the senior British representative to the Yugoslav Army of National Liberation, should direct an integrated organisation and that he should be in a position to make it clear to Tito that he did so.

For a period of a year, from May 1943 when the Canadian Croats were the first British mission to go to the Partisans, a curious situation prevailed in which British officers were attached to the main and subordinate headquarters of, and were engaged on actual offensive operations with, two rival resistance movements each dedicated to the extermination of the other. Increasing supplies of weapons, ammunition and equipment were delivered to both. The supplies were provided on the condition that they would be used only against the Germans and the Italians, but the condition was incapable of enforcement. Once the stores had been handed over for distribution they were beyond the control of the liaison teams. There seem to have been few, if any, instances of a British liaison officer with the Chetniks being involved in direct fighting against Partisans, possibly because Mihailović was careful to cover his tracks in case his supply lines were cut off. There were plenty of occasions on which British officers with the Partisans were about when Chetniks, usually operating alongside Germans or Italians, attacked or were attacked. Deakin himself became temporarily unpopular with the Partisans when he declined an offer to interrogate three recently captured Chetniks – he heard them being shot as he walked away. He was later presented with a bulky dossier of written evidence in the shape of acquired enemy operation orders and signals which established conclusively that there had been active collaboration by the Chetniks with both Germans and Italians. He passed a summary of the papers to Cairo, where it added further fuel to the case against Mihailović.

But Mihailović was still the legitimate Royalist government's Minister of War and Commander-in-Chief, and the leader of a numerically powerful force that, if properly used in loose co-ordination with Allied enterprises elsewhere, could make a valuable contribution to the combined effort. The fighting in North Africa had been concluded successfully in the spring. The British and Americans landed in Sicily in July. Italy was to be next. The campaigns in both would benefit from major diversions across the Adriatic. The mission to Mihailović and the mission to Tito were upgraded in status and size. Each was to be commanded by a brigadier, with an enhanced liaison and communications staff. The prime function of the mission to Mihailović was to persuade him to fight and to furnish him with extra materials to do so. No persuasion of Tito was necessary. All that was required in his case was an orderly, systematic and comprehensive scheme for the delivery of the materials.

In late September 1943, Brigadier C.D. Armstrong, a regular soldier of twenty-five years' service who had fought at Dunkirk and in North Africa, was parachuted to Mihailović's headquarters, which since the April and May excitements in Bosnia with the Partisans had been moved first to Berane in Montenegro, and then to Serbia. Colonel Bill Bailey stayed on as Armstrong's second-in-command and political adviser. This book is about British participation in wartime Yugoslavia, which from that time onwards had less and less to do with co-operation with the Chetniks and more and more to do with support of the Partisans. It might be as well to take the Chetnik connection out of sequence, and to follow it through to the end of its story.

For six weeks after the arrival of Armstrong, the Chetniks fought the Germans with enthusiasm in the Sandzak and in eastern Bosnia. Italy had capitulated on 8 September, and Mihailović was able to secure much Italian booty, although his anger at not being given advance notice of the capitulation was extreme. This brief flurry of constructive activity was checkmated by the Partisans. They moved in to the area which the Chetniks had cleared of Germans. Armstrong's instructions from the Commander-in-Chief, Middle East, were specific about the need to obviate clashes between the two resistance movements. Armstrong was insistent upon a Chetnik withdrawal. Mihailović complied resentfully, and after that, in Bailey's words, 'at once relapsed into stubborn obstructionism and inactivity'.

The commonest way in which these traits were demonstrated was in a failure to issue orders that he had agreed to issue, or in the covert cancellation of orders that he had in fact issued. A proposed operation would be discussed by the leader of one of the British sub-missions and the local Chetnik commander. The commander would agree to carry it out, subject to authorisation by Mihailović. Armstrong or Bailey would recommend approval to Mihailović, who would agree. Thereafter, nothing would happen. The local Chetnik, when pressed, would deny that any orders had reached him, or he would become truculently evasive about what they were.

While these processes of procrastination were being repeated continuously, reports from the greatly increased spread of British missions to the Partisans were of hard fighting and of the holding down in Yugoslavia of a very large body of German troops. All realistic military cost-effectiveness studies demonstrated beyond doubt that a logistic investment in the Partisans paid a handsome dividend. The Chetniks were a wasting asset. Military and political opinion in London and Cairo began to shift rapidly to the view that there was little or no point in persisting with the alternative-leaders policy. Mihailović was to be given a last chance. Unless he took it, he would be abandoned.

The last chance was framed in a request for the demolition by the Chetniks of two strategically significant railway bridges, one over the Ibar river, one over the Morava, before 29 December 1943. The bridges carried the railway which supplied the bulk of the German forces in Greece. If this supply line were to be severed, the thinking ran, Greek guerrilla operations could be expanded to an extent that might precipitate a German withdrawal from the southern Balkans. (This was not altogether consistent with the objective of tying down German forces in the Balkans.) Both bridges were in a part of Serbia that Mihailović claimed to control. He agreed to issue orders for the two blows. He discussed with Armstrong the details of what additional explosives would be required and of the covering force necessary to protect the layers of the charges. By 30 December the bridges were still intact. Mihailović was asked to blow them without fail by mid-January. Nothing happened.

The British War Cabinet approved a recommendation

agreed between the Foreign Office, the Middle East Defence Committee and the Supreme Allied Commander, Mediterranean, that all supplies to Mihailović should be cut off. His attacks upon the Germans had been sporadic and unsatisfactory. He had authorised, or connived at, the collaboration of some of his subordinate commanders with the enemy.

The next step was the potentially dangerous one of the extrication of Armstrong's mission and its outlying sub-missions. The fate of Atherton two years earlier suggested that at least some Chetnik leaders might express their disappointment lethally. For safety's sake neither the Royal Yugoslav government nor Mihailović himself were at first told of the decision. Some of the sub-missions were given discretion, confidentially, to join up with the nearest Partisan unit. Others were brought in to the mission headquarters. So were several escaped allied prisoners-of-war who had been succoured by various Chetnik groups.

After this concentration, both the Royal government and Mihailović were told of what was in the wind, Mihailović in a message from General Paget, the Commander-in-Chief, Middle East. Paget asked for Mihailović's full co-operation over the evacuation of the mission and the prisoners. To his great credit, Mihailović accepted the obligation without reservation. To his equal credit, he and his Chetniks, from the time that they were discarded until they finally disintegrated, continued to give help and shelter to further Allied escapers, and to several hundred baled-out aircrew who jumped into Chetnik territory from damaged aircraft during the long series of heavy raids on Central and Eastern Europe in 1944.

Armstrong's mission, and its acquired escapers, were flown out from a Chetnik-held airstrip in central Serbia in successive lifts on the last three days of May 1944. With them went Colonel Albert Seitz, the United States Army Liaison Officer attached to Armstrong. The Americans later sent back a purely intelligence mission to Mihailović. A Royal Air Force organisation known as BATS, or Balkan Air Terminal Service, which specialised in the preparation of airstrips in occupied territory, was given every help in the provision of strips in Chetnik country from which Allied aircraft could collect shot-down aircrew.

These two manifestations aside, Mihailović ceased to be a factor in Allied military calculations.

In the remaining year of the war his fortunes declined with cumulative rapidity. Many of his followers left him to join the Partisans. He became increasingly reliant upon German help, and towards the end was reduced to negotiating with Pavelić and the Ustashi for a safe conduct for Chetnik wounded. As the fighting drew to a close, Mihailović and a small part of loyalists made for the mountains of Serbia. The loyalists became fewer, the peasants they relied upon for food more hostile or frightened to give it. He stayed free, a hunted man, until the spring of 1946, when one of the groups of OZNA, the Communist secret police, who had been after him, at last caught him. He was half blind, physically debilitated, and had been living for weeks on snails and herbs. The doctors restored him to strength for his trial and sentencing to death. The last words of his speech in defence were: 'I wanted much. I started much. But the whirlwind, the whirlwind of the world, carried me and my work away.'

Colonel Bill Bailey, the British officer who with the possible exception of Hudson was longest in direct contact with Mihailović, and who carried the weight of most of the Mihailović wrath when he found British policies to be inconvenient or British supply drops to be inadequate, had no doubts about the rightness of the British decision to transfer support from the Chetniks to the Partisans. But Bailey's endorsement of the British decision did not carry the corollary of a condemnation of Mihailović's stance. British objectives and Mihailović objectives diverged. The Western Allies were simply looking for the Yugoslav body that 'was killing the most Germans', so that the fighting load could be spread, the war shortened, and British and American casualties diminished. Mihailović was a Serb nationalist who stood by his oath of loyalty to his king, whose experience of appalling Serbian battle casualties and of murderous German reprisals on civilians during the First World War had convinced him that premature action would be a betrayal of his responsibility for the safeguarding of Serb lives, and whose negotiations and accommodations with his enemies were within a hallowed Balkan tradition of justifiable temporary expediency. He was also a mystic, a fatalist and a stubborn, brave, rather muddled man, who could not see that the war was changing everything, and that his ideal of restoring an unchanged Yugoslavia to a returned King Peter had become an illusion. The whirlwind of the world indeed carried General Draža Mihailović away.

SEVEN

The Arrival of Maclean

Possibly the only stimulus to which Tito and Mihailović reacted identically during the war in Yugoslavia was the Allied failure to reveal that negotiations for an Italian capitulation were in progress. Mussolini, the Duce, the founder of the Italian Fascist Party, the ambitious dictator who in 1940 scented quick, rich pickings and put his country into what three years later had developed into a disastrous war, stood down in July 1943, soon after British and American armies landed in Sicily and brought the fighting to the Italian homeland. Mussolini's successor as head of government, Marshal Badoglio, correctly read the writing on the wall, decided to change sides, and instituted secret talks with the Allies through emissaries. Agreement in principle was soon reached. The timing of the conversion of principle to practice was crucial. It was agreed that it would precede by one day a major Allied landing on the Italian mainland at Salerno, south of Naples. If word of this planned defection by an ally were to reach the Germans, the dangers of an efficient German pre-emptive response, which aside from its wider consequences could prejudice the Salerno undertaking, were obvious. The fewer people who knew of the Italian intentions, the better. Balkan resistance leaders, of untested discretion and with dubious standards of communications security, would have to find out what was happening when it had happened and had become public knowledge.

Mihailović and Bailey, Tito and Deakin, first heard of the Italian switching of allegiance through BBC news bulletins. Mihailović upbraided Bailey furiously for concealing from him information that, passed over with advance notice, would have allowed Mihailović to make detailed plans for the swift acquisition of Italian weapons and equipment, instead of the improvisation that would now be necessary. Bailey could only reply that it was news to him too. Later in the day, 8 September, a signal from General Headquarters in the Mediterranean arrived. It provoked fresh rage, on two counts, in Mihailović. The first was that he was convinced that Bailey had had the signal all along, and had deliberately withheld it. The second was that it instructed Bailey in person to negotiate an armistice with Italian commanders and to supervise the disarming of their soldiers. That this task could not possibly be accomplished by one man was bad enough evidence of an absence of realism in whoever originated the instructions. What was much worse was that it ignored, insultingly, the rights of an Allied commander-in-chief to help himself in his own country to surrendered enemy property. He of course did help himself, with Bailey's whole-hearted assistance. But it was yet another example of an unnecessary difficulty thrust upon Bailey from above.

Deakin, in Jajce, was sent similar instructions. It was the only time in four months of daily association that he saw Tito lose his temper. Tito was not the constitutionally appointed commander-in-chief of his country's army, but he was the unquestioned leader of the largest and most effective anti-German fighting force in Yugoslavia. His old suspicions of Allied motives, suspicions that Deakin had hoped by now largely to have assuaged, resurfaced with bitterness. He was ironic about the idiotic notion that Deakin should personally walk down from Bosnia to the Dalmatian coast through Ustashi-held country, disarm a couple of Italian divisions and transfer their trappings to the British and Americans. Tito was more deeply concerned about the danger that the lack of warning of the Italian move might cause him to miss a rich haul of Italian weapons and equipment. The biggest concentration of Italians was in and around the Dalmation port of Split. The nearest German units could reach Split in about two days. The nearest Partisan force to Split, the 1st Proletarian Division, was at Bugojno, by normal marching standards three, possibly four, days away from the coast.

Deakin discarded his regrettable instructions, said that he

fully understood the implications for the Partisan future of the need to get their hands on the Italians' booty, and suggested that a study of the possibilities would be more profitable than continued recrimination. Tito recovered his temper. Maps were looked at. The 1st Division, decided Tito, would have to try to win the race for Split by forced marches. Deakin at once volunteered to go with them. He proposed to take with him Major Melvin O. Benson of the United States Army Air Corps, the first American officer to have been parachuted into Yugoslavia, who had joined Deakin a short time previously.* There would thus be both British and American witnesses of the Italian surrender to the Partisans, and reports of the event would be signalled back to Allied headquarters. By this means it would be made clear to distant Allied commanders, who seemed to be under the impression that their liaison officers in the field customarily gave orders to the leaders to whom they were attached, that Tito was in complete control of his own operations and intended to stay so.

Tito agreed that Deakin should go with the 1st Division, and that he should leave at once. Benson and the signaller would follow as soon as possible. The breach for the moment was healed. Deakin had a particular reason to be glad about the healing. His successor and commander-to-be, the new brigadier appointed to lead the British Military Mission to the Partisans and to broaden its work, was due to be dropped in within a few days. A soured atmosphere would have got the new man off to a bad start.

In the previous June, Captain Fitzroy Maclean had been in command of a detachment of the 1st Special Air Service Regiment. The detachment were for the moment based at Haifa, in Palestine, and were preparing for an operation aimed at the destruction on the ground of Luftwaffe aircraft which flew from an airstrip in Crete. Before the war, Maclean had been a professional diplomat. He had

*Benson was not under Deakin's command, although the two worked together in the closest of collaboration. His was an independent American mission. He was, however, reliant upon Deakin's wirelesses for his communications.

served in the British embassies in Paris and Moscow, and when war began in 1939 was working in the Foreign Office. His application to resign, so that he could join the army, was refused. He was told that a great deal of time and trouble had been invested in his diplomatic education, and that it was unthinkable that he should cast aside this expensive specialist instruction in favour of doing something that he knew nothing about, and that in any case could be taught to almost anyone. He was more useful to the country where he was.

Maclean was dissatisfied by this response. A careful look at the regulations of the Diplomatic Service showed that any of its members who wanted to stand for Parliament must leave the service. Maclean said that he wanted to stand for Parliament. This time his resignation was accepted. He enlisted as a private soldier in the Cameron Highlanders, was commissioned, heard rumours that his absence from politics had been noticed and that he was in danger of recall by the Foreign Office, and set about searching for a co-operative constituency committee. He found one in Lancaster, where a by-election was due. The Lancaster Conservatives readily accepted his precondition that, if chosen, his soldiering duties would take precedence over his political ones. He won the seat, and was posted to the Middle East.

There, in Cairo, he met an old friend – Maclean had a large number of helpful old friends – whose brother, Major David Stirling, was the progenitor, founder and leader of a small raiding unit that for deception purposes had been designated the Special Air Service. The Stirling concept rested on the vulnerability of the immensely long line of communications through the Western Desert between the forward Axis troops and the supply ports that serviced them from hundreds of miles to their rear. Attacks on these communications, and on enemy airfields, could do much material damage, which in turn would lead to a substantial diversion of Axis fighting strength from where it was most needed to static guard duties. The original idea was that the SAS would parachute by night to within a hard march of their chosen objectives, do their damage and make their own way back to the British line. Parachuting was abandoned after an early, expensive failure and was replaced by trans-desert travel in light trucks and, later, when they became available, in jeeps. (For a time the SAS were carried in the vehicles of the Long Range Desert Group, a reconnaissance unit that afterwards was to play a distinguished role in Yugoslavia.) Stirling was choosy over the acceptance of volunteers to the SAS. He wanted people of determination, initiative, versatility and mental and physical toughness. He accepted Maclean.

Maclean was engaged in these unorthodox desert operations over a period of about a year of intermittently planting explosive charges on parked aircraft, shooting up transport and generally raising merry hell. In the autumn of 1942, at a time when German successes in the Russian campaign might have led to a German thrust through the Caucasus into Persia, he was sent to Persia to raise a new SAS detachment from the small British force occupying that country in conjunction with a Soviet force. In the event, the Germans did not reach Persia. Maclean nonetheless contributed to its security by means of a kidnapping, carried out on the joint orders of the British Ambassador and the Commander-in-Chief. The victim was a disaffected Persian general named Zahidi, who seemed to be planning a general uprising against the Allied occupying forces. Maclean's instructions were to remove Zahidi in whatever manner he thought best, provided that Zahidi stayed alive and that there was no disturbance. Maclean's snatch met both provisos.

His preparations for the raid on the German airfield on Crete during the following June were frustrated when air photographs showed that the selected targets had flown away. He turned his thinking to a different branch of unconventional warfare, the liaising with guerrillas in occupied Europe. Another of his old friends, Rex Leeper, was the British Ambassador to the exiled Greek government in Cairo. Maclean asked Leeper about his prospects of joining the British Military Mission in Greece. Leeper telegraphed an enquiry to London. The reply was that Maclean was to fly to London at once to be briefed by the Prime Minister on a mission which Maclean was to undertake in Yugoslavia. Until that time, the only Yugoslav resistance leader of whom he had heard was General Draža Mihailović.

*

Churchill's interest in Partisan achievements, which was given its initial focus by the memorandum handed to him in Cairo by Colonel Keble of SOE, and was fortuitously stimulated further by his personal affection for Deakin, had led him in effect to remove the formulation of British policy towards Yugoslavia from the conflict of views between the Foreign Office and SOE, and between SOE London and SOE Cairo. The Prime Minister now made the policy himself. Its central plank was the giving of all possible support to the people who were doing the most fighting. For its implementation, he minuted to the Foreign Secretary, he wanted 'a daring Ambassador–leader to these hardy and hunted guerrillas'. Fitzroy Maclean, the experienced diplomat, SAS soldier and absentee Member of Parliament, clearly met the requirements of the job description. The fact that even at this stage of enhanced knowledge of Partisan organisation the word 'leader' was included demonstrated that the misconception that was to embarrass Deakin with Tito, and Bailey with Mihailović, at the time of the Italian surrender was not restricted to staff officers in the Middle East.

In the last week of July 1943 Maclean, summoned to Chequers, the official country residence of British prime ministers, was told precisely what was required of him. The resignation of Mussolini, word of which came in on that same night, had made the task planned for Maclean even more important. It was now vital to apply every pressure in the Balkans that would undermine the German position in Italy. Maclean was to go in to the Partisans, find out who was killing the most Germans, and help them to kill more. He was to be promoted to brigadier immediately, and would be the Prime Minister's personal representative. He had the entire army from which to pick his second-in-command and his supporting team. He was to leave at the earliest practicable moment.

There was one question on which Maclean wanted clear instructions. He had served in the Moscow Embassy during the pre-war Stalinist purges and the show-trials that had accompanied them. He had no illusions about Communist expansionism. He was a Conservative Member of Parliament. Was it accepted that if Tito and the Partisans came out on top in Yugoslavia, as seemed likely, the almost inevitable consequence would be a post-war Communist Yugoslavia closely tied to the Soviet Union? Churchill said that it was. While Western civilisation was under threat by Nazi Germany, long-term considerations of British policy must not divert British attentions from the prime objective of defeating Nazism. Politics were at present secondary.

With this reassurance Maclean went away to make arrangements for his mission. He found them to be more difficult than he had thought possible. There were those in SOE who regarded as unacceptable the grafting to their organisation of an outsider with a Foreign Office background and with direct access to the Prime Minister. Chief among these was the recently promoted Brigadier C.D. Keble in SOE Cairo, who had personally sown the seed and nourished the growth of British support for the Partisans, and who meant to keep the harvest under his own control. The methods that he chose were appropriately Balkan.

Maclean's preliminary call was to the headquarters of SOE London in Baker Street. He asked for, and was promised, the first available seat on an aircraft flying to Cairo. When nothing had come up for a week he telephoned to ask the reason. Bad weather, he was told. All flights had been cancelled. He was then sent for again by the Prime Minister, this time in Downing Street, and shown a personal signal signed by General Sir Henry Maitland Wilson, the Commander-in-Chief, Middle East, an old friend and patron from Maclean's SAS days. The message was that Wilson considered Maclean to be totally unsuitable for his new job. Churchill's reply, also shown to Maclean, was a curt injunction to Wilson not to argue.

On his way from Downing Street, Maclean met another of his friends who said that he was flying to Cairo on the following morning. Maclean went to this man's office and telephoned the Air Ministry branch that controlled flights to Cairo. They had his name, but had been told by SOE that he did not really want to go at all. Maclean booked his seat for the next day, and went to see SOE. They regretted that the weather was still unfit for flying. He said that he had heard differently, and was leaving within a few hours.

A Small War in the Balkans

He was taken to see Lord Selborne, the Minister of
Economic Warfare, responsible for SOE. Selborne
received him affably, congratulated him on the trust that
had been placed in him by the Prime Minister, and invited
him to swear an oath of loyalty to SOE. Maclean declined.
Selborne thought this a pity. He pointed to two leather
medal cases inscribed 'DSO', and said reflectively that that
was what was done for those who served SOE loyally. 'I
was beginning to wonder about SOE,' recorded Maclean
many years later.

The going got rougher when he reached Cairo. He was
immediately summoned by General Wilson, whose staff
wanted to know what had inspired the Prime Minister to
rebuke Wilson for sending a non-existent signal about the
new head of the British Mission to Tito. It soon became
clear that the signal had been counterfeit. General Wilson,
naturally enough, was not pleased when the news was
broken to him of the fraudulent misuse of his name. He
told Maclean that the originator of the signal would be
dealt with. In the meantime Maclean was to have himself gazetted as a brigadier, and to get on with the job.
If he had trouble of any sort he should report back to
Wilson.

He had trouble from the start of his first visit to SOE
headquarters in Rustum Buildings. Minds failed to meet in
the course of a crisp dialogue with Brigadier Keble, the
SOE Chief of Staff. Why was Maclean dressed as a
brigadier? Because that was General Wilson's instruction.
Why had he seen General Wilson? Because Wilson had
sent for him. Well, if Wilson sent for Maclean again,
Maclean was not to go. Maclean pointed out that he was a
serving soldier. If he were summoned by the Commander-
in-Chief he would certainly go.

Keble shifted the conversation (probably the wrong term
for it) to Yugoslavia. Keble would see to it that Maclean
would never get there, whatever the Prime Minister, the
Commander-in-Chief or anyone else had to say. SOE had
been against the appointment all along. In one way or
another they would stop it. Keble had already given orders
that Maclean was to be shown no files, signals or any other
material on Yugoslavia held by SOE.

All this clearly came within the definition of the sort of

trouble that was to be reported back to General Wilson. When Maclean reached Wilson's office there was more of it under discussion. A Colonel Vellacott was present. Vellacott's job was to spread misleading rumours among the bars and bazaars of Cairo, with a view to their being picked up by the large number of resident spies and agents for onward transmission to the Germans. A good, apparently well-grounded rumour could cause a great deal of confusion to the enemy. The latest rumour that SOE had asked Vellacott to put out was about Maclean. It was to travel in the usual bars and bazaars, but was also to be given a more elevated circulation in the Continental and Shepheard's hotels, and within GHQ itself. Its theme was that Maclean was a hopeless drunk, an active homosexual, and had been notorious for his cowardice and unreliability while with the SAS. Vellacott assumed that there were sound operational reasons for the spreading of this story. He had nonetheless thought it right to confirm with General Wilson that it was in order to go ahead.

Wilson put a freeze on the rumour, listened to Maclean's account of his talk with Keble, and called an urgent meeting. To this came R.G. Casey, the British Minister of State in the Middle East, Lord Glenconner, the Head of SOE Cairo, and Maclean. By coincidence, the staff of SOE Cairo had been purged for various reasons in August 1941 and again in August 1942. It was now August 1943. The outcome of Wilson's meeting was that August 1943 was added to the series, thereby converting a coincidence into a trend, an annual event. Keble was removed, and was shortly afterwards killed in action. Glenconner too was removed from Cairo.

There are some of Keble's SOE associates of those Cairo days who preserve for him a respect, well short of liking. They admired his drive, his corner-cutting, his ruthless efficiency. The drive and the corner-cutting had certainly brought the case for the support of the Partisans to the Prime Minister's attention, and had precipitated a change in British policy towards Yugoslavia. The ruthlessness was evident in his endeavours to dispose of Maclean. To the uninvolved, there seems in retrospect to be a question-mark about where the efficiency became overlaid by a ludicrously overblown self-confidence and self-importance.

How efficient was it to send a spurious telegram to the Prime Minister over the name of the Commander-in-Chief, to try to discredit the Prime Minister's nominee as head of the mission to Tito, and to hope to get away with it?

Whatever the answers are to these questions, the Keble preamble to Maclean's mission had started him off with one of the more unusual introductions in British military history to one of its more unusual episodes. One consequence was that Maclean was granted a status unparalleled in any other special operation of the war. He was already the Prime Minister's personal political representative. He was now made directly responsible militarily to the Commander-in-Chief, Middle East, thus by-passing SOE. Maclean insisted upon the setting up of a direct signal link with both, to supplement the SOE net, which he regarded as both suspect and unreliable. The time-lag in the decipherment of some signals from Yugoslavia, he discovered, was up to six weeks. The considered accounts from Deakin of Partisan strength, deployment and capacity had yet to be deciphered. It was no wonder that Churchill, impressed as he was by the intercept evidence, was still trying to find out who was killing the most Germans; and no wonder that Maclean's brief was an exploratory one, not far removed from Deakin's of four months earlier.

On 17 September 1943, the Maclean mission took off in two Halifax bombers from Plotsville, near Bizerta in Tunisia. Maclean had his top-level direct links to Churchill and Wilson, but for his routine administrative support he was still dependent upon SOE, a body in which his confidence had not been restored after the Keble imbroglio. Maclean refused the first parachute offered to him. He was taking no chances. With him were his second-in-command, Colonel Vivian Street, a gifted and experienced regular soldier; Major Peter Moore of the Royal Engineers, who had been prominent in the gapping of the Alamein minefields and whose new task was to help the Partisans with demolitions; Major Gordon Alston of the SAS as Intelligence Officer; Major Michael Parker for administration; and

Major John Henniker-Major. Major Linn 'Slim' Farish was the American liaison officer to the mission. The Halifax with Maclean in it found its way accurately to the signal fires and dropped its passengers and stores in the right place. The second aircraft got lost, returned to Tunisia and tried again successfully the next night.

Maclean was given the same sort of welcome as Deakin had experienced in Montenegro earlier in the year – a welcome of embraces by armed, ragged young men dressed in a medley of part uniform, part civilian clothing. Vlatko Velebit, smartly turned out in a well-cut uniform bearing badges of rank, arrived and introduced himself as a member of Tito's staff who had been sent to greet the party. They sat talking around one of the signal fires, heaped up with fresh wood to offset the cold of an upland night, Velebit, Maclean, Street, Farish and Maclean's old SAS orderly, Sergeant Duncan, while Partisans sought and collected the stores canisters. The canisters were loaded on to horse-drawn farm carts and taken away. Horses were brought, the sun rose, and they rode off beside a bubbling mountain stream in a green valley, accompanied by a large Partisan mounted escort. Breakfast of black bread and vanilla brandy was provided in a peasant cottage in use as a local Partisan headquarters. Velebit thought it unwise to continue further in daylight. There were too many German aircraft and foot patrols in the area.

At dusk the horses were replaced by a captured German truck, extensively bullet-holed, with a huge red flag fastened to its bonnet. In this vehicle, driven at speed, they were carried beside a lake, up a narrow valley and across a wooden bridge. Behind the bridge, high on a cliff face, was a ruined castle, Tito's headquarters in Jajce. Maclean was bidden to bring his Chief of Staff to the castle for supper with Tito. He at once appointed Street as his British, Farish as his American, Chiefs of Staff, and nominated Sergeant Duncan as his bodyguard. All four smartened themselves up and set out together for supper.

Deakin was still in Split. The 1st Proletarian Division, starting with a forced march of about forty miles in twenty-four hours, with brief halts of a few minutes at a time for snatched sleep, had beaten the Germans in the race to the coast for the Italian arms and equipment. On the way the division had chanced upon a Ustashi force, killed a few of its members, and captured some of its supplies. On the morning after this fight, a tiny Fiat car came up the zigzag road from Split to the mountains behind it. The driver said that the Italians in the city had already handed their arms over to the local Partisan committee and the students of the high school. General Popović, the divisional commander, his political commissar and Deakin squashed into the car and wound down the hillside, through groups of jubilant peasants proffering fruit and wine.

The 1st Division followed fast on foot and in captured Italian trucks, some to the city, most to defensive positions on commanding heights to the north of it. The Italian booty was already being sorted, before being loaded on to Italian vehicles. To extricate it, routes to the mountains were being selected and arrangements made to keep them open. Benson and the signaller Wroughton arrived with the truck convoy, which had been shot up from the air, and joined Deakin in a house on the waterfront at Kastella, a suburb of Split. A squadron of German Stukas dive-bombed the barracks in which the surrendered Italians were concentrated. An Italian general tactlessly asked Deakin what he was doing with 'these bandits', and was given a brisk brush-off. A surrender-signing ceremony was staged, with Popović and the Italian general subscribing as principals, and Deakin and Benson, neither of whom had any instructions on the matter, witnessing the signatures on behalf of the British and American Commands in the Mediterranean. There were further, heavier air attacks. A group of young Italian officers volunteered to fight alongside the Partisans, on the condition that they should do so in a distinctive unit of their own. Popović would not agree to the condition. The Italians could be spread among the Partisans, or not join at all. The Italians withdrew their offer. Popović's stipulation would breach their oath of loyalty to their king.

The three Partisan leaders – Popović, his commissar Lola Ribar, the Supreme Staff representative in Dalmatia, and Krstulović, the regional commander – stood with Deakin and Benson on a balcony overlooking the main square of the city, with an excited crowd swarming below. Speeches were made, and met with fierce applause. Deakin made one, translated by Ribar, in which he said that, since the Allies now held ports on the Italian Adriatic coast, aid in decisive quantities would soon be on its way to Yugoslavia. (This speech later attracted press attention of differing emphasis. *Free Dalmatia*, a Partisan sheet with a circulation of 20,000, printed the text in full. A German paper, published in Zagreb, reported that a local Jew disguised as a British officer had made an unfortunate speech from the balcony of the Split town hall.)

Deakin had done what he had intended to do when he made his spontaneous offer to Tito to accompany Popović's division into Split as an official British witness of the Partisan takeover of the Italian arms. His presence was an explicit British acknowledgement of the Partisan status as a well-organised, effective army in entire control of its own affairs in its own country. The harm done by the insensitive offending signal had, he hoped, been undone. There was nothing more for him in Split. The Partisans would hold on long enough to remove as much as they could of the surrendered Italian material, and would then withdraw to their familiar habitat of the forests and mountains. It was time for Deakin to go back to Jajce to meet the successor whom he had originally meant to welcome on the dropping zone.

He, Wroughton and a Partisan party of couriers with an escort left for Bosnia together. It was a prolonged journey which was begun in an Italian truck, involved some circuitous marching to avoid Ustashi-held positions, took in several tactically necessary pauses, one of them to await the departure of Chetniks on weekend leave in a village on the route, and ended comfortably on top of a load of straw in a farm cart. The farm cart stopped outside the municipal offices in Mrkonjićgrad. Inside were crowded tables. At the top table were six smartly dressed British officers. Deakin dusted himself down to get rid of some bits of straw, walked up to a tall man with the crown and three stars of a brigadier on his shoulder straps, and saluted Fitzroy Maclean. Then they shook hands.

*

Maclean's first impressions of Tito, confirmed by daily discussions of plans and the exchange of ideas, were identical with those formed by Deakin a few months earlier: the quiet and confident exercise of authority, the ability to cut through irrelevancies and to identify essentials, the humourousness, the willingness to consider a proposition on its merits, above all the easy decisiveness, had been manifest to both men. Because of his earlier background, Maclean was possibly even more deeply impressed than Deakin had been. It had been a pleasing surprise to Deakin to find that Tito was no cliché-ridden Communist fanatic, his thought-processes replaced by received dogma. Deakin had had little previous personal experience of Communists. Maclean had had plenty, during his time at the Moscow Embassy. There he had been accustomed to nervous Soviet functionaries, frightened to reach a decision in case it in some way contravened the Party line, referring the most minor matters upwards in the bureaucracy so that the responsibility for any decision could be laid on someone else's doorstep if it were unpalatable to the higher reaches of the management. There was no sign of that sort of hesitancy in Tito. He considered a problem, weighed the advantages and defects of differing courses of action, listened to, but did not necessarily take, the advice of his staff, and made up his mind himself.

He was already clear in his mind that what he wanted from the Western Allies was the heaviest tonnage of warlike stores that they could give him. He had earlier feared, as he told Deakin, that the long gap in British attempts to make contact with the Partisans had been because the British held the Partisans responsible for the murder of Atherton. Tito had long thought himself the victim of a British boycott. First Deakin, then Maclean, reassured him. The delay had been brought about entirely by the operational realities of misfortunes in the Western Desert, the need to concentrate upon overcoming them, and the consequent lack of weapons to spare and of aircraft of suitable range for their delivery. Later developments had changed all that. The Allies were now firmly in Italy, just across the Adriatic. Ports and airfields were within easy range of Yugoslavia. Stores of all sorts were now available, from British and American sources and from the vast amount of material that had come in with the Italian capitulation. What was now wanted was the devising of an efficient system for their despatch and distribution.

The pattern was soon agreed on the lines previously recommended by Deakin, but with some refinements. British missions, subordinate to Maclean, would be dropped to Partisan formations throughout Slovenia, Croatia, Bosnia and Montenegro – everywhere except Serbia, where Partisan strength was at the time meagre. The missions would indent for the supplies asked for by the various Partisan headquarters. Where possible, the Partisans should build airstrips, which would allow for the delivery of heavier loads than could be dropped free* or by parachute. In the many areas in which the preparation of an airstrip was out of the question, dropping would be the norm. The removal of the Italians from the board had opened up the altogether new possibility of the organisation of a substantial traffic by sea. The Germans had retaken Split and most of the other mainland Dalmatian ports, but they had yet to do much about the offshore Dalmatian islands. The islands were in Partisan control. The islanders were born sailors, their fishing schooners capable of carrying sizeable cargoes. If the British could run supplies from Italy to the islands, the fishermen of what was developing into a Partisan navy would see to their onward delivery among the islands and to some places on the mainland.

On 5 October 1943, seventeen days after his first meeting with Tito, Maclean, Vivian Street with him, left Jajce on the long, mountainous march to the coast. Maclean carried an itemised list of required supplies agreed between Tito's staff and his own, and a comprehensive report on the military and political situation within Yugoslavia, an assessment from the perspective of Partisan headquarters.

---

*The term 'free' drops, confined to such unbreakables as boots and battledress uniforms, meant that the bundles were thrown out of the aircraft without a parachute attached. A load of ammunition boots, dropped from a height, was potentially lethal to its recipients. Deakin and a reception party were lucky once not to be eliminated by British issue boots.

There was a need for much detailed discussion with higher British authorities. It could not be conducted satisfactorily by the exchange of coded signals. Maclean intended to go out by sea to Italy.

Before his departure he had wirelessed to Cairo a suggestion of Tito's that two senior members of the Partisan Supreme Staff should also go out to help to present the Partisan case for enhanced supply. (It later became clear to Deakin that they were also to argue for political recognition.) The two chosen emissaries were Lola Ribar (the translator of Deakin's impromptu balcony speech in Split, a son of the first president of the Yugoslav Assembly in 1920) and Miloje Milojević. No reply to this proposal had come in by the time Maclean left. After some hard marching, a considerable amount of dodging German patrols and posts, and a sea journey in a Partisan schooner, he reached the island of Hvar. In an exchange of signals he was told to get over to Italy as quickly as he could. A Royal Navy motor launch would pick him up from the island of Vis. He was urgently wanted for something unspecified but important in Cairo. No decision had yet been reached on whether the two Partisans should come too. If necessary, they could follow later. Maclean, reflecting uncharitably about far-off staff officers who seemed to think that journeys from Bosnia in 1943 were simple matters of catching the right transport on time, sent a message to Jajce for Tito, revealing this provisional postponement. Then he left by schooner for Vis.

The important something in Cairo was the preliminary to a meeting of the Big Three, Churchill, President Roosevelt and Marshal Stalin, each of whom would be accompanied by an entourage of his top-level military and political advisers. Maclean gave his written report on the significance of Partisan operations to the Foreign Secretary, Anthony Eden. Eden said that he would get it to the Prime Minister before he met Roosevelt and Stalin, and would also pass a copy to General Sir Alan Brooke, the Chief of the Imperial General Staff. Maclean was instructed to hold himself in readiness to return to Cairo a few weeks later, bringing the Partisan spokesmen with him. He flew back to

Italy, where he was told that the German squeeze on the routes between Bosnia and the Dalmatian coast was now total. There was no way through. Unless Ribar and Milojević could somehow be flown out, they were stuck. The Partisan case would not be presented by Partisans.

Deakin and the other members of the British Mission at Jajce, helped by the American Liaison Officer Slim Farish, had found a possible site for an airstrip on a plateau near Glamoč, a town bordering the Dinaric Alps. Technical advice on how to make an airstrip was sought, and obtained, from the Royal Air Force in Bari, in southern Italy. A young Sapper officer, Captain Donald Knight, with Deakin and Major Robin Wetherly as co-foremen, supervised the work of a Partisan-recruited labour force. The first snows of winter descended, but the strip was finally pronounced, on rather shaky amateur evidence, to be usable.

Maclean made three attempts to use it. The first, in a light bomber aircraft, a Baltimore escorted by a swarm of United States Army Air Corps Lightning fighters, crossed a sunny Adriatic, met an impenetrable snowstorm above the Bosnian mountains, and went back to Italy. The second, in the same Baltimore with a similar escort, ran into identical conditions. They too flew back to Italy. The third was an unescorted try by the New Zealand Baltimore pilot. Maclean, anxious to preserve the pilot from disciplinary sanctions, asked if there would be trouble if the flight went without the ordained escort. The New Zealander said comfortingly that it made no difference. If he delivered Maclean successfully, no questions would be asked. If they were shot down, no questions would be asked either. In the event, they were frustrated by thick cloud. Maclean was taken back to Italy.

The Partisans, conspicuously Lola Ribar, were un-instructed in the limitations of contemporary aircraft. They began to convince themselves that Maclean's extended absence was evidence of British duplicity. Deakin's improvisations about meteorology were ignored with progressive suspicion. Deakin, eventually persuaded in the interests of restoring acceptable relations that an enterprise in which he had no confidence must go ahead, concurred in a scheme of slap-happy hopefulness. The

Croat crew of a German Dornier had flown their plane from Banja Luka, crash-landed in Partisan-held territory, and defected. The Dornier was brought to Glamoč. If Maclean could not get in, the Dornier could get out.

The Dornier's preparations for take-off from the Glamoč strip were interrupted by the appearance of a small German Henschell, which bombed and machine-gunned. Deakin had another of his near misses. Ribar was killed. So were Wetherly and Knight. Milojević was wounded, for the seventh time. Most of the Partisan escort were killed too. Vlatko Velebit, who had been added to the Partisan delegation, was slightly wounded. A post-war Yugoslav enquiry, of whose conclusions Deakin, then a First Secretary in the British Embassy in Belgrade, was doubtful, found that the Dornier's radio operator had been coerced into the defection by the other members of the aircrew, and was transmitting detailed accounts of their aspirations to the Germans. True or false, he was a brave man. He was decapitated by one of the German bombs.

The poor weather, still regarded by the Partisans as a Western democratic excuse for inaction, broke on 3 December. It was a cold, sunny, clear day, all the way from southern Italy to central Yugoslavia. An RAF Dakota, escorted once more by American Lightnings, got through. It bumped to a halt on the rough surface of the Glamoč landing strip. Maclean was aboard with reinforcements for his mission. The reinforcements got out. In climbed Velebit, the wounded Milojević, Deakin and a bemused German intelligence officer, recently captured, named Meyer, preserved by Deakin for interrogation at the cost of much acrimony with the Partisans, who had favoured instant shooting. The turnover was done at speed. The pilot kept his engines running. Maclean said goodbye to the reinforcements and climbed back into the aircraft. It was in Brindisi by nightfall. The New Zealand aircrew, assured by Maclean that he would attend to any disciplinary repercussions, obligingly evaded the need to get the endorsement of their commanding officer for further travel, and delivered the party to Alexandria by way of a refuelling stop in Malta.

*

Yugoslavia was only one of a large number of items on the Cairo agenda of the Big Three, but the Prime Minister gave it his detailed personal attention. He had studied the continuing intercept evidence and Maclean's report. He cross-examined both Maclean and Deakin, at length. He was confirmed in his belief that the case for powerful military support of the Partisans was watertight. He gave approval for the provision of sufficient aircraft, to operate from Italian bases, to give the Partisans a really effective supply service. Maclean was told to enlarge his mission to a size suitable for the proper co-ordination of the supply arrangements.

The difficult political question of how to square British obligations to the Royal Yugoslav government with a policy of running guns to an organisation held in abhorrence by it was set aside for future resolution. One preliminary step was taken. Deakin was instructed personally by Churchill to tell the young King Peter, now also in Cairo, of the British conviction that Tito was fighting Germans hard and that Mihailović was drifting further and further into collaboration with them. Deakin did so at a private luncheon, given by Ralph Stevenson, the Minister to the Royal government. Deakin enjoyed neither the task nor his lunch.

PART TWO

Vis

EIGHT

Coastal Forces and the Commandos

The Italian capitulation on 8 September 1943 was as much of a surprise to the German Command in Yugoslavia as it was to Tito, Mihailović and to most of the Italians themselves. The initial German reaction to the news that yesterday's allies were now on the other side was uncharacteristically slow. In the 1941 carving-up of the post-invasion spoils Dalmatia had become an Italian prize, to be exploited, administered and defended. About eight Italian divisions were deployed along the coast. To the Partisans these now became a fruitful source of weapons, ammunition and supplies of all kinds, along with a scattering of recruits. The German problem was not one of reinforcement, but of reconquest.

They faced this with their customary thoroughness. Early hesitancy switched to forceful action. They put two divisions into Albania, one into southern Montenegro, the Prinz Eugen Division along the Neretva river to Mostar and thence to Dubrovnik, and the 114th Jaeger Division into Knin, Šibenik and Zadar. It was no part of Partisan military policy to try to fight it out in set-piece battles against fully equipped and trained German divisions. The Partisans harassed, held up, sabotaged and demolished. When holding on was no longer profitable, they withdrew to the hills and forests to fight another day.

By 26 September all the major ports along the coast were in German occupation. Three Italian divisions, 1st Alpine, 19th Venezia and 41st Firenze, fought against their old partners for a short time, but were soon suppressed. There remained, for the Germans, the matter of the Dalmatian islands, the rocky chain of peaks of a submerged limestone mountain range that in clusters of various shapes and sizes fringes the coast of Yugoslavia from Istria in the north to the Albanian border. The southern islands, from the town of Split downwards, were the subject of the most immediate German concern. They were all Partisan-held. To get at them would require a series of amphibious operations across famously inconstant waters that could be either enchantingly blue and placid or a churning mass of white-capped waves, thrashed into wildness either by the bura, the wind from the north, or by the yugo, the slightly less destructive wind from the south. If crossings were successfully made, and were followed by equally successful landings, there were other problems to be faced. Aside from a few small coastal towns, fishing ports with a charming Venetian architecture, and some narrow stretches here and there of alluvial plain, the former mountain peaks had all the distinguishing qualities of mountain peaks. They were a tangle of rocky valleys and hills, some of them more than 2500 feet high. It was hard country to fight in, with the additional advantage to the Partisan defence that the defenders were remarkably tough and enduring fishermen and hill-farmers, familiar with the contortions of the land and the local habits of the sea.

Once taken, these islands would have to be held, an expensive tying up of troops in an undertaking of negative value. But the alternative, of simply leaving them as they were, was potentially even more expensive than the commitment of a large number of soldiers to what seemed likely to be little more than a police role. Several ports in southern Italy, a hundred miles or so to the west across the Adriatic, were now in British hands. Light craft of the Royal Navy were known to have visited recently several of the islands and to have run in supplies for the Partisans. If this trade were allowed to expand, it could soon be extended into a dangerous and substantial replenishment of Tito's military larder on the mainland, with the islands, or some of them, used as entrepôts and the goods put ashore at remote parts of the coast by Dalmatian schooner. The balance of German advantage lay in the occupation of the islands.

It was a job which took the Germans several months. It was never entirely completed. By 20 October the

Germans had taken about half of the Pelješac peninsula, the long finger of land that points north-west from its mainland base until its tip runs close and parallel to the north-east shore of the island of Korčula. The Partisans held on hard to the other half. In late September they had fought off a seaborne attack on Hvar, and in October they did the same to similar attempts on Brač and Mljet, and to a second attempt on Hvar. But German pressure was increasing all the time. It was clear that German strength, and superior resources including generous air support, would prevail. Other considerations aside, the defence of islands against conventional attacks was not what Partisans were for. They were guerrillas.

While the Germans were forcing their way down the Pelješac peninsula, and were making their first tentative attempts on the islands, the Royal Navy's contribution to future operations in the eastern Adriatic was being shaped in the south-eastern Italian port of Brindisi. Two flotillas of mixed motor torpedo boats and motor gun boats were allocated the tasks of helping the Partisans by landing arms and ammunition in the Dalmatian islands, of patrolling the channels between the islands by night to break up German attempts at landings, and to disrupt German inter-island sea traffic. Lieutenant-Commander Morgan Giles was in overall command of the naval force. It was fast and manoeuvrable, bore a formidable armament and was led and manned by men of spirit.

The MTBs and the MGBs were of similar basic design, seventy feet from stem to stern, powered by three Diesel engines; the MTBs were capable of speeds of twenty-eight knots, the MGBs of twenty-one knots. Each boat was crewed by three officers and twenty-seven ratings. The MTBs mounted two torpedo tubes. Otherwise they, like the MGBs, were fitted with quick-firing pom-pom guns forrard, a 6-pounder aft, and twin Vickers machine-guns on either side of the bridge. The Vickers were backed by 20-mm Oerlikons. Depth charges were carried aft. In their earlier trips to the islands the commanding officers of these craft quickly identified two ways of enhancing their operations. The first was to take a plentiful supply of spare fuel, carried in forty-gallon drums. The second was to make use of simply designed camouflage netting. Coastal Forces interceptions were almost invariably undertaken by night. By day, as was found by experiment and investigation, conditions were perfect for the mooring of the craft in concealment at any one of a large range of suitable places among a large choice of islands. The Mediterranean is tideless. There were innumerable small creeks with rocky steep-to shores. A craft moored close to the rocks, its outlines disguised by the spread of a cloth-mesh net, painted to match the greys and browns of the rocks and fastened asymmetrically to bamboo outriggers, was indistinguishable from its background at 500 yards in broad daylight. From these lying-up berthings, observers could disembark, climb convenient hills and, if in luck, note German sea movements for attention after nightfall.

Many of these night patrols were uneventful and routine, with no contact made. Moving ahead in time a little, to December 1943, there was a not untypical sequence in the life of MTB 649, commanded by Lieutenant Hughes, a South African Naval Force Volunteer Reservist. In the early hours of 10 December Hughes, who had been patrolling the Neretva Channel north of the Pelješac peninsula, closed the small port of Trpanj. All civilians had been evacuated. MTB 649 shelled its harbour and the adjacent buildings from a range of 300 yards. Three nights later Hughes did it again, as a diversion to a Partisan landing near Loviste. This time there was a heavy return fire. Hughes withdrew, went off to shoot up Crkvice, and sneaked back again for another go at Trpanj. An old Austrian steam torpedo boat next blundered into the shooting, joined in, was hit several times and took shelter in Loviste, where during the next few days it was attacked by the RAF and finally sunk by Partisans using limpet mines.

On 19 December, 649 was lying at her moorings off Hvar. The naval Liaison Officer then based on Hvar reported a sighting of two small ships, lashed together and making about four knots between the islands of Brač and Hvar, proceeding towards Drvenik. It was one of the rare daylight opportunities. Hughes slipped his moorings, gave chase and caught up after thirty-five minutes. Two German ensigns were lowered from their mastheads and were replaced by a white flag. Hughes put over a boarding party who came back with the prisoners (plus a collection of automatic weapons, rifles and pistols), having checked that the schooners had no demolition charges planted. He towed both craft back to Hvar, as a present for the Partisans. The prisoners displayed an emotion that was to become familiar: they were delighted to be told that they would stay in naval hands. They had feared that like their schooners they would be handed over to the Partisans.

The third week in December was a busy one for the MTBs based on Hvar. On the night of the 19th two of them, 637 commanded by Lieutenant Davidson of the Royal Navy Volunteer Reserve, and 297 commanded by Lieutenant Woods of the Royal Canadian Navy Volunteer Reserve, with Lieutenant Lancaster as Senior Officer embarked in 297, covered a raid by Partisans carried in schooners to the mainland port of Omiš, north of the island of Brač. The MTBs shepherded the schooners, put in diversionary shoots while the Partisans were landing, and followed the progress of the land battle by watching streams of tracer and soaring Very lights. It was a brilliantly moonlit night. The two boats separated and patrolled close in to the wooded shoreline. Those in 297 saw a sudden eruption of tracer from 637 and then heard a massive explosion. The explosion was followed by a fire, burning low on the water. At once 297 hurried over; 637 had torpedoed a Siebel ferry, sunk an E-boat (a German motor gun boat) and damaged another. She herself had suffered some casualties and some damage. Lancaster sent her back to Hvar, and continued the patrol in 297.

At 1.30 a.m., concentrated study of an eccentrically shaped large rock at the foot of a cliff-face showed it to be a camouflaged ship of about 200 feet length, with a large superstructure and two gun turrets aft. From a range of a thousand yards, 297 fired torpedoes, and scored two hits. Clouds of debris were thrown high into the air, and for half an hour the area was obliterated by thick smoke.

Two nights later, on the 21st, Partisans reported that the former Royal Yugoslav Navy cruiser, *Dalmacija*, which had been used by the Germans as heavyweight support for attacks on the islands, was aground off Silba island.

Dalmacija had been a great nuisance to the Partisans. Two MTBs, 298 (Lieutenant Shore, RNVR) and 226 (Lieutenant Hyslop, RNVR), left Hvar at maximum speed shortly after darkness fell. They slowed, to reduce the noise, as they closed with the target. A German destroyer and E-boats had earlier been seen near the cruiser, and a cautious approach was necessary. Both MTBs fired their torpedoes from 500 yards at 2 a.m. There were violent explosions, and columns of wreckage and water were flung up against the silhouette of the island. A vivid flash cut through the smoke that swathed the cruiser as the MTBs withdrew at high speed home to Hvar. The Partisans later confirmed that *Dalmacija* and a small craft alongside had been totally wrecked and then gutted by fire, although some of the cruiser's armament was subsequently salvaged by the Germans.

Ever since the Eighth Army's advance in southern Italy (following the landings at Reggio in September) had brought Yugoslavia within comfortable range of the Royal Navy operating from Italian ports and the Royal Air Force operating from Italian airfields, Fitzroy Maclean had been giving thought to a scheme for the establishment of an offshore advanced base that would simultaneously fulfil several functions. Ideally, it would be a stronghold from which amphibious raiding parties could emerge to harry the coast and the German-held islands. It would be a rallying point for the island Partisans and a distributing centre for their supply. It would have one or more defensible harbours for the use of RN Coastal Forces who could then more easily get in among German coastal shipping. And, most ambitious requirement of all, it would have an airstrip from which the RAF would be able to penetrate more deeply, and for longer periods, over the mainland in support of Partisan operations. A glance at the map suggested that, geographically at any rate, the most promising candidate for the meeting of these desiderata was Vis, the westernmost of the southern Dalmatian islands. Vis stood well back on its own, was the nearest island to Italy (the source of all Allied support and supplies), and was centrally placed for the mounting of offensive forays.

Maclean, on his way out from Bosnia in October for the preliminary meeting with the Foreign Secretary before the Cairo conference, had made his way to Vis by Partisan schooner for subsequent collection by the navy. Vis's functional attractions, in all but one respect, matched its geographical ones. There were two small but serviceable fishing harbours, one at Vis town at the north-east of the island, the other at Komiža at the west end. Both were suitable for the accommodation of motor gun boats, motor torpedo boats, landing craft and possibly ships of up to the size of a destroyer. Inland the island seemed to be as hilly and as rocky as all the other islands. Maclean abandoned any notions of looking for a possible site for an airstrip. He had not found everything that was wanted, but he had found enough. Tito had already endorsed with enthusiasm the idea of setting up an Allied/Partisan base. If the British could be similarly persuaded, Vis seemed the obvious place.

During an interval among the press of other business in Cairo, Maclean hawked around a proposal that British troops should be sent to Vis. He was after an infantry brigade, to match a brigade that the Partisans had promised to provide. Maclean was listened to sympathetically, but without result. There were no British infantry available. All those in the Mediterranean were needed to meet the insistent demands of the Italian campaign, from which large numbers of experienced troops had been subtracted and sent back to Britain to prepare for the Normandy landings. There were fewer difficulties about the acquisition by Maclean of extra officers for his expanding British Military Mission. One of the recruits was Major Randolph Churchill, the Prime Minister's son, who had been with the Commandos of the Special Service Brigade at Salerno. Later, at a loose end, he had gone to Cairo to see his father. Randolph Churchill was an old friend of Maclean's, and had once been with him on a rather chaotic SAS raid to Benghazi in Libya.

When Maclean had flown back to Italy from Cairo and had studied reports of steady German progress in the Dalmatian islands, he decided to see for himself what was happening there before rejoining Tito's headquarters in Bosnia. A Royal Navy MTB took Maclean, Vlatko Velebit of the Partisan Supreme Staff and some others (including an RAF officer unnamed in Maclean's account of the journey in his book, *Eastern Approaches*) across the Adriatic at high speed. They landed first on the island of Korčula, which was garrisoned by Partisans from the mainland. It was being shelled sporadically from the Pelješac peninsula, and clearly could not be preserved for long from a powerful German incursion.

The MTB took them next to Vis, where they were met by Vivian Street, who had remained on the island when Maclean went to Cairo. They consulted maps and did a lot of walking around. One of the walkers, the unnamed RAF officer, reported at lunchtime on the following day that after the examination of a long, central valley, currently under vines and olives, he had satisfied himself that it was capable of conversion to a usable airstrip. The professional judgement of this anonymous expert, coupled fortuitously to the recent personal history and social leanings of Randolph Churchill, led to the commitment of a relatively small but formidable British fighting force to operations alongside the Partisans. Americans were to join in too.

Randolph Churchill's contribution to this end was to take Maclean to a New Year's Eve party at Molfetta in the south of Italy, given by officers of No. 2 Special Service Brigade. The guests were a number of people 'who had been kind to us'. The host, Brigadier T.B.L. Churchill, met them hospitably and later listened to Maclean's account of his present insistent preoccupation, the urgency of providing a British garrison for Vis. Churchill and Maclean withdrew from the noise of the party to a quiet room where maps could once again be consulted. At the end of this discussion there was provisional agreement. Island operations were admirably suited to the training and outlook of the Commandos. If Maclean's influence in high places were sufficient to engineer the posting, Tom Churchill was in full accord. Three of the four Commandos in his brigade were committed to planned operations in Italy. The fourth, his brother Jack's No. 2 Commando, was at present recruiting throughout the Middle East, in search of volunteers to replace its high losses at Salerno. It would be some time before the unit was up to full strength, but about 200 men were available immediately. These could go to Vis at once.

Should Maclean be able to square the thing with General Alexander, the Allied Commander-in-Chief in Italy, Tom Churchill would gladly stiffen the original 200 of No. 2 Commando with their new reinforcements, and later feed in other units of his brigade when they were free of their obligations in Italy.

Maclean was in reach of something rather better than he had hoped for. Instead of a conventionally trained infantry brigade, which would doubtless defend Vis against German assault with efficient dedication, he had been offered the services of experienced and rehearsed raiders, who could certainly look after the island, but who knew a thing or two about what to do to its German-occupied neighbours. It all depended upon the success of Maclean's advocacy. Maclean had to deliver it in two stages.

Stage One was an interview with General Sir Harold Alexander and his Chief of Staff, General John Harding, at Allied Forces Headquarters in Caserta, twenty miles north of Naples (AFHQ was to supersede GHQ, Cairo, as overseer of Allied activities in the Balkans). Maclean's status was peculiar. He was a recently promoted brigadier who had skipped three ranks in the promotion. He was also the irregularly accredited ambassador to Tito, the most effective guerrilla leader in Europe, but a man held in abhorrence by his own government, the legitimacy of which was recognised by all the Allies, Western and Soviet. Moreover, Maclean was the personal representative of the Prime Minister. Senior generals, not normally disposed to enter into discussion at short notice with importunate brigadiers, did so with Maclean unquestioningly. Alexander and Harding listened with interest to his proposal that the Commandos should go to Vis, said that offensive operations in the Dalmatian islands could usefully complement Allied military progress in Italy, and invited Maclean to make his pitch at a higher level than theirs. The future conduct of the war in the Mediterranean was to be discussed at a conference at Marrakech, in Morocco. Winston Churchill, who had contracted pneumonia after the Cairo meeting, was convalescing there. A few hours later Maclean, whose living standards were alternating eccentrically between the peasant simplicities of guerrilla soldiering and the sybaritic consolations attendant upon international high-level politico-military consultation, was flying comfortably to North Africa in the Commander-in-Chief's personal aircraft.

Maclean came back to Italy with two things to be pleased about. One was a personal letter, phrased in terms of encouragement and admiration, from the Prime Minister to Tito. Although it further complicated the diplomatic curiosities of British relations with Yugoslavia, it simplified Maclean's task of promoting mutual military co-operation. The other was the confirmation of the commitment of the Commandos of No. 2 Special Service Brigade to the defence of Vis – more significantly, to a remit to raid from it.

Commandos, in the form in which they existed in 1944, had evolved from one of the many improvisations that had followed upon the brilliantly successful German blitzkrieg against France and the Low Countries in May and June of 1940. France, Belgium and Holland had laid down their arms. The British Expeditionary Force, evacuated from Dunkirk, had had to abandon most of its weapons, vehicles and heavy equipment. It had left behind it much of its small arms. Britain, supported by the distant Dominions and Colonies of the then British Empire, was the only European country still in the fight against Nazi Germany and its recently acquired opportunist ally, Fascist Italy.

A German invasion of Britain seemed to be imminent. Its essential preliminary, an attempt by the Luftwaffe to dominate British air space, was soon under way. British troops, the majority of them recently recruited, under-trained, under-armed and under-equipped, were deployed throughout the island to build and man defences against a German landing. During this time, any trained and fully armed body (that is, any that had not been physically and materially depleted before and during Dunkirk) was committed to Home Defence as its priority task.

While defensive preparations were being attended to urgently, consideration was given to what offensive land operations could be mounted with the least delay. These, for the time being, could only be on a small scale. There were obvious opportunities for amphibious raids on the

German-held coast of Western Europe, where German responsibilities now stretched from the Arctic Circle to the Pyrenees. Even the massive German military resources were inadequate to man this vast shoreline with full effectiveness. Clear candidates for the role of harassing the occupiers were the Royal Marines, traditionally charged with the provision of 'a striking force . . . immediately available for use under the direction of the Naval Commander-in-Chief for amphibious operations such as raids on the enemy coastline and bases. . .'. But the Royal Marine Brigade had not been at Dunkirk, had lost neither men nor weapons, was well trained and intact, and was judged to be indispensable to the country's counter-invasion precautions. The raiding task was allotted to the army.

The army authorities decided that it was a job that called for picked volunteers, who were invited to put down their names for unspecified 'special service of a hazardous nature'. Applicants had to be fully trained soldiers of sound physique who knew how to swim. There were several times as many volunteers for the new force as there were vacancies. Colonels interviewed and selected their own officers, who in turn interviewed and selected their own men. Training was rigorously tough. The maintenance of discipline was simplified by the introduction of the ultimate sanction of dismissal. The unsatisfactory, the disillusioned, the troublesome, were 'RTU'd', Returned to Unit, and replaced from the throng of volunteers anxious to get in. At their inception, the new units were known as Special Service Battalions. The name was soon changed to Commando, with the enthusiastic endorsement of Winston Churchill, who had sound personal reasons to recall the self-reliance, hardiness and initiative of the Boer Commandos of the South African War of forty years before. The force's headquarters, however, retained the title of the Special Service Brigade.

The original ambitions for early action of both the progenitors of, and the volunteers to, the first army Commandos were largely frustrated. A few small raids amounting to seaborne patrol actions were mounted against the French coast and the Channel Islands, but none was conspicuously successful. There were shortages of everything from suitable landing craft to Tommy guns. Imaginative and impractical operations conceived by Churchill in his capacity as Minister of Defence were argued out of court as militarily pointless by the Chiefs of Staff, after much ill-tempered wrangling. Plans were repeatedly made, and as repeatedly cancelled. The first reasonably sized Commando operations took place not against occupied Europe but in the Middle East, where Colonel Robert Laycock arrived with 'Layforce' – Nos 7, 8 and 11 Commandos – in early 1941. Different parts of Layforce raided Bardia, fought the Vichy French in Syria, tried unsuccessfully to shoot General Rommel of the Afrika Korps, and suffered heavy casualties in Crete. The force was then disbanded, but it left a notable legacy. From some of its survivors were formed the Special Air Service and its seaborne counterpart, the Special Boat Section.

Small-scale raiding, of useful reconnaissance value and minor destructive impact, skilfully publicised to boost public morale, continued from Britain throughout 1941 and 1942. There were also some much larger combined operations, involving all three fighting services, in which the army commandos furnished the ground force element. Two of these, unopposed, were against the Lofoten islands, where oil installations and some shipping were destroyed. A landing at Vaagso, in Norway, strongly opposed, led to similar results and considerable casualties. The most lastingly significant enterprise in this series was at St Nazaire, on the Atlantic coast of France. Its harbour basin held a dry dock and associated facilities capable of refitting major German surface warships which, if based there, could have caused chaos among the trans-Atlantic convoys upon which Britain relied for survival. No. 2 Commando, helped by demolition teams from other Commandos, were landed by the basin and blew up everything that they could get at. An old destroyer, HMS *Campbelltown*, was packed with explosive and run by the navy against the gates of the dry dock. Delayed fuses set off the charges on the following morning, and put the dry dock out of action for the remainder of the war, killing a large number of German naval and military spectators who had come to take a look at *Campbelltown*. No. 2 Commando's casualty list was long, and included the commanding officer, Lieutenant-Colonel A.C. Newman. Newman's successor was

112

Lieutenant-Colonel Jack Churchill, who had already distinguished himself at Vaagso.

As time went by, and Britain acquired first the Soviet Union and then the United States as allies, there was a fundamental change in the nature of the Western Allies' planning. The rash German embroilment in the invasion of the absorbent vastness of Soviet Russia eliminated any realistic possibility of a German invasion of Britain. The requirements of Home Defence moved well down the priority list. Thought and preparation were turned to the retaking of territory occupied by the Axis powers. This change of emphasis led in turn to changes in both the employment and the composition of the Commando force. The Commandos became in effect specialised assault infantry, fast-moving and highly trained, capable of taking objectives of importance at a speed beyond the reach of a more cumbrous conventional infantry battalion. The speed carried with it a built-in handicap, more evident in some circumstances than in others. Speed was achieved by the sacrifice of nearly all the support and supply arrangements universal in standard military organisations. Commando soldiers carried everything needed to sustain them, from ammunition to food, on their backs. When, as in a spectacular action on an otherwise disastrous day during the raid on Dieppe in August 1942, No. 4 Commando got ashore, speed-marched to the German flank battery which they were to neutralise, assaulted it, destroyed it and re-embarked within a couple of hours, the absence of a long-term maintenance structure was irrelevant. Things were very different for Nos 1 and 6 Commandos in Tunisia during the following winter. For months they were used as ordinary infantry to man a sector of the line. They were organised and equipped for an intensive operation lasting not longer than forty-eight hours. They survived by dedicated, and sometimes amoral, improvisation.

The change in the composition of the Commandos was brought about by the return of the Royal Marines to one of their traditional roles. The Royal Marine Brigade had expanded to the Royal Marine Division. From this, and from a variety of shore establishments, was formed the first of the Royal Marine Commandos. It was originally named 'A', subsequently given the number 40. Like the army

Commandos, 40 Commando was an all-volunteer unit. Its first action was at Dieppe, where its casualties were heavy. One of the more lightly hurt was a young captain, 'Pops' Manners, who was blown from his craft into the sea by shellfire, but returned to England to fight again. A second Royal Marine Commando, No. 41, also composed entirely of volunteers, was formed shortly after Dieppe, in late 1942.

In the year following, there came a decision that illustrated a basic philosophical difference in approach between the army and the Royal Marines. The Corps of the Royal Marines were indifferent to the volunteering ethos upon which the army Commandos set such store. They produced seven new Royal Marine Commandos by the elementary process of slimming down and converting seven of the existing battalions of the Royal Marine Division.

The first of these to go through the constructively devised ardours of the Commando Basic Training Centre at Achnacarry, the ancestral home in the Scottish Highlands of Cameron of Lochiel, was No. 43 Commando, late the 2nd Battalion, Royal Marines. The process was exhausting, but it was new only in detail. Cross-country marching over mountains, cliff climbing, river crossings in which a simulated enemy fired live ammunition just above the heads of the attackers, and speed marches in which the marchers, carrying weapons, ammunition, full packs and water bottles, covered seven miles in one hour and twelve miles in two, were well within the abilities and experience of the marines. They had been rehearsing similarly for the past three years. The Royal Marine Division had been arguably the best trained, and the most physically fit, military formation in the United Kingdom.

One of the outcomes of this thinking in high places, and exertions in lower places, was that Tom Churchill had at his disposition four Commandos of similar strength and organisation, but of differing collective personality. Three of the four were to fight in Yugoslavia for varying periods. No. 2 Commando, formed from volunteers from a wide spread of most corps and regiments in the British army, and leavened by a vigorous element of continental Europeans, was commanded by Brigadier Tom Churchill's elder brother, Colonel Jack Churchill of the Manchester

Regiment. The leader of No. 40 Royal Marine Commando, the original marine volunteers, was Lieutenant-Colonel Pops Manners, whose individual style of leadership inspired in his followers a feeling that years later was to be described simply by one of his former troop commanders as 'love'. No. 43 Royal Marine Commando was a transmogrified battalion of mixed volunteers and pressed men with a workmanlike and unsentimental approach to their task. Their commanding officer was Lieutenant-Colonel R.W.B. 'Bonzo' Simonds, an orthodox, militarily highly educated regular and a firm disciplinarian, much respected but not always looked upon by his followers with warm affection. All three Commandos were well suited to what lay ahead of them.

NINE

First Raids from Vis

After the discussion between Fitzroy Maclean and Brigadier Tom Churchill at the New Year's Eve celebration in Molfetta, and after the prime ministerial endorsement issued at Marrakech, matters moved forward rapidly. On 6 January 1944, less than a week since Maclean had first floated his ideas to Tom Churchill, Jack Churchill was ordered to make a reconnaissance of the island of Vis. 'The Commanding Officer', reads No. 2 Commando's war diary, 'and the adjutant [Captain Ray Keep] departed to recce an island off Yugoslavia, which it is intended we should garrison for the Partisans and use as a base for raids on enemy harbours.' It was a false start. Intelligence reports suggested that the Germans might have got there first. The journey was deferred until the true position was established. The delay was beneficial. Jack Churchill was given more detailed briefing, and acquired some unexpected allies.

The briefing came from Brigadier 'Bonzo' Miles, who commanded the advance element of Force 133, the local branch of Special Operations Executive from which the commandos were to take their orders, and from Major McKenna, the Combined Operations planner attached to the force. They listed for Jack Churchill specific proposed tasks. They took note of his requests for the additional equipment his Commando would need.

On that same day in Molfetta, McKenna introduced to Jack Churchill the commanding officer a specially trained group of about twelve American officers and 120 men, second-generation Yugoslavs and Greeks who spoke, or claimed to speak, their ancestral languages. Known as

117

the Operations Group, they were available for deployment on Vis alongside No. 2 Commando. No. 2 Commando found them refreshingly frank. The Americans said that they regarded themselves as very good. They were definite in their ideas. Since, however, they admitted cheerfully to complete inexperience, they would put themselves in the hands of Jack Churchill. If he thought their concepts sound, well and good. If not, they would do whatever he advised. Jack Churchill, a hospitable man, took their leader to dinner, along with McKenna. Between them they drew up a training programme: 2 Commando would give the Americans an intensive course in weapon training, followed by another in fieldcraft, field firing and minor tactics in a suitably bleak area near San Michele. American open-mindedness and enthusiasm continued to impress, despite the fact that their executive officers were almost all approaching forty years of age, amazing venerability to young, wartime Commando soldiers. One particular American deed was much admired. They insisted on assembling a representative collection of all the special weapons and equipment with which they had been provided, for inspection and uninhibited appraisal by Jack Churchill.

On 10 January came firm news that Vis was still in Partisan hands, and that although the Germans were by now swarming through the other islands, they had not completed their occupation of all of them. Churchill and Keep set out at once for Vis. On the following day they were joined there by Brigadier Miles. Keep stayed on Vis, reconnoitring defensive positions and making arrangements for the unit's future accommodation. Miles and Churchill left on a Partisan-conducted tour of Brač, Hvar, Korčula and Šolta, all still holding out, just, and all clearly about to fall. It was a useful preview of ground over which there would be much assorted fighting in the months to come.

A Royal Navy motor launch took Miles and Keep to Bari three days later. On 16 January, Keep and a thirty-strong advance party of No. 2 Commando embarked on a Landing Craft, Infantry, at Molfetta, the first body of British soldiers committed specifically to a fighting role alongside the Partisans in the Second World War. The nature of their journey did not measure up to the historic significance of the occasion. For naval reasons the sailing time was advanced unexpectedly. The troops clambered aboard in a hurry, carrying one of their jeeps by hand. A storm blew up. One of the LCI's engines broke down. Her captain put her in to Manfredonia, another small port along the Italian Adriatic coast. On the next day the Adriatic was crossed successfully, but things began to deteriorate again when the craft reached Vis harbour. Darkness had fallen. Partisan sentries opened a brisk rifle fire on the LCI. The LCI ran on to a submerged rock and holed her bows. Partisan machine-guns thickened up the fire of Partisan riflemen, while the LCI doggedly and repeatedly flashed the recognition signal. This was at last recognised. The shooting stopped, and was replaced gratifyingly by music from a brass band and by a Partisan refusal to let any of their new friends do any work. Partisans unloaded the stores.

The rest of the available 200 men of No. 2 Commando followed within the next few days. They were deployed in three main groupings. Komiža, the tiny port at the western end of the island and the nearest port to Bari, was chosen for Commando headquarters and as the supply base. The medium machine-guns and the 3-inch mortars of the Heavy Weapon Troop were put into the central plain of the island, the one certified a few weeks earlier by Maclean's travelling RAF adviser as suitable for conversion to an airstrip. It was also clearly suitable for a German airborne landing, and it was the role of the heavy weapons to deal with any attempt at one. A mobile strike force was based in Vis town, the other little port in the north-east of the island.

In the making of domestic arrangements the Commando found the Partisans to be refreshingly direct and incisive. There was none of the interminable paperwork and argument that had attended upon the requisitioning of buildings in Italy. If the Commando wanted a house in which to billet troops or to store equipment and ammunition, they told the Odbor, the Communist Party committee. The Odbor at once sent an adjudicator, with full powers of decision. If he said No, it was pointless to contest the issue. If he said Yes, which is what he usually said, the building was allocated on the spot, a squad of cleaning women was sent to tidy it up, and the troops or stores were installed within a few hours. It was a ruthlessly high-handed disposition of other people's private property, but Vis after all was under direct German threat. Many a house-owner on the south coast of England had found himself similarly dispossessed during the dangerous days of 1940.

No. 2 Commando were impressed by more than the co-operative efficiency with which their living requirements were attended to. They admired the fighting spirit of the Partisans. These were dressed in a ragged miscellany of Italian and German uniforms, taken from the bodies of enemies whom they had killed, and their weapons were as heterogeneous as their clothing. Women, carrying guns and slung about with grenades, served in the ranks alongside the men and performed identical duties, in battle and out of it. All were inspired improvisers. They were generous sharers of what little they had. They were admirably disciplined. They marched fast, long and tirelessly, humping their loads of weapons and equipment along the steep, stony tracks of the island. They sang beautifully, in a lovely Slav harmony, traditional Dalmatian airs, most with the words adapted to carry a message of unit pride or Communist solidarity.* There was, in those early days, a warmth, generously expressed and uncomplicated by differences of political philosophy, in the Partisan welcome for foreign soldiers who had travelled a long way to help keep the German invader out of Vis and to make life as unpleasant for him as possible on the other islands.

The Commando's settling-in process, the detailing and study of defensive tasks, and the adjustments of domestic life in a new setting, lasted a week. On 23 January Colonel Jack Churchill, accompanied by his second-in-command Major Ted Fynn, his adjutant Captain Ray Keep and an

---

*There can be few among the several thousand British, and many fewer American, servicemen who were on Vis at one time or another during the next year, who have forgotten the strain and some of the words of 'Dalmatinska', the rousing song of the Partisan 1st Dalmatian Brigade. British old-timers on nostalgic visits to their old haunts still sing it with sub-tuneful affection. A loose translation of its opening words gives its flavour: 'Our First Dalmatians . . . Hail to our own Shock Brigade.'

officer from the Maclean Mission, paid a call on the Partisan senior commander, whose *nom de guerre* was Crni, the Black One, or Darky. Crni was found to be a pleasingly robust and aggressive operator, who agreed briskly to a sensible division of responsibility for the defence of Vis, and who joined with constructive enthusiasm in discussion of a British raiding programme from Vis to the other islands. With an officer of Jack Churchill's qualities in control, there were unlikely to be many moments when something out of the ordinary was not going on.

Jack Churchill's career had been a strange mixture of the conventional and the unorthodox. For ten years he was a regular officer in the Manchester Regiment. The rigidities and limitations of peacetime soldiering bored him. He discovered that an officer who resigned his commission after ten years' service was entitled to a gratuity, and further discovered that an officer who timed his resignation to the precise day when the ten years was up, and then demanded that the cheque be handed over without delay, was not viewed with favour either by his colonel or by the War Office. Churchill fought a vigorous verbal battle. He pointed out that it was an unarguable fact, verifiable from published records, that he had indeed served for ten years, that there was no reason whatsoever for any bureaucratic vacillation, and that he intended to take the matter step by step up the military hierarchy until he was given satisfaction. His commanding officer and his brigadier were successively unhelpful and reproachful. His next stop, his divisional commander, listened carefully to the case put to him and said that Churchill was quite right. Payment was made on time. He used it to repair to the south of Italy.

After an interlude on the isle of Capri he decided to walk to Paris, exercising one of his many skills, the playing of bagpipes, as he went. He piped his way to Paris, where he improved his finances by piping in restaurants. In one of these he was approached by a brother-musician, a Thai prince who was a virtuoso on the mouth organ. The prince was being fleeced by rapacious hoteliers, night-club proprietors and wine merchants, who heavily overcharged him

for everything. Churchill was appointed to the post of
Royal Financial Watchdog on the spot, but when bailiffs
foreclosed on the fur coat of the prince's Swiss mistress,
Churchill gave up financial advising and went back to
England to become a film extra.

In this new trade his piping once more served him well.
So did his talents at archery (he had been in the British
Olympic archery team), at rowing, swimming, riding
horses, and similar healthy and filmable outdoor pursuits.
He was the piper in *The Drum*, an epic about the North-
West Frontier of India, filmed in Wales. He rowed for the
Dark Blues in *A Yank at Oxford*, which is still re-run from
time to time in the Old Movie slot on television. He spent a
happy and reasonably profitable few years in front of the
cameras, until he went back to the army when war broke
out in September 1939.

He was with the British Expeditionary Force in France,
and came back through Dunkirk in 1940. He was with the
first batch to volunteer for 'special service of a hazardous
nature' without knowing what it was. (He suspected that it
was something to do with going to Ireland in civilian
clothes, disguised as an artist, and poised to take on any
Germans who landed there.) He was at once made second-
in-command of No. 5 Commando, was with No. 3 on the
Vaagso raid in Norway in 1941, and took over command of
No. 2 when its previous colonel was captured at St Nazaire
in 1942.

The Churchill personal kit list for battle was idiosyncratic. He carried, and when appropriate played, his pipes.
He wore a claymore. His choice of gun varied according
to forecast circumstances, and was either an American
Garrand repeating rifle, a German Schmeisser machine-
pistol or a lightweight American carbine. The claymore was
more than just an eccentric item of private decoration. It
had been put to good practical use at Salerno during the
previous September. Jack Churchill, accompanied by a
corporal, had got out ahead of the troop that he had been
marching with on its way to attack a village at the upper
end of a valley. Churchill and the corporal reached the
village alone. Some of its German occupants were sleeping,
some were digging in and some were resting. By the time
the troop arrived Churchill was in possession of thirteen

prisoners, three of whom were drinkers who had swiftly given themselves up when approached menacingly by an aggressive-looking man waving a claymore at them; the other ten were the sleepy crew of a mortar who had been awakened noisily and confronted by the same sight. There were more to come. A selected prisoner was taken on a tour of German sentry posts. When each sentry challenged, the prisoner gave the counter-sign, Jack Churchill made threats with his sword, and each sentry surrendered in turn. The total on the scoreboard was more than thirty. Most colonels did not behave like that. Jack Churchill was an unusual colonel, as the Partisans were to discover to their pleasure.

In nine days of heavy fighting at Salerno during the previous September No. 2 Commando and No. 41 Royal Marine Commando had had 367 killed, wounded or missing out of a committed strength of 738. It was a loss rate of 50 per cent. The percentage fell when many of the wounded recovered sufficiently to return to work, but a large intake of replacements was still necessary. The Royal Marines found theirs from within the resources of the Corps. No. 2 sought theirs from army volunteers, and at once found themselves facing difficulties that had been barely noticeable in the past. Commanding officers of units with the rest of the Italian campaign ahead of them, or earmarked for the imminent landings in north-west Europe, had no interest in letting go of what by definition would be the pick of their best officers and men. A crisp series of 'Nil Returns' suggested that the question had not been put, and never would be put, to the potential clientele. Colonel Jack Churchill shifted his attentions to the Infantry Replacement Depots of North Africa.

These soulless transit institutions housed an inconstant population of recovered sick and wounded, military criminals who had completed their sentences in detention centres, former belongers of units that had been disbanded for one reason or another, and the miscellaneously lost and strayed. Churchill was given permission to recruit among them. There were four times as many applicants as he had vacancies. Some were wildly unsuitable. But he and his officers found enough excellent material to fill most of the gaps. He also found that there were in the Middle East a sizeable number of fit and versatile continental Europeans who were employed as Pioneer Corps road makers or drivers in non-combatant units. These people, German Jews and German trade unionists whose families had suffered under Hitler, Poles and anti-Franco Spaniards, were inspired by a deep hatred of Nazism and all that it stood for. He took them on in numbers, and never regretted the decision. They were hardy, enduring and dedicated. Of them all his preference was for Germans. They all spoke good English; of course, to a fighting unit engaged against Germans there were clear advantages in having a proportion of soldiers who were bilingual in English and German.

It was because of the need to train these replacements up to acceptable Commando standards that No. 2 Commando arrived on Vis only 200 strong. The training, in Italy, was long and thorough. But it at last came to its end and the Vis garrison was soon strengthened by fresh drafts of reinforcements from almost every regiment in the British army,* and with the foreigners distributed among every troop and treated like everyone else. Two additions of foreigners in formed bodies added further to the island's strength. These were the Americans of the Operations Group, their training in Italy now also completed; and the Yugoslav Troop of No. 10 Inter-Allied Commando, one of the more colourful of the army Commandos made up of individual national troops of exiled Norwegians, Belgians, Frenchmen and so on. The Yugoslav Troop was to give No. 2 Commando its introduction to the labyrinthine complexities of Balkan politics.

*

*The nominal roll of No. 2 Commando's officers at about this time gives an indication of the wideness of the spread. There were representatives, more than one in some cases, of the Manchester Regiment, Gordon Highlanders, King's Regiment, South Wales Borderers, Herts, Lincolns, Cameron Highlanders, Reconnaissance Corps, Royal Artillery, Royal Welch Fusiliers, Northumberland Fusiliers, the King's Royal Rifle Corps, the Somerset Light Infantry, Royal Signals, the Coldstream Guards and the King's Shropshire Light Infantry.

The training did not stop when the newcomers left Italy. Both they and the old hands were kept at it incessantly, stripping and reassembling weapons, shooting, cross-country marching, speed marching, map reading, tactics, anti-invasion dry runs, landing exercises. On 27 January Jack Churchill put in his first raid, on the island of Hvar. It was a carefully planned affair, designed primarily as a 'nursery-slope test' for members of the new intake. The force was carried in Partisan schooners, which, despite the patent enthusiasm of their crews, were a less than satisfactory means of transport. Two schooners lost contact, one holed on the rocks, and half the force failed to land. The half that did so found disembarkation from a schooner to be a slow and awkward process, and re-embarkation to be similarly clumsy. But they killed two Germans, and brought back three prisoners and a captured heavy machine-gun. There were no Commando casualties. It was small-scale stuff, but it was innovatory – the first fight of the war on Yugoslav soil of British and American troops against Germans. The highly efficient Partisan intelligence-gathering network soon reported signs of German perturbation. With the exception of some coastal observations posts, which were doubled in strength, all German troops in outlying posts on the island were called in and concentrated in a strongpoint in the lovely old Venetian Hvar town.

The primary role of No. 2 Commando was to preserve Vis as a safe base through which supplies from the Western Allies could be channelled to the Partisans. No chances could be taken with this defensive priority, which was honoured to the full. Enough people, and in those early days there were always far too few people, had always to stay on the island in rehearsed readiness to repel attempted German landings by sea, air or both. But the German prospects of making a realistic attempt on Vis would clearly be diminished if German attention could be diverted economically to contrived irritations elsewhere, on land and at sea. As we have seen, motor torpedo boats and motor gun boats of the Royal Navy had been operating in Dalmatian waters since the middle of the October of the previous year, 1943, harassing and sinking German coastal shipping. (The Yugoslav Navy museum in Split lists the tally of RN Coastal Forces successes for 1943–4 as one German destroyer, *Neouwa*, and eighty-four other miscellaneous craft sunk, twenty-four captured and thirteen damaged.) The capturing of boats required boarding parties. The navy had earlier provided their own, but in action every man on an MTB or an MGB had essential functions to perform, and it would clearly be helpful if the boats could carry boarding parties additional to their crews. With the warm endorsement of Lieutenant-Commander Morgan Giles, the Senior Naval Officer, Vis, the job was taken on by the Commandos, almost from the moment of their arrival. In the weeks following the nursery-slope raid on Hvar, Jack Churchill retained the bulk of his force upon Vis, sent out boarding parties with the navy, and despatched small reconnaissance parties, authorised to attack targets of opportunity, to the other islands. In the meantime he and his staff worked upon plans for a major raid, to be sharp and short because Vis could not be left exposed for too long.

One of the oddities of life in German-occupied Dalmatia was that although the Germans carried out spot checks and searches of fishing craft, they put no ban upon fishing by night. There was thus always a lot of legitimate (from the German point of view) movement of sea traffic, distinguishable by bobbing acetylene masthead lights. Partisan craft on less pacific missions merged unobtrusively and with little interference among the fishing fleet, much of which in any case doubled when required as components of the Partisan navy. The sea part of the journeys of reconnaissance parties was almost without exception uneventful, and so long as a storm was not blowing and the stars were bright, it was one of the more restful and attractive ways of going to war yet devised. The schooner crews knew their home waters and the coves suitable for landing with experienced intimacy. The landing party, by prior arrangement made with the Partisan staff on Vis, were met and guided by local Partisans as knowledgeable about the ways around their home island as the schooner crews were about the sea. The civilian islanders detested the Germans, kept their mouths shut about British visitors, provided food, and contributed information about German habits, locations and strengths.

In the first half of February small parties of varying size were ashore on Hvar, Šolta and Brač. They were replaced from time to time, but in essence a permanent study was in progress of German dispositions and routines, and a permanent eye was kept open for exploitable offensive opportunities. Captain Bare and Lieutenant Parsons led the current team on Hvar. Three American officers were on Šolta, becoming enthusiastic about the chances of putting on an all-American operation. Lieutenant Barton was dreaming up something remarkable on Brač.

By 3 February, Bare, on Hvar, had identified the opening that he had been looking for. He signalled to Vis to ask that his whole troop should be sent over for an assault on the strongpoint in Hvar town. They were brought in schooners by Lieutenant Benn on that same night. Colonel Jack Churchill went with them, as an observer. He was not the sort of commanding officer to adjust arrangements made by a subordinate in whom he trusted. He wanted to see for himself how Bare handled his troop in battle, and to assess the risks attendant upon the slow re-embarkation into schooners of the attacking force during a period of full moon.

Bare's attack went in on the following day. Four Germans were killed. Four more were taken prisoner. Bare himself died while leading an assault on a house. Private Tuck was too badly wounded to be evacuated, and was left behind in the care of Partisans. Two other men were missing when the time for evacuation came. Bare's body was brought back for burial in the little British naval cemetery near Vis town, a relic of the Napoleonic wars, when a British naval force commanded by Captain William Hoste had been based on the island in circumstances with close similarities to those of 1944. The cemetery had been overgrown and neglected. Captain Ray Keep, the 2 Commando adjutant, asked that it should be cleaned up. The Partisans willingly provided a working party. Bare's burial is described in 2 Commando's war diary:

Captain Bare was buried in the afternoon in the British naval cemetery in Vis, the first British serviceman to be interred there for a hundred and thirty years. . . . A simple, unostentatious service was decided upon. The body was draped in a White Ensign, a Union Jack not being available, and was carried by six brother-officers. A piper from No. 5 (Scottish) Troop played a lament. The body was placed on the deck of a schooner. Many wreaths were sent by Partisans, and by representatives of all British services. . . . The schooner set off across the bay, and a volley was fired by Partisan guns. There was a simple impressiveness about the scene as the white-topped waves broke over the bow of the boat, and the smoke of the guns giving their salute to an Englishman who had fallen fighting in Yugoslavia curled lazily in the clear blue sky. The body was disembarked and interred near that of the Hon. Richard Anson, killed in action on his frigate in 1811. The Partisan company fired a volley, and the C.O. conducted the service in the absence of a padre. Our own men then fired the usual three volleys. . . .

One of the prisoners taken by Bare's troop was an unusually useful catch. In March 1942, he had been one of the defenders of St Nazaire during No. 2 Commando's raid on the dock there. He had detailed information, not known to Combined Operations Headquarters, on the extent of the damage that had been done during the raid. He was sent under escort to Italy for further interrogation. Shortly after Bare's funeral Private Tuck, thought to have been mortally wounded when he was left behind on Hvar, was delivered home, very much alive, by Partisans. With Tuck were the two men who had missed re-embarkation. It was the first of many instances of Yugoslav civilians risking German reprisals (that is, death) to succour wounded or left-behind British troops on the islands, until they could either be evacuated by Partisans or recovered by British search parties. It was a matter for admiration and gratitude that endured after later frictions soured relations.

The first boarding party to have a success was led by Lieutenant Stillwell. On earlier forays the navy had been unable to make contact with a suitable target. On the night of 3/4 February the MTB bearing Stillwell's boarders closed with a schooner impressed into German service. Stillwell's team was brought alongside, boarded, and after a sharp rough-house accepted the surrender of seventeen disconsolate prisoners on the first leg of a journey home to Germany on leave. Stillwell wanted to bring the prize back to Vis. The MTB's captain did not agree. He sank the schooner by gunfire. When it had gone down the prisoners disclosed casually that it had carried a cargo of chocolates and cigarettes, rare luxuries on Vis. The boarding party in their turn became disconsolate. It was some time before boarders brought off another capture. There was much searching for prey, and a series of laconic reports of No Contact.

On Brač, Lieutenant Barton was assembling a great deal of knowledge and experience of the intricacies of island warfare, as currently practised in Dalmatia. His party was ten strong, and included a Partisan interpreter and a redoubtable German Jewish corporal named Haussman, recruited in North Africa. The group was of a size that was easy to control and administer. Barton intended to spend the first of his two weeks on Brač in looking around and assessing the opposition, and the second in attacking it. As was customary, they were met by Partisan guides on disembarkation from the schooner that had taken them to the island. The guides led them on a four-hour march to Partisan headquarters, a small stone hut in the middle of a wood in the western end of the island. This suited Barton's purposes admirably. There were horses to carry loads, Partisan guides to take him and his followers to any part of Brač, and a wide range of up-to-date information.

Almost immediately, however, there was a turn for the worse. On the day after Barton's arrival, Partisans elsewhere on the island took their first offensive action against the Germans since the German landing of a few weeks earlier. It was a minor affair, the ambush of a German staff car in which two or three officers were wounded, but it led to a general tightening up of German security and to a general spread of alarm. Small, vulnerable, casual patrols gave way to large, heavily armed, alert ones. As on Hvar, outlying posts were pulled in to central garrisons. The Germans attributed the ambush to British troops, and publicised a colourful account of the action in which they claimed to have caused several British casualties. Early on in this furore, a captured Partisan disclosed under torture the whereabouts and use of the stone hut, the location of the beach where Barton's party had been put down, and particulars of its size and armament. The Partisan leader with Barton was warned of this just in time. He led their combined groups to safety through and around a force of 150-odd German soldiers who had been sent to beat through the area of the hut.

From their new headquarters, Barton began his pro-gramme of the study of dispositions and arrangements, as revised since the staff-car ambush. The overall pattern was of a total garrison of about 450 men, grouped in bases in a few of the larger villages. From these, strong patrols left by day to scour the neighbouring hills, valleys and vineyards, leaving observation posts on heights with commanding views. All were withdrawn to their central keeps before dusk. It was an efficient and comprehensive arrangement, and Barton had to adapt his own movements to circumvent it. He marched his party by night to within range of what he wanted to look at, laid up and observed by day, and marched on again the next night. It was hard marching. Brač is as hilly and rocky as anywhere else in Dalmatia. The upland massif rises to nearly 3000 feet. In February there were frequent patches of frozen snow, and a bitterly cold wind was usually blowing. Barton added a further, self-imposed constraint. He was not prepared to risk compromising the location of the new Partisan head-quarters. Approach marches aside, he did not operate within ten miles of it.

Almost from the beginning Barton for most purposes integrated his soldiers with the Partisans. They ate together, stood guard together and patrolled together. Barton developed a high admiration for the Brač Partisans. Their stamina and toughness were remarkable. They were gifted movers by night. Their scoutcraft was exceptional. Barton's party learnt a lot from them. In one respect they were, however, 'hopeless'. They had no fire discipline. The moment that they saw a German they shot at him with everything they had, regardless of how far away he was or of the advisability of keeping still and quiet until a larger target could be lured into range. This absence of restraint was conspicuously irritating on an occasion when a joint Partisan/Commando patrol went out for a planned ambush. Its preliminary was a thirty-mile cross-country march lasting for two nights and a day, and with no food for thirty hours. After this marathon ('Very good training', in Barton's view), the Partisans ruined everything by banging away too soon.

But this one category of backsliding excepted, the Barton respect for the Partisans stayed undented. He was greatly taken with their commissary system, the passing of word on the island grapevine that a meal was wanted at X for Y people at Z o'clock, and its unfailing delivery by a small boy or a woman. Most of all, he was impressed by the thoroughness with which the islanders collected information about the Germans and passed it to the Partisan Commandant. This intelligence was in constant flow. Some of it was detailed enough to list the rooms in which individual named German soldiers slept. It was a piece of information of this sort that stimulated Barton to reflect upon the definition of the targets of opportunity that he had been encouraged to engage. Barton concluded that the most opportune target in the vicinity was the German Commandant at Nerežišće. Barton decided to kill him.

Nerežišće is a small hamlet lying among the rocky hills in the centre of the western half of the island. It housed a German garrison about 200 strong. Defensive positions had been dug, and were manned erratically. A curfew was imposed from six o'clock every evening until six o'clock the next morning. During curfew hours sentries were posted on all approaches to the village, and the roads and the perimeter were constantly patrolled. The Commandant, whose name and rank were unknown to the Partisans, was something of a recluse. He was rarely seen by the civilians. He passed most of his time in the house which he had sequestrated as a billet. He usually dined in this house with four or five other officers at about 7 p.m., but his guests, who slept elsewhere, invariably left after dinner. For

Barton to get undetected anywhere near this set-up was, in the Partisan view, impossible.

The Partisan commander was nonetheless intrigued by Barton's stated intentions and nominated two of his men as helpers. The helpers were well known in Nerežišće, and were not suspected by the Germans of hostile sentiments. Barton at once sent one of them in search of specific additional information. Was the Commandant's house guarded by a permanent sentry? What was its layout? The helper came back on the following day. He reported that there was no sentry. Occupancy of the house was variable, but in addition to the Commandant there was a small Yugoslav domestic staff and, sometimes, three German batmen. The house was of simple, rectangular design. A corridor ran along its length. At one end was the dining room. The Commandant's bedroom adjoined this. There were three other unused bedrooms with doors opening on to the corridor. Across the corridor from the dining room was an extension which housed the kitchen. At the other end of the corridor from the kitchen was a small hall with an inner glass door, and an outer door that opened on to the street.

During the afternoon of 18 February, while his Partisan assistant was assembling his data, Barton from unobtrusive cover made a close study of the geography of the village and of its assorted comings and goings. It was, he concluded, an easy place to guard, and it was being guarded efficiently by sentries and patrols. There was, however, one exploitable flaw in the defensive precautions. Shortly before dusk, all the shepherds on the adjacent hills rounded up their flocks and drove them into Nerežišće. It was clear that familiarity with this routine had diminished German alertness. The sentries let the shepherds through the roadblocks without questioning them.

Barton made an unsuccessful attempt to get at the Commandant on that same night. He ran into both sentries and patrols, was forced to withdraw, and turned his mind to shepherds. He decided to become one. His two Partisans were helpfulness itself. They enlisted a genuine shepherd as a collaborator, who would make himself and his sheep available two days later, on the 20th. In the meantime Barton refrained from washing and shaving. On the morning of the 20th he smeared his face and hands with a mixture of dampened flour and mud, put borrowed civilian clothes over his uniform, and hid a Sten gun fitted with a silencer under his greatcoat. At noon, he and the two Partisans set out to meet their friendly shepherd. They found him in some pasture about two miles from Nerežišće. Here, the silenced Sten was stripped down by Barton, secreted in a bundle of cut brushwood, and taken on the back of a mule by a woman firewood-gatherer to a hideout prearranged by the Partisans in a barn in the village. After an interval, the two Partisans followed the woman. After a further interval Barton, the shepherd and his flock of sheep followed the two Partisans. 'This part of the show', recorded Barton, 'was very good fun and amused the shepherd immensely.' It amused the shepherd so much that it nearly brought fatal embarrassment. Barton, 'whistling furiously', was conscientiously ushering sheep past a German post when the shepherd suddenly turned, slapped Barton admiringly on the back, and shouted 'Bravo!'

Barton and the shepherd managed to negotiate this self-generated little contretemps with aplomb, and headed for the rendezvous in the barn. It was by now 5.30 p.m. By 6.30 darkness had fallen. Barton had recovered and reassembled the Sten and its silencer, and was reunited with his two Partisans. He had also discarded his temporary shepherding outfit, and was once more dressed as a British officer. There was trouble from a persistent dog which barked and sniffled outside the door of the barn. The Germans ignored the dog. Barton and the Partisans left for the Commandant's house, and reached it after a twenty-minute journey through the narrow streets of the curfewed village.

At the house Barton posted one of the Partisans, armed with a Sten, as a guard in the street. The other, also carrying a Sten, went in with Barton. They burst through the front door, turned left and ran along the corridor straight to the kitchen. Barton had intended to shoot the German batmen before he dealt with the Commandant. The batmen were absent. Present were the Yugoslav female domestic staff, one of whom, understandably enough, immediately broke out into hysterical shrieking. The Partisan told the rest of the women to hold her down and keep her quiet. They did so. Another woman spoke to

Barton in French. He explained that he was a British officer, that he had come for the Commandant, and that the women would not be harmed. The French-speaker said that the Commandant was dining elsewhere that night. One or other of the women would guide Barton to the house where this meal was being held. Barton accepted the offer, but before acting on it decided to search the house for anything that might be useful or interesting.

He started in the Commandant's bedroom. He had collected the Commandant's automatic pistol, binoculars, compass and Mauser rifle, and was looking around for papers, when he heard the sound of a movement in the dining room next door. Barton ran back into the corridor. The Partisan covered the dining-room door. Barton jumped through the doorway. The room was dimly lit by one candle on a table. Barton's initial impression was that there was nobody there. He revised this swiftly when he saw the glint of an Iron Cross, reflecting the candlelight, in the shadows by a connecting door on the right-hand side of the room. Barton gave the Iron Cross 'a burst of about 8 rounds, and as the body fell to the floor, another burst through the head. He was a big man of about 180 lbs, and well over 6 feet tall. He was definitely dead.'

An extensive commotion ensued. The Partisan coverer pulled Barton from the room. The hysteric in the kitchen began to scream again. A dog barked. There was a developing hubbub in the village outside. Barton and the Partisan ran from the house, picked up the guard from the road, jumped a wall into a field and sprinted for open country in a retreat that 'was unplanned and somewhat undignified'. They were through the perimeter and away before the guards had understood what had happened. Barton and his two companions listened to a great deal of shouting and the sound of a few shots in Nerežišće. On the following morning Partisan sources confirmed that it was indeed the Commandant whom Barton had killed.

Barton wrote some helpful advice about the mechanics of shooting German commandants. Any automatic weapon would do, he thought, but there was doubt about whether a successful disengagement was feasible without the use of a silenced Sten. The hint was disregarded. There were no emulators.

TEN

Liaising with the Partisans

Reconnaissances, schooner journeys by night, boarding parties on the MTBs and MGBs (alert but more often than not disappointed), training, more training, island defence exercises and operational planning continued with unabated intensity throughout February. There were diversions, some of them greatly enjoyed. Among these were the haunting, swelling harmonies of Partisan choral concerts, and the stamping, rhythmic abandon of the *kola*, the wheel, the traditional Dalmatian folk dance in which a circle of men and women alternately put their arms around one another's shoulders and swing round together as the music progressively increases its tempo. The Commando soldiers were often invited to join in, and did so, with brio. An 'International Soccer Match', Yugoslavia versus England, attracted a large crowd of wildly enthusiastic spectators. Yugoslavia fielded two genuine and much capped internationals, both of whom before the war had indeed played against England. No record survives of the composition of the England side, but it is fair to assume that there must have been some doubt about the national credentials of some of the players provided by a unit recruited from English, Scottish, Irish, Welsh, South African, German, Polish and Spanish sources. The band of the 1st Dalmatian Brigade was in attendance, and played 'Dalmatinska' for a Yugoslav goal and 'It's a Long Way to Tipperary' for an English one. Yugoslavia won by five goals to two. There was great local rejoicing when the final whistle blew, and much subsequent conviviality between the two teams and their supporters.

No. 2 Commando also introduced Rugby football to

Yugoslavia.* The Komiža group of the unit played the Vis town detachment. Play was fluent, there were some spectacular three-quarter movements, and the tackling was thumpingly hard. The tackling and hand-offs occasioned tremendous excitement to the large turnout of Partisan spectators. A hot debate, words supplemented by gestures, was conducted about hand-off techniques by critics standing beside No. 2 Commando's doctor, Captain Brian Lees. There was mimed puzzlement about why the opened palm of a hand was used when a clenched fist would clearly be more effective. Lees left the match pondering upon the total of non-battle casualties that he would have to treat if the Partisans took to playing Rugby.

One traditional military recreation, sex, was decidedly not available on Vis. Under the puritanical Partisan code, sexual relations, and the even more heinous military crime of pregnancy, were capital offences. The rationale behind this harsh ukase lay in the nature of Partisan warfare. Men and women marched and fought side by side, and slept side by side, without distinction. Physical and emotional entanglements would affect efficiency and diminish the survival prospects of the whole. A pregnant *Partisanska* would be even more of a liability to the group. Some executions by firing squad of pregnant Partisan girls were actually carried out in the presence of witnesses from No. 2 Commando, and were met with profound shock and disgust by the unit. But the lesson was absorbed. Very few British soldiers and sailors were prepared to risk putting sexual partners in peril of their lives. One, genuinely in love, was reported to have taken his, very small, future wife out of the island by putting her in his kit-bag and carrying it, and her, up the ramp of an LCI when he embarked for Italy. Many years after the war a marine or two claimed to have managed successfully discreet liaisons, and, in one case, to have kept in touch with the lady for over forty years. But, for most, celibacy reigned.

---

*That, at any rate, is their claim. Whether or not they were the pioneers, the game has certainly caught on in Yugoslavia since the war. By the 1970s clubs like Split were sending teams on tours to Australia, and there was a knife attack on a referee in Zagreb by a player dissatisfied with a decision.

There were other distractions of the time from the task of fighting Germans. One was revealed from small beginnings. A soldier of the Yugoslav Troop of No. 10 Inter-Allied Commando was put on a charge of disobeying an order by the commander of the 2 Commando Heavy Weapon Troop. When the case was heard, the accused said that he did not know that he had been given an order. He did not know what had been said to him. Indeed, he understood almost no English. In the discussion that followed upon this reasonable defence, Lieutenant Tripović, the leader of the Yugoslavs in the British service, took the opportunity to say a few things about Partisan attitudes to himself and his men. When his troop had first arrived on Vis they had been fêted as returning heroes. This approbation had not lasted. They were now regarded as spies sent by King Peter, the Chetnik's constitutional head, and had been told by the Partisans that they would not leave the island alive. Tripović said that all his detachment were fanatically patriotic, and most of them were very Partisan-minded. Several had asked for permission to join the Partisans. He was convinced that if the contingent were to be posted from the island, there would be mass desertions and re-enlistments in the Army of National Liberation, an eventuality that would leave him with some awkward explaining to do to King Peter.

Tripović was, of course, in a classic contemporary Yugoslav dilemma of irreconcilable loyalties. The 2 Commando management of Jack Churchill and Keep were straightforward soldiers anxious only to get on with the war, with an instilled and instinctive belief that soldiering and politics were things apart and should be kept apart, and with no training in, or experience of, endemic Balkan political imbroglios. They understandably dealt with the problem in a crisp military manner. They told the local Partisan commander that Tripović and the Yugoslav Troop were an integral part of No. 2 Commando, and that no outside interference would be tolerated. As an additional measure the troop were moved to within the protection of the area of Commando Headquarters. A short time later Tripović was sacked, classified by the British as a failure. He was sent away from Vis (and the Yugoslav Troop were themselves to be sent back to Italy). In retrospect, it is hard not to feel sorry for him. He was, at a junior level, a replica of many of his seniors in the Royal Yugoslav Army. Draža Mihailović chose to stay loyal to his oath to his king, and was shot as a traitor by a Partisan firing squad. Arso Jovanović chose the Partisans because he thought that they offered a better future for his country in association with the Soviet Union, and was shot by Partisans when they broke with Russia and he stuck to the old, orthodox Party line. Tripović's problem, like those of Mihailović and Jovanović, was only capable of solution by a mixture of crystal-gazing and luck.

On 22 February 1944 there was a further ruffling of Partisan feathers. 'A celebration of something Russian was held by the Partisans, a sort of August Bank Holiday with bands and drinking.' No. 2 Commando declined to have anything to do with it. So did the American Operations Group. The danger of a German landing was still paramount in Jack Churchill's mind, and he kept his defensive positions fully manned. It became clear on the next day that serious offence had been taken. The British and Americans had boycotted Red Army Day, the anniversary of the Soviet organisation that was the fount of all Partisan military and much of its political philosophy. Amends were hastily improvised. Selected British and American officers were sent to follow-up ceremonies in Vis town and Komiža at which there were long speeches, elaborate cheers and the reading out of telegrams from Vis to Stalin, Churchill, Roosevelt, Eisenhower and Alexander. To British and American eyes it was strange that this sort of manifestation should be organised by the leaders of a threatened garrison in the middle of a blood-soaked campaign. British troops by nature and inheritance were cynically rhetoric-proof, did not take kindly to long speeches and had never been in the habit of telegraphing messages of encouragement and support to Allied commanders and national political leaders, domestic or foreign. But from then onwards it was accepted that differences of approach must be recognised and respected, and local protocol requirements honoured. The ceremonial side of Partisan warfare was not again ignored.*

---

*With some surprising consequences. Later in the year, for example,

Two other bothersome necessities eroded the concentration of 2 Commando's attentions. One of the tenets of Commando soldiering was that the number of people in a unit employed upon administration should be trimmed to an absolute minimum, 'teeth not tail' in the jargon of the day. Jack Churchill, as the Commanding Officer of the Commando, had a small staff that dealt with the unit's affairs admirably. Jack Churchill, as the Allied Force Commander on Vis (the Allies being the British and Americans; the partisans were an entirely separate entity), had no staff at all. There was considerable additional work to be done, from continuous operational liaison with the Partisan command and Morgan Giles's naval headquarters, to such small but time-consuming details as arranging for the meeting, transport and accommodation of a growing flow of officers from Italy calling on essential business. The extra work fell to the pared-down headquarters staff of No. 2 Commando. They attended to it, but they were pressed to their limits.

The second extraneous commitment was to the guarding, feeding and interrogation of German prisoners taken on raids and reconnaissances by Commando parties, by boarding parties, or through the recovery of survivors after the navy had sunk enemy shipping. From these sources, prisoners were accumulating all the time. Barton, to quote but one example, contributed five when he returned from Brač. There were soon well over a hundred. Some of those pulled out of the sea by the navy had no clothes. There were no reserve blankets to give to any of them, and Dalmatian winters can be cold.

Despite the hardships, the prisoners had been in luck when they fell into British hands. Tom Churchill had been commanding the British and American force on Vis for

---

Lieutenant Stevens, of 43 Commando, marched a load of explosives carried on mules over the mountains of southern Montenegro to blow up a bridge. The Germans had already left when he got there. Instead of blowing the bridge, the crumpled and begrimed Stevens found himself standing on the balcony of the old Royal palace in Cetinje, taking the salute alongside a Partisan corps commander at a mass parade.

only a few weeks when he was brought up sharply against a problem that was never resolved satisfactorily during the entire period of over a year of operations by British troops, ships and aircraft in direct contact with the Partisans. This was the manner in which the Partisans treated captured Germans.

The dilemma came to the fore in April 1944, after some notably successful Partisan attacks on Korčula and Mljet. Five hundred and five German prisoners were taken. The operations were strongly supported by the Royal Navy. Wireless communications were British, the operators speaking *en clair* in English. The BBC gave prominence in its news bulletins to these successes, gave exact details of the numbers of Germans killed and captured, and stressed the importance of the part played by the navy. None of the prisoners was brought back to Vis. The Partisans took them to Biševo, a tiny island to the south of Vis. Reports soon began to reach Vis from Biševo that many of the prisoners had been shot, and that more were about to be shot.

There were several aspects of this news which bothered Tom Churchill. The first was his moral and Christian abhorrence at the killing of unarmed prisoners. It was an abhorrence shared by many of his officers, who took up much of his limited time, as he explained in a long signal to Brigadier Miles of Force 133 (now transmogrified into Force 266), in requesting interviews with him to express their disquiet. Morality aside, there were practical implications to consider. Churchill listed these in the same signal to Miles. He was concerned that the attitude of his officers to the killings might diminish their respect for the Partisans to a point at which co-operation would be affected. There was, it seemed to him, a real danger, particularly in the light of the emphasis in the BBC's accounts of the actions on the British contribution and of the likelihood that the Germans had listened in to the British signal net, that the Germans would reciprocate by shooting captured British sailors, commandos and baled-out aircrew, and by refusing to restrain the Ustashi from doing likewise. There was the related and larger issue, outside his personal responsibilities but requiring urgent consideration by higher authorities, of whether the Germans might take reprisals on British prisoners-of-war held in camps in Germany and Poland.

140

Tom Churchill made a number of recommendations, the first of which was that a public statement should be made at the highest possible level repudiating any suggestion that British troops had any hand in the shooting of German prisoners, or held any responsibility for those in Partisan hands. This should be followed by the negotiation of an agreement between the Commander-in-Chief, Mediterranean, and Marshal Tito that whenever joint British/Partisan operations were undertaken, all prisoners should be handed over to the British; that Partisan prisoner-of-war camps on Biševo, or anywhere else, should be open to inspection by observers from a neutral power; and that neutral observers should also be present at the trials of any Germans accused of war crimes. Tom Churchill felt so strongly about the issue that he suggested that the future availability of British troops for island operations should be made dependent upon a satisfactory response, and that Tito should be told of this. He had discussed the points raised in his message with all senior navy, army and air force commanders on the island. All concurred with its contents.

On 5 May, Miles replied that the Chiefs of Staff in London agreed that a public statement should be put out. Before it was drafted they wanted to know the circumstances in which the Partisans had shot prisoners in April, whether any attempt had been made to try them, and if so on what charges. Churchill put the questions to Commander Crni, the Partisan commander on Vis. Crni replied that a number of executions had been carried out on Vis itself. The site chosen had been an isolated one. The Partisans had not wanted to cause embarrassment to their allies. Trials had been held in all cases. The charges had included the killing of, or cruelty to, Partisan men, women and children, rape, the burning of Partisan houses, and wanton robbery. Specific instances were given by Crni of the mass killing of 150 people, the pouring of petrol over seven old men who were then set on fire, the mutilation of Partisan prisoners prior to their killing, the enforced evacuation of people of both sexes and all ages from the areas where they lived, after which no more was heard of them, the abduction of young girls for service in German army brothels, and of a variety of rapes. Crni conceded that at the trials it had not always been possible to establish an unambiguous connection between the accused and the crime with which he was charged. In some cases soldiers belonging to a unit known to have committed war crimes were executed. Categories who had in the past qualified for automatic conviction numbered among them gauleiters, possessors of photographs of mutilated Partisans, kidnappers of girls for army brothels, 'sub-human types' and truculent or fanatical types. Crni asked Churchill to have the question of future practice raised through British channels with Marshal Tito. If there were to be changes, Crni wanted clear orders from Tito himself.

In addition to his talk with Crni, Tom Churchill ordered British unit commanders to make enquiries among their men about any evidence that they might have seen of the killing of prisoners. One contributor was close to home. Earlier in the year a blood-soaked, muck-stained German had made his way by night to No. 2 Commando Headquarters in Komiža. He had been one of a group of Germans who had been made to dig a common grave, and were then lined up beside it and shot. This man was only slightly wounded. He fell into the grave, shammed dead, survived the partial filling in of the grave, and escaped after nightfall. Colonel Jack Churchill had him smuggled back to Italy by the Royal Navy.

Written statements came in from several sources. Corporal J.G. Stickney, of 43 Commando, was present when thirty-four German prisoners were shot in the backs of their heads by a Partisan firing squad. The bodies fell, or were dropped, into a previously dug pit, and were then treated to heavy fire from automatic weapons. Lance-Bombardier C.J. Dunton, of the Raiding Support Regiment, went to look at a recently crashed Liberator bomber of the United States Army Air Force. A Commando soldier who was there ahead of Dunton took him to an open pit, guarded by a Partisan sentry, about sixty yards from the wreckage of the Liberator. There were several German bodies in the pit. They appeared to Dunton to have been mutilated, although it was possible that the excessive damage that they had suffered had been caused by a close-range *coup de grâce* with automatic weapons of the kind witnessed by Stickney. Lieutenant

Abbott, of 43 Commando, came across four open graves with uniformed Germans in them. He recognised one of the bodies as that of a prisoner whom he had last seen in the POW cage at Poselje. There were other similar submissions. Tom Churchill attached copies to the letter that he sent to Italy reporting upon his conversation with Crni.

After the receipt of this letter there was an urgent exchange of correspondence by wireless between Vis, Allied Forces Headquarters at Caserta, near Naples, and London. Maclean had temporarily left Yugoslavia (where he now spent most of his time, based at Tito's headquarters) on one of his periodic excursions for consultations in Italy and England. Colonel Vivian Street was left in command of the British Mission at Tito's headquarters, which had newly moved from Jajce to Drvar, also in Bosnia. Street was sent instructions to raise the matter with Tito, which he did. Tito at once issued orders that there were to be no more executions in Dalmatia, but pointed out to Street that in the peculiar conditions of the Partisan war, and given the revolting cruelty with which the Germans had treated Yugoslav civilians and captured Partisans, in particular captured Partisan wounded, he could not agree to defer the trials of German prisoners accused of war crimes. What he would do was to arrange that all those suspected of war crimes would be transferred to the area of his own headquarters for properly supervised trials under central direction. Crni, on Vis, confirmed shortly afterwards that he had received this directive, and would of course conform to it.

On 14 May, the Prime Minister intervened with a forthright personal message to Tito, to be passed to him by Street. Tito was asked to ensure that in all operations in which British troops were engaged alongside the Partisans, Germans who had surrendered should be treated in accordance with international law. The trial of war criminals could wait until later. The British adhered strictly to the Geneva Convention, and not only because 120,000 British prisoners were in German hands. It was a point of strict principle, and he could not have the British position in the matter impaired. 'It would be a great pity if our operations in the islands, and along the coast, could not broaden out as General Wilson* is planning and be made important and effective, simply by disagreement [*sic*] between us on this essential matter.' This not very veiled threat of sanctions was followed by a sweetener. Brigadier Maclean was in London and had given very good accounts of Partisan achievements. Churchill sent his good wishes.

Six months earlier, on 29 November 1943, the Assembly of the Yugoslav Communist Party, meeting at Jajce, had promulgated the 'symbolic nomination' of Tito as Marshal of the Army. On 28 May, Tito replied in a formal and conciliatory message in which he addressed Churchill as 'Your Excellency'. In sum, Tito took the point. He had, he said, already issued orders to all his commanders operating with the Allies. As Churchill had wished, the trials of all war criminals would be postponed to a later date. Meanwhile, those against whom there was 'indubitable proof' would be kept under Partisan or British guard until the time for trials was right. A second paragraph rehearsed briefly the German record of atrocities in Yugoslavia, and commented that it was no wonder that these sometimes inspired revenge. It was essential that the guilty should ultimately be punished. Marshal Tito fully understood Churchill's engagement in the matter, and assured him that 'you will have no inconvenience from our side.' The message was signed J.B. Tito, Marshal of Yugoslavia and Supreme Commander of the Army of National Liberation.

The British did in fact have a certain amount of further inconvenience on this score from his side, notably later in the year in Montenegro. There were a number of incidents there, in one of which, at Grahovo, 200 German prisoners were shot on the ground that they had not surrendered early enough when called upon to do so. The moral side of the problem continued to trouble many British consciences until the end of the campaign. It was complicated by an intrusive, distorting thought. How many prisoners would British troops have taken if captured British wounded had been run over by tanks to save German ammunition, if British fathers had been soaked in petrol and ignited, if British girlfriends and sisters had been taken for use in

*General Maitland Wilson had become Supreme Allied Commander, Mediterranean.

German brothels, and if a few more of the things on Crni's list had had British, and not Yugoslav, victims? It was perhaps as well for British consciences that the matter was never put to the test.

The care of prisoners-of-war remained yet another diversion of effort from the overriding task, the defence of the Vis base and the mounting of offensive operations from it, with which Colonel Jack Churchill had been charged.

During the last week of February and the first week of March there was a marked change for the better. Things became better still not long afterwards.

The three Commandos left to Brigadier Tom Churchill in Italy in the opening weeks of 1944 were committed to operations in the Anzio beach-head and in the mountains beyond the Garigliano river, on the southern approaches to Rome. One of the three, No. 43 Royal Marine Commando, was free of its Italian responsibilities by the middle of February. Tom Churchill sent it to Vis. Its advance party, led by Lieutenant-Colonel R.W.B. Simonds, reached the island on the 27th and the rest of the unit followed a day or two later. The British garrison of Vis was thereby doubled. It had earlier been strengthened by the arrival of some Bofors light anti-aircraft guns of the Royal Artillery, brought in to counter the increasingly frequent Luftwaffe attacks on Komiža harbour, and by the acquisition of a troop of the Raiding Support Regiment, equipped with Browning 0.05 heavy machine-guns. The Raiding Support Regiment, formed in the Middle East from volunteers, parachute-trained and designed to add the muscle of heavy weapons and light artillery to guerrilla operations, were further reinforced later and were to take part in every major island raid, and in some smaller ones of their own.

Along with this accretion of trained, armed strength came relief for Jack Churchill from his extra-mural command responsibilities and administrative chores. Brigadier Tom came over with the advanced headquarters of 2 Special Service Brigade, assumed command of the Allied force, and took over the planning, liaison and administration.

Tom Churchill also brought with him the oldest commando

ever, aged seventy-two. This was the five-foot high Admiral Sir Walter Cowan, who had been recruited by Jack Churchill in the bar of the Officers' Club in Bari, the Imperiale Hotel. The Admiral had a long and distinguished record of service. He had been the naval ADC to Lord Kitchener during the South African War. The colourful spread of medal ribbons on his left breast testified to both gallantry and variety of experience in the First World War and after it. He had been long retired when the Second World War started, but he exploited past influence to get himself into it. He soon found himself being courteously moved on from ship to ship in the Mediterranean Fleet's equivalent of the children's party game of Pass the Parcel. He had one land interlude, when an Indian Cavalry Regiment took him on for a stretch in the Western Desert. This ended unhappily. The Cavalry Regiment, and the Admiral with it, became prisoners when the Afrika Korps took Tobruk. The reverse was compounded by insult: there was an exchange of Italian and British prisoners-of-war too badly wounded to be of any further fighting value. The Italians threw in Cowan free, as a sort of make-weight.

The Admiral deeply resented this rebuff, but it did not daunt him. He was soon on his way round the Fleet again. In between ships he was with a naval officer in the bar of the Imperiale when the naval officer saw Jack Churchill's Commando insignia and had an idea. He went over to Churchill and asked him if he would like to meet an extraordinary old admiral. Churchill said that indeed he would. The Admiral, 'a midget', sprang to his feet, there was an affable exchange, and Churchill invited Cowan to come and see his Commando, then still at Molfetta, 'for a day, a week-end, or as long as you like'. The Admiral stayed for seven months.

He became greatly admired. His stamina, for a man of his age, was exceptional. So was his fearlessness. He went on almost every island operation in the charge of Jack Churchill's batman, who was detailed off to keep an eye on him. The Admiral made himself useful by performing two functions not covered in the list of duties laid down for a Commando's establishment. He was an assiduous brewer of cocoa. He took over the equitable distribution of loot, a source of contention to forward troops from time immemorial. The people who actually did the work in the taking of an enemy position were customarily so busy in a follow-up, or in standing by to repulse a counter-attack, that the acquisition of captured binoculars, cameras, watches and miscellaneous articles of domestic use became the prerogative of later arrivals who might not have heard a shot fired in the action. The Admiral imposed order and justice upon this distributory system.

With the provision of these valued welfare services went a capacity for entertaining conversation in a reminiscent manner. His most appreciative listeners were the Churchill brothers in their joint mess in Komiža. The best flow of talk was after dinner, which the Admiral, a slow eater, always began long before anyone else. This was probably as well. He offset a shortage of teeth by a simplified method of eating. Whatever the meal was, he was given a base of porridge, served in a soup plate. On to the porridge he poured or piled his share of everything else, soup, coffee, vegetables, fish, meat, custard. This he stirred up until he considered it to be digestible; then he digested it. Some of the more fastidious guests of the mess who saw the middle or final stages of this feast discovered that they were less hungry than they had thought.

ELEVEN

Assaults on Šolta and Hvar

In terms of cost-effectiveness, both cost and effect being
expressed in the squalid but militarily necessary terms of
the relative shedding of blood, the two most profitable
operations run by the British in the Dalmatian islands in
1944 were the first and the last, in March and September.
Each was on the island of Šolta. Each benefited from
closely interrelated co-operation between the fighting
services. The end product of both was the total elimination,
through death or captivity, of the island's German garrison.
Preparation and execution of the first, code-named Detained
1, involved a sizeable American element.

Colonel Jack Churchill, a convinced follower of
Napoleon's dictum that time spent in reconnaissance is
seldom wasted, had included Šolta within his elaborate
coverage from a few days after the arrival of No. 2
Commando upon Vis. Šolta is one of the smaller islands in
the Dalmatian archipelago. It is ten and a half miles in
length, running from east to west, and, at its widest, three
miles from north to south. Narrow, winding tracks join a
central plateau to a number of small coves along the shore.
There are the characteristic Dalmatian profusion of rocks,
a close network of stone walls and a lack of trees. In 1944
the only motorable road was a rough and unpaved track
between the villages of Grohote and Gornje Selo. (In
translation Gornje Selo means the higher field, an apt
indication of the island's topography.)

One of the more comprehensive and detailed reconnais-
sance reports to have been preserved was signed on 14
February 1944 by Walter F. Ruthowski, First Lieutenant,
Infantry, US Army. It encapsulates graphically the curious

structure of contemporary life upon the islands, the limitations, physical, geographical and of morale, that constrained the German garrison, the reaction of the islanders to foreign occupation, and the relative impunity with which the Partisans and their Western allies could visit, and move about in, what was technically enemy-controlled territory.

Ruthowski was not the sort of officer to pad his recorded observations with generalities. He was a conscientious noter of statistics, measurements, menus, meteorological phenomena and timings. His opening sentence gives an accurate foretaste of his style: 'Four Americans (3 officers and an interpreter) and one British captain, departed the town of Vis by fishing boat (about 50 ft in length and powered by Diesel engine) at 1900 hrs on 6 Feb. 1944, landing on Šolta in a small cove near Gradac, two miles S.E. of Grohote, 3½ hours later; distance travelled: 18 miles.' The party was rowed ashore, picked up by Partisans and taken to a well-hidden cave, halfway up a hill ('It lies directly on line with a stone hut at the water's edge . . . and a prominent boulder near the top of the hill').

The next day was passed in three separate reconnais- sances. Captain Bliden of the US Army took a circumspect look at the German garrison in Grohote. The British Captain examined Stomorska, and found that the Germans had left it for Grohote. Ruthowski himself went to Gornje Selo, which seemed to be on the verge of evacuation. Bliden, finished at Grohote, spent the rest of the day interrogating civilians from all over the island, who came to report to him in the cave. That night Bliden, the second American officer, and the British Captain went back to Vis, leaving Ruthowski and the interpreter, a US Army enlisted man, on Šolta. They stayed for six further days.

On the first of these they witnessed the move of the Gornje Selo Germans to Grohote. 'We were forced to seclude ourselves behind a stone wall within 150 yds of the road, to permit the party to pass. We were three, a Partisan, the interpreter, and myself. We carried an Italian carbine, an American carbine, Thompson sub-machine-gun, 2 Colt 0.45 Automatic pistols and an Italian Beretta, 6 British grenades, perhaps 250 rounds of ammunition.' Ruthowski enumerated the opposition with care: '. . . 16

men, 4 horses laden with ammunition, and 4 native women. It moved slowly, stopping frequently while the soldiers loudly harangued the women in order to get the horses moving faster . . . no march security was posted and weapons were slung. A heavy machine gun was broken into a two man carry.'

After that it was back to the cave for three days of 'rain and raw, cold wind', and a series of interviews in which 'natives reported odd bits of information.' On the fifth day Ruthowski, on Partisan advice, abandoned the cave. It was becoming too well known. The entire population of Šolta wanted to see the Americans. They moved to Gornje Selo and were put up in the house of a Partisan named (Ruthowski's spelling) Yurko Garbin, 'small, wiry, tough, and unofficial i/c group. Aged 30. Wife in Egypt.' A large turnout of villagers assembled at Garbin's house, and in the subsequent festivities a meal of boiled octopus, boiled cabbage, and (surprisingly) doughnuts was washed down with *vino*. The celebration lasted until 11 p.m., at which time, wrote Ruthowski with one of his rare ambiguities, 'we were bedded.' Whatever the nature was of the bedding, Ruthowski and his interpreter were up at 5.30 a.m. They moved at once to an isolated stone hut, one-and-a-half miles to the east of the village.

The peace of the hut was disturbed on the seventh day by the arrival of a small boy, running. The whole German army, screamed this lad, was after Ruthowski. Ruthowski, the interpreter and six Partisans who were with them grabbed their weapons, ran 200 yards south to the rocky shore and, once again to use a favourite expression of Ruthowski's, secluded themselves. It soon became evident that the small boy was less precise in the counting of heads than was Ruthowski. Six German soldiers, all drunk and vomiting as they went, were embarking shakily in a rowing boat at Livka Point, prior to crossing to the island of Brač. Ruthowski let them be. At 3.30 a.m. on the following morning he and his interpreter were back on Vis. He had much to write about.

From personal observation and painstaking enquiry of Partisans and civilians he had accumulated enough material to produce what amounted to a socio-military survey of life, on both sides of the divide, on Šolta. His findings

151

ranged from an informed estimate of the German numerical strength, through an analysis of who composed it and with what degree of enthusiasm, to detailed personality reports on the few resident Partisans and an assessment of civilian attitudes.

The German garrison, concentrated at Grohote since 'Feb 8th 1944 at approx 1530 hrs', was composed of between 150 and 160 troops, commanded by a second lieutenant. At least twenty-five of the soldiers were Poles. Others were Czechs and Slovaks. These reluctant conscripts from German-occupied satellite countries spoke freely to the islanders of their belief that Germany could not win the war. Given half a chance they would surrender, but only to the British or to the Americans. If they tried their luck with the Partisans they were afraid that they would be butchered. The Poles in particular were so clearly disaffected that they were actively discriminated against by the second lieutenant and his NCOs. On the march the Poles were always put in front of the column to prevent their running away. In Grohote they were segregated into one billet, the most prominent building in the town and the likeliest target for aerial attack. Unlike the German soldiers, who wore on the left breasts of their tunics the insignia of either a spread eagle over a swastika or an emblem depicting a helmet and rifles, the suspect Poles were permitted no martial symbols at all.

This unhappy force lived in five requisitioned houses in Grohote, the location of each, and the number of its occupants, being helpfully marked on a sketch map by Ruthowski. Every fourth man carried an automatic weapon. In addition they had at their disposal twelve heavy machine-guns, eight small mortars and an anti-aircraft gun. Ruthowski was rather apologetic about his ignorance of the size of the German stock of ammunition. He called it an undetermined quantity. It was about the only thing on Šolta that he had neither counted nor measured. The habits of the garrison were lethargic, possibly because one part of it had to keep an eye on the other. By day five pairs of sentries and a two-man wireless watch stayed in the town. The rest withdrew to the reverse slope of a hill to the north of the town, partly because they feared Allied air attack, and partly for 'rest and relaxation'.

152

Ruthowski's census figures put the civilian population at 1200 in Grohote and 700–800 in and around Gornje Selo. They were united in a bitter resentment of the German intrusion, then of only four weeks' duration, and they continually asked when the Allies would arrive and throw the Germans out. Meanwhile they monitored all German activity and provided the Partisans with a constant flow of up-to-the-minute intelligence, in the form of oral reports, notes and sketches delivered by men, women and children. One of these informants was actually employed by the Germans as an interpreter.

The permanent Partisan nucleus on Šolta was of four men only. In addition to the hospitable Yurko Garbin there was Yadran Ursić ('stocky, handsome, aged 23. The best man in the group, married, 2 children, wife in Egypt'), Pero ('30. Dark and swarthy. 2nd i/c') and Miro ('25, slightly built, pleasant nature'). These were supplemented on a rotating basis by a further four provided by the Partisan 4th Sector on Vis. They lived in hideaways on the south-east coast, overlooking one or two coves suitable for the landing of Partisan schooners. The Partisans' main functions were the passing out of intelligence to Vis by way of the schooners, and the forwarding and delivery of incoming and outgoing mail. Their catering arrangements presented no problem. A handy well supplied fresh water. Townspeople and fishermen delivered *vino*, fish and bread.

Given the situation described by Ruthowski, with the German garrison self-quarantined in Grohote and rarely sending anyone out from there, No. 2 Commando's reconnaissance parties were able to come and go by Partisan schooner to Šolta, and move about on the island, pretty well as they wished. In early March, however, there was a sharp demonstration that immunity from German interference was less than total. Its longer-term consequences were less serious than they might have been.

During the night of 2/3 March a party landed led by Captain S.L. Jenkins, once a Welsh Rugby international. With Jenkins were Lieutenant McMenamin, Lance-Corporal Wright and Trooper Scholem, one of 2 Commando's Germans. They passed what was left of the night in a Partisan hideout, and on the following day were led by a Partisan named Karlo towards Grohote. Karlo knew his way around. He took the party, undetected, to within about 130 yards of a house occupied by twenty-five Germans, and pointed out the locations of the anti-aircraft battery, the church, the signal centre and other items of tactical interest. Jenkins took compass bearings on each of these, selected a forming-up position for his troop in the forthcoming attack, and recorded it all in his field service pocket-book. The group withdrew, still unseen, and were taken by Karlo to his house for refreshment.

Over the wine diluted by water, Jenkins asked Karlo, through an interpreter, whether he would be willing to guide a large body of troops along the route taken earlier in the day. Karlo said that certainly he would. Jenkins wrote Karlo's full name in his notebook. In addition to Karlo's name, the notes now included the information logged in at Grohote, and labelled sketches of proposed landing beaches with comments upon their suitability. At 1.30 in the morning Jenkins, after warning everybody in Karlo's house to say nothing of a British visit, set out for a viewpoint from which he would be able to see Grohote from a fresh angle at dawn. They marched in single file. Two Partisan guides led. Scholem, Jenkins and McMenamin, in that order, followed. After about ten minutes, while they were walking along the road between Donje Selo and Grohote, Jenkins said that he could hear the sound of people approaching. Scholem asked him from which direction the sound was coming. Jenkins said, 'Behind you, you bloody fool.' Then they all heard quite clearly the tramp of marching boots and of soldiers whistling. Jenkins's team dispersed abruptly. The two Partisans, one of whom made a great deal of noise, broke right and kept going. McMenamin, more circumspectly, also went right. Jenkins and Scholem went left. McMenamin last saw Jenkins crouching behind a bush a few yards from the road.

McMenamin was about five yards from the road when the whistled tune ceased, there was a loud challenge in German, and a red Very light was put up to illuminate the area. A second Very light was followed almost immediately by a protracted burst of Schmeisser fire. There was nothing that McMenamin could do about it. Accompanied by the only member of the party with whom he was still in touch, the Partisan guide Miro ('25, slightly built, pleasant nature': Ruthowski), McMenamin headed for the Partisan hideout by the beach on the south coast of the island.

There, the Partisans were greatly upset when they heard the story from Miro. They were concerned that if, as seemed to be the case, Jenkins was in German hands, his elaborate notes and sketch maps might include a pointer to the whereabouts of Partisan hideouts and the names of the Partisans themselves. On the next morning Juraj, the other Partisan guide, reappeared. He was followed by Garbin, Ruthowski's old host, the leader of the Šolta Partisans. Garbin had been told by a woman that she had seen two British prisoners being taken into Grohote that morning. One was a badly wounded captain.

That this report could not have been entirely accurate was shown twenty-four hours later when Scholem arrived at the hideout. He had a broken ankle and had travelled for thirty-two hours without food. The ankle had been broken when he caught his foot between two rocks. When the group had dispersed, Scholem had stopped about forty yards to the left of the road, had cocked his Tommy gun, and had turned to watch developments. Jenkins was still behind the bush, two or three yards from the road. The German patrol was searching either side of the road. Scholem heard one of them shout: 'I see one against the wall.' Shooting ensued at once.

A few hours after Scholem had rejoined McMenamin, Garbin, who had gone off to scent around for news, arrived to say that there was only one British prisoner, the wounded Captain, rather than the two that the woman had earlier spoken of. The Captain had been sent to Split. There was further confirmation of this a few days later. A boatman from Split told the Partisans that a British officer, taken from Šolta to Split, had died there on the night of his arrival.

There can be no doubt that the Germans took a close look at the notes and maps made by Jenkins. They made no difference to the fate of the Grohote garrison.

*

On Saturday, 18 March, the strongest force yet to sally forth from Vis went to attack Grohote. Colonel Jack Churchill was in command. His sources of information, channelled and refined through observers like Ruthowski and Jenkins placed in the eastern end of the island, had given him all that he needed to know. There had been a continuous watch, replaced at intervals, of one officer. Night patrols, day observation through binoculars, and a mass of information contributed by islanders, mostly women who lived in Grohote, had helped Churchill to limn a clear picture of the size, dispositions and morale of the opposition. He had been less well served by maps. A pre-war Yugoslav government map in the scale of 1:100,000 showed too little detail. (British Ordnance Survey maps of one inch to the mile were at the time of a triangulated accuracy of 1:63,360.)

Air photographs were available. They had been taken at 29,000 feet by a 20-inch camera. They were inadequate unless scrutinised by an expert. One was on hand. Tom Churchill was a specialist in the interpretation of aerial photography. He had spent three years of his pre-war life as a lecturer on the subject to the Royal Air Force. A mosaic was made from the photographs, and the whole was re-photographed, enlarged and gridded. The end-product was 'a very fair sort of map'.*

The raiding force embarked in two Landing Craft, Infantry, one at Komiža, the other at Vis town. A spare LCI, loaded with reserve rations and ammunition for use if the force were marooned by bad weather on Šolta, also went from Komiža. Each LCI towed a Landing Craft, Assault. Two of these carried three Italian 47-mm anti-tank guns and 600 rounds of ammunition. The third took more reserve food and more ammunition of all kinds. The Vis LCI was the first to reach Šolta. It put into Tatinjak cove at midnight. It was moonless and very dark. Lieutenant McMenamin, who had been the duty reconnoitrer on the island for several weeks, and who had with him two signallers equipped with an 'S' radio–telephone and four

---

*It was still less than perfect. One of my personal memories of the second Šolta operation is of being disconcerted by a reproduction of one of these sheets: a number of contour lines simply stopped dead.

Partisan guides, was waiting at the cove to shepherd the craft to its landing place. The 'S' set failed to make contact. McMenamin blamed the navy. The navy blamed McMenamin. The craft was ushered in successfully by flashlight signals. The beach was small, rocky and awkward. Disembarkation took a long time.

When it was completed Jack Churchill had ashore with him one rifle troop, fifty-two strong, from No. 2 Commando; seventeen officers and 138 other ranks of Yugoslav and Greek origin of the United States Combat Group; three 47-mm guns, two of them crewed from 101st Light Anti-Aircraft Regiment, Royal Artillery, and one from No. 2 Commando; the four Vickers medium machine-guns of the Heavy Weapons Troop of 43 Royal Marine Commando; and the headquarters party of Churchill himself, Lieutenant Webb of the Royal Navy, and the spry old salt with the death wish, Admiral Sir Walter Cowan. Led by McMenamin and the Partisan guides these all moved across rough country in the black night to their preselected assault positions in a loose crescent strung around the west, north and east of Grohote.

The Komiža LCI beached at a separate cove five minutes after midnight. It put ashore three other rifle troops of No. 2 Commando, numbering 126 between them, two 3-inch mortars and their crews from the 2 Commando Heavy Weapons Troop, and a protection party to safeguard the LCAs. The three rifle troops marched off to thicken the semi-circle around Grohote. The mortar-men carried their weapons to high ground, where the three Italian guns and the four Vickers were grouped centrally under the control of Major Thomas of the Light Anti-Aircraft Regiment. With Thomas was Flight Lieutenant Hardy of the RAF. Hardy had a fighter–bomber-control wireless set. Hardy, and what he represented and could conjure up, was the trump in a well-endowed Churchill hand. A loud-hailer borrowed from the navy, was another essential instrument in the plot.

By 5.30 in the morning everyone was in his correct position. A troop of 2 Commando, and twenty-five Americans, who had been employed as porters ('slaves', in the Jack Churchill idiom) to lift up the ammunition and stores of the concentration of heavy weapons, had sweatily done their job and were placed in reserve, ready to carry out a fighting task. Desultory shooting began. Soon, all the attackers, less one rifle troop and the Heavy Weapons Troop, were firing away. They had been given strictly defined objectives. They were to make no attempt to get into Grohote. They were to take in whatever looked good locally, without exposing themselves to unnecessary casualties. During this phase they captured fifteen prisoners, and were reminded by wireless that they would be unwise to press too far ahead. The Royal Air Force was due shortly.

Jack Churchill, by means of the naval loud-hailer, and through the agency of one of the Germans whom he had recruited in North Africa, now addressed the defenders. Churchill wrote down his harangues in English. The interpreter broadcast them in flawless German. The Churchill advice was that the garrison should surrender. They responded with a combination of mortar and machine-gun fire that caused him to shift the position of the public-address system. A few minutes later, thirty-six Kittyhawk fighter–bombers of the RAF appeared in the sky above Grohote. They created a profound impression upon both the garrison and its assailants. Jack Churchill, whose personal experience at the delivery end of the products of air power had embraced the Dunkirk beaches, Vaagso and Salerno, was full of cynical praise. 'It was the first time that almost anyone in the assaulting ground force had seen the RAF attacking an objective that was of any real interest to them.' The Kittyhawks, bearing two, three or four bombs each, and machine-gunning as they made their runs-in, dive-bombed Grohote comprehensively.

When the hideous screaming, crashing noise of the bombing had faded, and the fragmented splinters, and fractured stone and rubble and dust, had subsided, Churchill's public-relations advocacy came on the air again. This broadcast announced an interval in the aerial bombing of ten minutes. Civilians, it was recommended, should leave the town, fast. Many did. The ranting directed at the German military was more specific. They should come out of their houses and posts with their hands up, displaying a white flag if suitable material were available. Those, however, who during the next half hour wanted to die for

Hitler should please indicate their preference by firing a rifle or Spandau at the nearest British or American troops. The last-ditchers would then be eliminated by further dive-bombing.

Churchill ordered a general advance into the town, all troops to fix bayonets. There was to be a minimum of shooting, but lots of shouting. Germans came out in groups, and were rounded up. The only firm resistance was from a couple of posts at the far side of the town, the occupants of which either were genuinely devoted to the Führer or, more probably, were unable to hear the loud-hailer. These were killed by Captain McCallum's troop of 2 Commando, and by Lieutenant Blidon's (presumably this is a misspelling and misranking of the Captain Bliden of Ruthowski's adventures) Americans of the Combat Group. There was no further shooting to be done.

The prisoners were sent off to collect their greatcoats, washing and shaving gear and personal belongings, and were then assembled in a group. Wounded were brought in. There was a final search of the town. German weapons and German papers were stacked. Six German dead were buried. A Partisan leader borrowed the loud-hailer, and used it to tell any of the civilians who wished to be evacuated to Vis to ready themselves. The second instalment of Kittyhawk dive-bombing, planned for 10 a.m., was cancelled through Flight Lieutenant Hardy's set. There was another row with the navy. The LCIs had returned to Vis after landing Jack Churchill's force during the previous night. The force had by now cleaned up Šolta. There was nothing left for them to do, and they were a sizeable component of the Vis garrison. It was time to go home, to meet their other responsibilities. The navy declined to take them off in daylight.

Churchill moved them down to the beaches, and set up beach-head defences. Brigadier Miles, the commander of Force 266, who had accompanied No. 2 Commando Headquarters as an observer, wirelessed Commander Morgan Giles, the Senior Naval Officer, Vis, to send the craft as soon as was possible. The wind was increasing and the sea rising. After further signalled exchanges the LCIs arrived at about 5.30 p.m., and embarked the force, a large number of civilians and one captive German second lieutenant, ninety-seven captive German rank and file, and six captive Croat policemen.

It had been a very satisfactory little victory. Šolta was denuded of all its occupying Germans. The cost had been light. Corporal Hallitsis of the United States Operational Group had been killed. Corporal Cox of No. 2 Commando died of his wounds. The Americans Captain Prescott and Lieutenant Manusos, the British Lieutenants Parnell and McMenamin, and ten other ranks of 2 Commando were wounded. Four others of 2 Commando, and two American enlisted men, were lightly wounded.

There was also confirmatory news of an earlier Šolta casualty, Captain Jenkins, wounded and captured on the reconnaissance two weeks earlier. Lieutenant Marvick, the German commanding officer of the Grohote garrison, told his captors that Jenkins had been shot through one eye and had four cross-chest wounds. He was still alive when he was carried on a stretcher to the boat that took him to Split. Marvick thought that there was little hope that Jenkins could have survived.

On the Šolta raid 43 Commando had been represented by their Vickers Medium Machine-Gun Section. Like the other heavy weapons taken to the island, and carried by hand up hills with much shedding of sweat, they had few shots to fire. A little time after the Šolta operation the whole Commando became embroiled in a complicated series of events upon Hvar, chosen by Tom Churchill and his planners as the next objective for a major attack. The top planners appointed were Colonel Bonzo Simonds of 43 Commando and Major Ted Fynn, the second-in-command of No. 2 Commando. When concentrating upon planning, a full-time job which involved the making of detailed arrangements and the co-ordination of timings with Morgan Giles's naval headquarters and with Partisan commanders, Simonds handed over 43 Commando to his second-in-command, Major Neil Munro, a young South African. Similar arrangements were made on operations when the force landed was accompanied by a large number of Partisan allies and British supporting arms. Simonds acted as Force Commander. Munro ran the Commando.

Hvar is a long, thin island with its length running from east to west, and its thinness from north to south. It has a slightly bulbous western end, where the coast breaks up into a series of creeks, bays and inlets. The ground, it need hardly be said, is hilly and rocky. On the north shore, about one-third of the way from the western tip of the island, is the small port of Jelsa. It held a German garrison of a size about which there were conflicting Partisan estimates. The highest figure on offer was 450, the lowest 120. As matters turned out, the best guess seemed to be about 200. The orders to 43 Commando were to destroy the German garrison of Jelsa.

An unusually large reconnaissance party left Vis harbour aboard a Partisan schooner at dusk on 12 March. Neil Munro, who was to command in the assault, took with him a total of five officers, one from each of the fighting troops, Colour-Sergeant McCartney of the Heavy Weapons Troop, Lieutenant Roberts, a naval officer whose job was to assess the merits for landing purposes of two alternative beaches, two Partisan interpreters and two Partisan guides. The journey was made on a calm sea in brilliant moonlight. The schooner reached its destination and anchored offshore. The party was ferried in in dinghies, made a rock landing and climbed, leaving Roberts in the schooner to go off to inspect his two beaches.

After a night at Partisan headquarters in a very large cave, Munro's team split into groups and went to look at the Germans. The viewers were protected by a screen of Partisan lookouts, to give warning of any attempted German interference. This co-operative Partisan contribution was to some extent cancelled out by the insouciance with which the Partisan commander led the entire party over a skyline, exposing them to the gaze of anyone in Jelsa who chanced to be looking in their direction. At least one alert German was. An investigative German patrol fell in. A head count by the visitors put it at sixty-six men. In mid-afternoon the patrol set out towards the mountains where Munro's people were. There had, however, been ample time for everyone to make a thorough study of what he was looking for. There was a clear view of German defensive positions, billets and administrative buildings in Jelsa, and of about 200 German soldiers, who could be heard as well

as seen 'strutting about the town'.* Approach routes for
the attack were noted. All work completed, the tourists,
less Captain John Blake and Colour-Sergeant McCartney,
who went for one last look at something of particular
interest to them, moved down to Blue beach, the second of
the two under examination by Roberts. There the Partisans
supplied them with an excellent meal, washed down with
vino. The German patrol closed in on the hills overlooking
the beach. The Partisan sentries stood to. There was
concern about what had happened to the absent Blake
and McCartney. Shortly before midnight the schooner
reappeared and put in to the beach. Blake and McCartney
were already aboard. The German patrol had still done
nothing offensive, but the Partisans wasted no time. The
party were hustled into the schooner and were back in Vis
by 3 a.m.

Afterwards, Neil Munro considered that he had taken
too many people with him. With a few exceptions, future
43 Commando reconnaissance parties were restricted to
two or three men. One of these small patrols, of Lieutenant
Gregory, a wireless operator and two marines, embarked at
Vis in a schooner bound for Hvar on the night of 20 March.
Fellow passengers in the schooner were Lieutenant
Odendaal and a sub-section of a dozen NCOs and marines.
Their destination was a tiny island to the south of Hvar
named Šćedro, upon which, it was thought, there might be
a German observation post with a radio. If so, Odendaal
was to dispose of it.

Gregory was dropped off on Hvar, where he was met by
Partisans. Odendaal landed on Šćedro, searched it, found
no hostile wireless station, and was hospitably received by
the inhabitants (total population, twenty-eight). Some of
the Šćedro men visited Hvar twice daily, and brought back
interesting reports to Odendaal, who wirelessed them to
Vis. Gregory, similarly well served with information on
Hvar, was also reporting to Vis. If the information were
true, and both Odendaal and Gregory were getting
identical accounts, the Germans had removed all their

*Whether they really strutted, or just walked about like anyone else, is,
in the light of hindsight, open to question. In the mythology of the times,
German soldiers moved themselves on foot by strutting.

Hvar garrisons with the exception of the one at Jelsa, which they intended to evacuate in turn on the night of 22 March.

Lieutenant Frost, 43's Intelligence Officer, was sent urgently to Hvar from Vis in 'a very small craft' to get more elaboration of this news than Gregory could send in coded wireless messages. Frost brought with him an American radio and its crew from the US Operations Group, whose sets were infinitely better than anything the British had yet produced. After a fifteen-minute, very informative briefing by Gregory, Frost headed back to Vis at 2.15 a.m. on the 22nd. A high sea had risen, visibility deteriorated, and the very small craft missed Vis altogether. But at 6.45 a.m. Vis was found again, along with two German Messerschmitt 109 fighters that flew close overhead but made no passes. Frost landed in Vis harbour soon after eight o'clock.

Tom Churchill called a conference at ten. The objective of the Hvar operation was changed from the destruction of the garrison of Jelsa *in situ*, to the destruction of the garrison of Jelsa before it could leave the island of Hvar. The job was to be done by 43 Commando, 280 strong, working in collaboration with 400 Partisans of two battalions of 1st Dalmatian Brigade. A bombing attack on Jelsa by RAF aircraft based on the Italian mainland was part of the plan. Simonds was overall commander of the force. Munro led the Commando. Captain Bogdan, a well-liked figure with a fierce moustache, commanded the two battalions of Partisans. It was the first large-scale joint British/Partisan operation.

The troops embarked in Vis harbour in the early afternoon, the Commando in LCI 260, the Partisans in five schooners. The navy provided an MTB escort and motor mine-sweepers, who picked up at least one mine in the Korčula Channel, south of Šćedro. The marines were landed dryshod at an excellent beach at Coromin Dolac, earlier checked by Roberts, on the south coast of the island. The five Partisan schooners arrived at 8 p.m., two-and-a-half hours after the LCI.

Gregory and Odendaal were waiting on the beach when the LCI touched down. Odendaal had brought his sub-section over from Šćedro in four rowing boats, rowed by the helpful islanders. The latest word about Jelsa was that the Germans planned to move out at 10 p.m. The RAF bombing raid had gone in during the afternoon, and by all accounts had done no good to German morale. Simonds ordered the Commando to press on with all speed to surround the town, and to prevent German embarkation. The Heavy Weapons Troop were to occupy a spur overlooking the harbour. The Partisans were to go to a position in the hills commanding the town, there to stay in reserve until matters became clearer at dawn.

The force marched across the spine of the island, 1500 feet high, tramping amid the rocks, weapons at the point of balance on shoulders, ammunition, food and water in pouches and water bottles slung from waist belts, spare kit and mess tins in packs on their backs. They were in their positions surrounding Jelsa by 10 p.m. Nothing much seemed to be happening in the town or harbour. Things started to happen on the hill tracks outside the town about half an hour later: the Germans were trying, not to evacuate by sea, but to break out by land.

About 150 of them, accompanied by a mule train, blundered in the dark into Commando Headquarters and 'A' Troop, commanded by Captain Jock Hudspith. There was a short, noisy, confused mêlée. When it eased the German column had split into two groups, one clattering away to the south-east, the other to the south-west. They left with Hudspith five dead, four prisoners and the mule train. The train was loaded with wireless equipment, ammunition and personal baggage.

The German south-east party, about a hundred of them, next ran into the Partisans on the high ground at Juraj. There was another mêlée, at the end of which ten more Germans were dead and thirty more had been captured. The Partisans lost four killed and had fifteen wounded in this fight. The remaining Germans made back towards Jelsa again, and once more found themselves among Hudspith and 'A' Troop, who killed a further six and took two more prisoner. Two marines were wounded in this second clash. The Germans, in small groups, broke north. The rest of the night was passed in the reshuffling of the various troops of the Commando to block tracks on likely German escape routes. The 3-inch mortars, on their spur above the harbour, banged away at German movement seen in the town near the church. Three more dead Germans were found there the next day.

By morning the contest had become something of a hunt. One of the Partisan battalions was sent to sweep the western end of the island. One was told to stay in reserve. Meanwhile 43 Commando searched eastwards and made contact several times with dispersed bands of opponents, who further split themselves up and went into hiding in the woods. The mortars caught one larger than average group in the open on a track near the north coast. A concentrated shoot killed fifteen of them. Ten others surrendered to the Commando, and another twenty, chased by the Commando, surrendered to the Partisans. At four o'clock in the afternoon the hunt was called off. The Commando reassembled at the beach. The Partisans stayed on Hvar. After a six-hour passage with a high sea running, 43 disembarked at Vis harbour at five o'clock on a bleak, wild morning.

Simonds added up the balance sheet. No. 43 Commando had three wounded and two missing. The Partisans had four killed and fourteen wounded. The bodies of fifty German dead had been counted, and there might have been some uncounted ones. Eighty German prisoners had been taken. So had seventeen Italians, who were not included in the count because 'they did not fight'. Simonds, like every other British soldier who had seen it at first hand, was full of praise for Partisan fighting spirit. Partisan assaults during the night action had been determined. A woman Partisan had been killed in one of these attacks, an event still sufficiently strange, and impressive, to British troops to be recorded in Simonds's official report.

On the mechanics of co-ordinating operations between British and Partisan forces he was cautiously sceptical: 'They [the Partisans] were a little difficult to control. After landing, they were with difficulty stopped from going down into the Jelsa–Stari Grad area, where they would have got involved in a shooting match with the Commando. As it was, there was a certain amount of firing on their part against British troops. The Partisans were too ready to believe information received from civilian sources. . . . In one case, a Commando Troop was reported as German.'

*

The cost to the Germans of the Šolta and Hvar raids had been high. The British and American forces on Vis, already formidable, were to become stronger still.

TWELVE

Naval Traffic

The clandestine schooner traffic between Vis and the other islands continued undisturbed by Germans, sometimes disturbed by weather. The chief purpose of these little expeditions was, of course, the close observation of German dispositions, but all sorts of ancillary information that might be of future use was logged in too: the suitability of coves for the beaching of LCIs; the state of tracks; the location of wells; the nature of civilian sympathies. Support on the islands for the Partisans was extensive, but not unanimous. Some islands were solidly pro-Partisan. On others there was a variable number with loyalties to the Ustashi or to the Chetniks, or who wished a plague upon all householders. The intricacies of internal Yugoslav strife were beyond the understanding, or interest, of most British soldiers. The prevalent simplification was that if you were allied to the Partisans, then it followed that the Partisan's enemies were your enemies. This sentiment omitted a few convoluted ideological intervening levels, but it made practical sense. A pro-British Chetnik backer, say, might not want to betray a British recce party to the Germans, but if he could he would certainly tell all about Partisan visitors, with whom the British were inextricably mixed. The potential consequences were the same for both Partisan and British.

These extracts from the patrol reports of spring 1944 give the flavour of what life was like on enemy-held islands, and of the type of information that was sought. Captain R.G. Schooley and Lieutenant Abbott, 43 Commando, travelled to Hvar:

13 April: 2300 hrs. Arrived beach below Zarac. Met by
Americans. . . . The Germans have mortars at Borovik
with an O.P. [observation post] on the NE slopes of
Hum. There is constant patrolling on this line. The bulk
of the German forces . . . is about 800. . . . 14 April: On
our return to Sveta Vedelia we learned that a German
patrol had passed through our O.P. at about 1100 hrs,
and proceeded by the track to Vrishir, and had
confiscated furniture and livestock there. . . . 15 April:
. . . we were able to observe a long stretch of the road
Selca–Brusje. At 1500 hrs we heard the sound of MT
[motor transport], and a few moments later a 3-ton open
truck came round the corner and stopped. . . . About 10
Germans jumped off the truck carrying a light machine-
gun, and deployed on the high ground left of the road.
Fire was opened at us from a range of 200–250
yards. . . . we succeeded in moving to another position
about 500 yards SE of Grablje. . . . On our return to
Zarac we learned that the Germans had entered Grablje
on foot, and were drinking heavily and confiscating fowl.
Remarks: We noticed that the Germans were very slow
in getting in to action, and appeared erratic and
indiscriminate with their fire. . . .

On 27 April Captain J.P. Blake and Lieutenant D.B.
Clark, 43 Commando, arrived on Uljan (an island far to
the north, well beyond the normal operational radius of the
Vis force):

Enemy positions: Town of Preko; Germans, 3 officers
and fifty men. Ustachi, 1 officer and thirty men.
Weapons: 6 machine-guns, No mortars. Positions: They
had bunkers with two single strand wire fences around
their whole position. The nearest fence was approx. 50
yards from the German bunkers. Mines between the
fences. Main exits from the German occupied part of the
town had wire barricades, which were drawn across at
night, or during alarms. . . . Some nights 14 men patrols
either went to Kali or Lukoran. . . . Hill Post 942992
[the figures are a grid map reference]: All German. 1
officer and 50 men. 4 machine guns. 4×81 mm mortars.
2×2 inch mortars. Bunkers with single strand wire fence

with 'S' mines. Had cleared field of fire on top of hill. . . .

Just as there had been on the outward voyage, there was much hitch-hiking between islands on the way home. Blake and Clark finally reached Vis on 3 May, in a Partisan ship bringing back wounded from central Bosnia.

If a major operation were planned, gunners might join the team, in search of gunlines for their own artillery, but most expeditions were smaller, concentrating on German gun positions, wire entanglements and minefields. There were many of these schooner trips, but only a very small proportion of them led to raids.

Another sort of naval traffic emanating from Vis was not so shy of attracting German attention. The Coastal Forces crews of the motor torpedo boats and motor gun boats seldom missed a night of freebooting from their 'advanced' advance base in Komiža harbour. Their normal tour of duty was sixteen days, after which they were rotated with replacement boats and returned across the Adriatic for maintenance, repair, resupply and relaxation at their advance (single advance only) base, HMS *Vienna*, at Brindisi. During their sixteen-day tours they were almost entirely responsible for their own maintenance. When a boat left Vis at the close of its tour, it was stripped of every possible spare part and item of stores that might be of use to its replacement.

Naval forays from the Komiža base during the first half of April 1944 are fairly representative of a pattern that had been devised some months before, and that was to continue for some months to come. An essential component of the pattern was the depth of the Adriatic close in to the shore of the islands and to that of the rocky capes and bays of the mainland. It was possible for MGBs and MTBs to lie silent and in concealment a few yards offshore. The most productive tactic was to approach selected prey suddenly and at speed from astern, and then to board her.

MTB 651 (Lieutenant Horlock, RNVR) and MGB 647 (Lieutenant Mountstephens) slipped from Komiža on the night of 2 April. The Senior Officer, Lieutenant-

Commander T.G. Fuller, one of several Canadians who were outstanding in Coastal Forces actions in Dalmatia, was embarked in Horlock's MTB. After some fruitless prowling along the shore of Mljet, they sighted a small schooner. She was boarded, captured and taken in tow within fourteen minutes. Booty taken included explosives, land mines, a jack hammer drill, cigarettes, cigars and eight bags of delayed Christmas mail for the German garrison of Korčula. There were four German prisoners.

On the next night the same two craft took two more schooners, and their crews and cargo, near Prsnjak island. One carried a deck cargo of 20-mm cannons. Each had a defensive armament, captured unused, of four machine-guns and boxes of stick grenades.

Two nights later MTB 651, this time in company with MGB 661 (Lieutenant Cole, RNVR) towed home a schooner laden with wheat, boarded, again without resistance, off Murter island. Fuller was out again with MGBs 661 and 647 on the night of 6/7 April. This time he had with him a Partisan interpreter and a ten-man Commando party. After some of the customary conversation with fishing boats – one fisherman who had previously run a fish shop in Los Angeles was given a present of a tin of soya link sausages – a 400-ton schooner came into view. Both boats closed fast to within 150 yards and trained their guns on it. The Partisan made sinister threats over the loud-hailer about instant torpedoing and throat-cutting unless her crew surrendered. Cole brought his MGB alongside, using as a fender the schooner's dinghy in its davits at the rail. The Commando boarding party swarmed over the rail in the manner of the old-time Spanish Main. The schooner's crew made no attempt to use their 20-mm Bredas or their light machine-gun. The schooner was towed back to Komiža by MGB 647, carefully negotiating a minefield on the way. The rations of the garrison of Vis, Partisan and British, were supplemented by 125 tons of butter, flour, barrels of sauerkraut, and goulash.

On the 11th, Fuller, in MGB 647, accompanied by MGB 661, and with Commando boarding parties again embarked in both, lay twenty yards offshore in Kosivina Cove, Murter island. At 11 p.m. the moon rose and gave a visibility of fifteen miles. There was no phosphorescence. It was an ideal night for a cutting-out action. This began shortly after two o'clock in the morning, when a north-bound convoy of three German I-lighters, an Italian assault craft, two small schooners and a motor launch came slowly into view. The most heavily armed of the I-lighters was towing the assault craft and one of the schooners. The two MGBs closed in at speed, blaring threats in Italian over their loud-hailers of immediate mass sinkings if there were any resistance.

The threats were ignored. The centre I-lighter opened a heavy fire when the MGBs were thirty yards away. A violent few minutes followed. An I-lighter was hit by 6-pounder fire from each of the MGBs and blew up in a great explosion. One of the MGBs rammed the Italian assault craft. The schooner which had been on tow was attached to the assault craft's bows, and caught the concentrated fire power of an MGB firing at about ten yards' range. The MGBs cut the German line, swung hard-a-port and circled the tail-end of the convoy. The convoy ceased fire. Two of the I-lighters had already sunk. MGB 661 went alongside the third, prior to boarding, but the Commando boarding party had been deafened by the gunfire, and did not hear the order to board. The first lieutenant of 661 found himself alone on the I-lighter, whose commander tried to shear off. The first lieutenant shot him. Then 661 put another short burst into the I-lighter, and its surviving crew surrendered. It sank a few minutes later.

The MGBs returned to Komiža with the motor launch and the two schooners in tow, all heavily shot about, and with thirty-five prisoners, assorted tool kits, several crates of German and British uniforms, and personal possessions packed for travel. The Germans among the prisoners all spoke excellent English. They were from a sabotage unit, and had been on their way home on leave.

MGB 661, with Fuller again aboard, and in company with MGB 646 (Lieutenant Knight-Lacklan, RNVR), returned to Murter island three nights later. Their first task was to land a Commando reconnaissance party. These were put ashore without incident, and the two boats lay close inshore, awaiting passing German traffic. A tug towing a tanker, which in turn was towing a lighter, appeared shortly before midnight. The tug was very close to the tanker, and their unified silhouette seemed to be that of an elderly destroyer. Fuller took no chances. He left out the loud-hailer announcements, and opened fire from both boats when the convoy was within each range. Nothing came back at him, and he realised that he had been mistaken. He stopped after two minutes. All three enemy vessels were boarded, in the hope of a further delivery of prizes to Komiža.

The hope was largely frustrated. The tug was by now incapable of manoeuvre, and the tanker was holed so badly that she was on the verge of sinking. MGB 646 towed the lighter and its cargo of hay back to Vis. MGB 661 stayed behind to sink the other two. The tug went down without difficulty. The tanker remained afloat after it had been further riddled by repetitive shelling and a boarding party had tried to blow a hole in her bottom with a depth charge. So 661 fired the last of her ammunition into the hulk, assumed that it would not last, and hastened back to Komiža, bearing the tug's guns and everything else of use that had been stripped from its deck.

An Admiralty assessment of the time had this to say: 'It would be difficult to find in any theatre an area better adapted to Coastal Forces than the Dalmatian coast, and the successes of the Flotillas which have operated there show that no opportunity of action is missed.' It is a summary that, deprived of its tone of satisfaction, might well have been made by the German naval staff.

THIRTEEN

Vis Reinforced

Nightfall and spring arrive abruptly in the Mediterranean. With spring came beauty, never entirely obscured by winter, but now abundant, and more evident to the eye. The rain diminished. The wild winds abated. The sun generated a benign warmth. Wild flowers – cyclamen, gentians, purple orchids – blossomed lavishly on the grey–white hillsides. Vis was only eighteen miles long and eight miles wide, and its hills rose craggily to its highest point, Mount Hum (1926 feet). From almost anywhere on the island there were vistas of twinkling blue–green sea, framed in the irregularities of limestone cliff. To the east could be seen a lovely panorama, the sunlit sea studded by the other islands, Hvar, Šolta and the looming heights of Brač, white when the light was at its brightest, but after dawn and before dusk a pattern of shifting mauves and blues and ochres, with black outlines. Behind them all, on the mainland, stood the towering backdrop of the Dinaric Alps, gleaming with snow in winter and early spring, still gleaming in summer because the reflections from the jagged white limestone mountains gave the illusion of snow. Spring and summer skies were almost unfailingly blue. The air was pure, scented as the days grew hotter by wild thyme. Amid these pervasive beauties, the Vis garrison developed its capacity for lethal aggression. In this they were greatly helped by a visit and inspection by Major-General G. W. R. Templer.*

*Later, in the 1950s, he was High Commissioner in Malaya, where he brought about the defeat of Communist insurgency during 'the Emergency', after which Malaya was able to achieve independence as a constitutional democracy. He ended as a field marshal, and Chief of the Imperial General Staff.

Templer had been sent in February 1944 by General Alexander, the Commander-in-Chief in Italy, to make recommendations for the provision to Vis of a properly constituted, balanced British force that would ensure the island's safety from attack, and enhance its value as a base for raiding. The initial despatch of No. 2 Commando had been almost casually opportunist, the product of the chance meeting between Fitzroy Maclean and Tom Churchill at the New Year's Eve party. Later came the arrival of 43 Commando, and of 2nd Special Service Brigade Headquarters. Later still, in May, Tom Churchill was able to call over to Vis the third of the four units in his brigade to fight in Yugoslavia. No. 40 Royal Marine Commando, led by their modest, enterprising and outstandingly brave colonel, Pops Manners, was not at full strength. It had incurred heavy casualties at Anzio, and had lost a further 25 per cent of its effectives during a subsequent period of a month when it was used, or misused, as ordinary infantry of the line on the Garigliano river. Many of its recovering wounded had yet to rejoin. The replacement of those who would never rejoin was a slow process. But the surviving nucleus was battle-hardened and formidable.

Tom Churchill's freedom to concentrate three-quarters of his brigade on Vis had owed as much to the absence of outstanding Commando tasks immediately available in Italy as it had to a considered study of the value to the Italian campaign of Partisan operations in Yugoslavia. An unsentimental analysis at Allied Forces Headquarters at Caserta of reports from Maclean's mission on the Yugoslav mainland, reports supported now by evidence from a spread of subordinate missions with Partisan formations throughout the country, and confirmed convincingly by Ultra intercepts of German wireless traffic, was focusing the attention of the Allied Command upon a military reality. German divisions had been sucked into Yugoslavia in an attempt to contain the Partisans. Should the attempt be successful, those divisions would be freed for commitment elsewhere, some at least to Italy where the British Eighth Army and the United States Fifth Army, facing fierce German resistance, were incurring heavy casualties. Military arithmetic suggested that stepped-up help for the Partisans would pay a good return. Greatly increased air supply to the mainland Partisans was one obvious form of sound investment. The strengthening of Vis, and the further exploitation of the opportunities that it offered, was another. The early *ad hoc* improvisation was to be replaced by a more powerful, fully integrated organisation, with its resources tailored to meet its functions.

The fruits of the Templer recommendations took time to mature, but by May 1944 they had transformed the condition, and in one respect the physical appearance, of Vis. An infantry battalion, initially of the Queen's Regiment, later relieved by the Highland Light Infantry, came from Italy to take over the role of island defence. The Commandos still had their defensive tasks, but they could now concentrate upon their proper job, raiding. No longer, as was the case with Jack Churchill on the Šolta operation, would the Commando leaders have to keep one eye on their watches to make sure that they could get home in time to frustrate a German landing attempt. Next came No. 111 Field Regiment of the Royal Artillery, with three batteries each of eight 25-pounder gun-howitzers, along with the squat armoured quads that towed the guns, the limbers that carried the shells, and a plethora of jeeps and other wheeled vehicles.

The gunners brought an immense improvement to the defensive fire-power of Vis. Colonel J.S. Elliott, their commanding officer, 'a bloody fine soldier' in Tom Churchill's assessment, soon became impatient with standing by to resist a German assault. He experimented, to discover whether a 25-pounder gun could be loaded into a Landing Craft, Assault. He discovered that the gun could not, as he had hoped, be simply wheeled up the ramp. It did not fit. It could be made to fit by temporarily removing its wheels and other protuberances, and could soon be reassembled after landing. Elliott took his findings to Tom Churchill and offered artillery support for future raids. Churchill accepted with pleasure, adding that he hoped that Elliott's Gunner boss in Italy would not be too offended by this bending of instructions. Elliott was unconcerned about what his Gunner boss in Italy thought.

Further troops of the Raiding Support Regiment joined,

175

with heavy Browning machine-guns, 75-mm mountain artillery, mobile anti-aircraft guns and, later, heavy 4.2-inch mortars. A heavy anti-aircraft battery was sent to supplement the light Bofors. Luftwaffe attacks on Komiža harbour were becoming more frequent, and on 28 March had been extended to new targets in Vis town, where a 500-pound bomb scored a direct hit on the only building there used by 43 Commando. Lieutenant Hancock, the assistant adjutant, and two signallers were killed. Other air attacks aimed at the airstrip area of the island's central valley killed several civilians, and one on 1 May, during which sixteen bombs fell in the headquarters area of 43 Commando, destroyed or damaged several vehicles.

The airstrip itself had by now changed the face of the centre of the island. Fitzroy Maclean had conceived it. No. 2 Commando had helped its gestation along by suggesting to the Partisan command that the vineyards on the floor of the valley should be uprooted, the separating stone walls knocked down, the stones removed and the ground levelled. The Partisans mustered a large labour force, and the work was done by pick, shovel and muscle. Even so, 2 Commando had not thought seriously that any aircraft would ever fly from it. They wanted only to con the Germans into thinking that it might be operational, and so make them more wary.

By the middle of 1944 the airstrip was the permanent base for a small section of Spitfires or Hurricanes, with its own flight control and servicing component, and with a ground guard provided by the RAF Regiment. The fighters flew their sorties from the strip, and made the most of the additional range that its advanced position gave them. Other aircraft, in trouble after misadventures over the Yugoslav mainland and unable to reach their Italian bases, made emergency landings there. Later in the summer, the United States Army Air Force began a concentrated programme of raids from Italy by heavy Liberators and Flying Fortresses on the Ploesti oilfields in Romania and on other strategic targets in Eastern Europe. (Anyone who has read Joseph Heller's novel *Catch 22* will recognise this sequence.) Many of their damaged stragglers headed for the Vis airstrip. Some achieved successful landings on a short, scratched-out earth strip that barely met the much

bove Captain D.T. Hudson (foreground) with Chetniks. Hudson landed in Montenegro from a *bmarine* in September 1941. He was the first, and longest-staying, British operational soldier in *:cupied* Yugoslavia.

elow General Draža Mihailović (centre), pre-war regular officer, leader of the Royalist Chetniks.

Above Mihailović, mounted, on the march with one of his columns in Montenegro. Mount Durmitor is in the background. Captain F.W.D. Deakin, with a party of six, parachuted on to it during a major battle in May 1943 and established the first enduring contact with Tito and his Partisans.

Below Mihailović (bottom left) dispensing what Hudson called 'fairly ceremonial hospitality' to his subordinate Chetnik leaders during a planning conference in Montenegro. On Mihailović's right is Major Ostojić, one of two Royal Yugoslav Air Force officers who came in with Hudson by submarine.

above Stores from the Western allies in Italy being landed for the Partisans at Komiža, in the Dalmatian island of Vis.

below 'Jugboats' – Dalmatian schooners adapted to warlike purposes by the Partisans – making ready in Vis harbour.

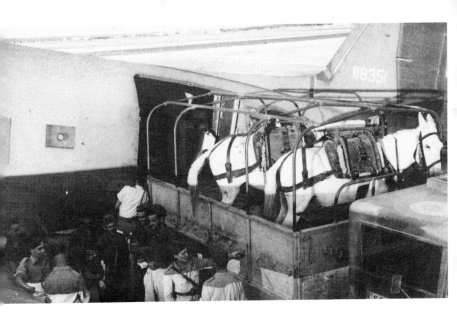

Partisans, in August 1944, embarking on a schooner for a raid from Vis. Most of their hauntingly ... ly singing was unaccompanied. This group has an accordionist.

ve Part of the massive British logistic support for the Partisans: pack mules being loaded into a ...al Air Force Dakota in Italy for flying in to a Partisan airstrip on the Yugoslav mainland.

ow Vis harbour, one of the two in the island (Komiža was the other) in constant use in 1944 by ...ish and Partisan craft embarking on raiding, boarding and reconnaissance parties. This was a ...racteristic scene on Vis, normally a peaceful backwater, in the summer of 1944.

Left Josip Broz Tito, pre-war outlawed Secretary General of the Communist Party, wartime leader the Movement of National Liberation, and Marshal of Yugoslavia.

Below Gunners of 111 Field Regiment, Royal Artillery, manhandling a twenty-five pound gun-howitzer towards a tank landing craft after a raid on the island of Korčula in September 1944.

ve Brigadier J.P. O'Brien-Twohig, Commander of Floydforce in Montenegro during the winter of
4, discussing operational progress with the Partisan General Vukanovic.

w Partisan girls helping in the Royal Air Force officers' mess on the island of Vis.

Above left   Lieutenant M.A. McConville in Montenegro, 1944.

Above right   A German 105mm gun, captured during the fighting around Risan in Montenegro in the early winter of 1944, repaired by 111 Field Regiment, Royal Artillery, and presented to the Partisans for further use.

Below   Brigadier Tom Churchill, the Commander of No. 2 Commando Brigade, escorting Marshal Tito prior to an inspection by the Marshal of British Commando troops on the island of Vis.

more modest requirements of fighters. Some crashed on landing. More circled the island and were then abandoned to ditch in the sea while their crews parachuted down, with luck to arrive on a not too rocky bit of Vis, with less luck to drift into the Adriatic from which most, but by no means all, were recovered by schooners or Royal Navy craft. The Yugoslavs have preserved statistics of the uncovenanted use to which the strip was put. In the few months of its existence it accommodated 215 forced or crash landings, from which 1936 British and American aircrew stepped, or were carried, alive.

Sea transport for amphibious operations also showed a happy improvement. Gone were the days of the first two raids on Hvar, when 2 Commando had to clamber ponderously in and out of Partisan schooners. Schooners continued to be used for reconnaissance parties, but this was for convenience and to facilitate liaison, not because there was no available alternative. A flotilla of Landing Craft, Assault, flat-bottomed, rectangular, their bow a ramp that was lowered when they beached, and capable of carrying about thirty fully equipped troops, was stationed permanently on Vis. The crews were Royal Marines, trained soldiers as well as sailors. This duality was on occasion put to good use, as in an operation on Brač when a landing-craft crew went ashore and shot it out with German infantry to cover the withdrawal of a Commando party.

Of larger size were Landing Craft, Infantry, shallow-draft ships with twin ramps on either side of a stubby bow. The ramps were lowered on beaching, and were used to discharge two parallel single files of troops. The insides of LCIs reeked nauseatingly of Diesel fumes. At a squash a whole Commando could be fitted into their troopdecks. Two LCIs per Commando was more comfortable. LCIs and LCAs had been made available for 2 Commando's raid on Šolta, and LCIs took 43 Commando on their first operation to Hvar. But they were on temporary loan from Italy. Until the Anzio beach-head was relieved in late May, landing craft of all descriptions were busy with its maintenance. After Anzio, the position was much easier. Many craft returned to Britain to help in the support of the Normandy beaches, but enough stayed in the Mediterranean to provide a handsome service for Vis. Some LCIs stayed in Vis for short periods. More often they were stationed in the southern Italian Adriatic ports of Bari, Barletta and Molfetta, in easy reach at short notice of the Dalmatian islands.

Later still there was another luxury, of great convenience to Colonel Elliott and 111 Field Regiment. The ingenious stripping down of 25-pounder guns in order to fit them into LCAs became redundant. Landing Craft, Tanks, put in an appearance. LCTs were big and ugly, and had cavernous holds with plenty of room for the guns, the quads, the limbers and the supporting vehicles. When the ramp at the bow was lowered the vehicles and guns could simply be driven on or off, in the manner of a modern car ferry (of which LCTs were, in fact, the precursors).

Along with the guns, and the reinforced fighting strength, and the fighter aircraft, and the landing craft, came detachments of army specialists: sappers, a transport pool and so on. The standing orders for the defence of the North Eastern Sector of Vis, revised periodically, and allocating responsibilities for the countering of enemy 'air and/or seaborne landings, either in an attempt to seize the island, or in the form of a raid', give a comprehensive picture of the resources available by mid-June. In addition to 43 Commando, whose colonel, Simonds, would be in overall command if a defensive fight became necessary, there were in the sector the United States Operations Group; a battery of the 25-pounders of 111 Field Regiment; a section of the Raiding Support Regiment; a platoon of No. 579 Field Company of the Royal Engineers; detachments of No. 64 Heavy Anti-Aircraft Regiment, No. 31 Light Anti-Aircraft Regiment, and No. 567 Searchlight Battery, all of the Royal Artillery; and detachments of the Royal Army Service Corps, the Royal Army Ordnance Corps, and the Royal Electrical and Mechanical Engineers.

Also in the sector were four battalions of Partisans, each about 300 strong, two companies of Partisan light artillery, and a further force of 400 Partisans committed to the local defence of Vis town. By now the Partisans were for the most part dressed in British battledress and wore British boots, while a high proportion of the weapons they carried were British. The capitalist provenance of these acquisitions was counteracted by indigenous fore-and-aft side-caps, with a five-pointed red star stitched on the fronts. Commissars, and very senior officers, bore a hammer and sickle emblem attached to the red star.

A great deal had happened since Colonel Jack Churchill first set foot on Vis in January.

The strength – though not the efficacy – of the forces gathered on Vis was displayed on 22 May 1944 on the island of Mljet. This was the scene of Operation Foothound, by common consent of those who took part in it the most exhausting test of endurance of all the British Commando operations mounted in wartime Yugoslavia. 'It was probably the most concentrated fatigue ever experienced by the Commando,' wrote Major Neil Munro in his report. This assessment should be considered in the light of the background and training of the people who experienced the fatigue. For years they had been practised in marching long distances, carrying heavy loads over rough country. They were among the fittest troops in the British armed forces. They had come successfully through the contrived rigours of the Commando depot at Achnacarry in the Highlands of Scotland. None of these preparations could compete with Mljet.

The essence of the difficulty was that too much was attempted over too hard country in too short a time. Brigadier Tom Churchill, who led it, regards the Mljet operation as, simply, a failure. The lie of the land aside, there was an unusual defect in the quality of the Partisan guides provided. On the other islands they had seldom fallen below the level of the superb. They knew every track, mapped and unmapped, every short cut, every obstacle, every inch. On Mljet they got lost.

The force that embarked in six LCIs in the Vis ports on 21 May was the largest British and American expedition that had yet set out from the island for battle. Tom Churchill brought with him his Brigade Headquarters, the whole of No. 2 Commando, the whole of No. 43 Commando, a troop of the newly arrived No. 40 Royal Marine Commando, a company of the Highland Light Infantry, nominally island garrison troops but with a flexible and co-operative colonel, the whole of the United States Special Operations Group, and the four 75-mm pack howitzers of No. 11 Troop of the Raiding Support Regiment. The six LCIs had a naval escort of motor gun boats. Support from Spitfires, carrying bombs, was on call. The object of the raid was to destroy the German garrison, estimated to number between 200 and 250 men, distributed among four wired and mined strongpoints on hilltops, two of which were about 1500 feet high, and two about 1200 feet. The plan was to land shortly after midnight. No. 2 Commando would head east for the two higher hills, No. 43 for the two lower. The 40 Commando troop and the Highland Light Infantry company would move to the east coast of Mljet to put a Stop above Sovra Bay, to cut off any German attempt at escape by sea. The hilltop objectives would be softened up by Spitfire bombing before the two Commandos attacked, and the assaults would be shot in by the RSR pack howitzers. The entire job was to be completed, with the troops re-embarked, by the late afternoon of the day of landing.

The convoy mustered at sea off Komiža, made course for Mljet and arrived in front of the selected beach half an hour before midnight. A beach party from the US Operations Group were the first ashore. They confirmed that it was the right beach, and that it was clear of enemies. The beach, about seventy-five yards wide, was of shingle, in a cove surrounded by high wooded hills, with only one narrow footpath as an exit. Next to land were 43 Commando, who found it to be harder than was customary. One of the ramps on LCI 281 was out of order. The other nearly broke off, and had to be held manually in position by two seamen. LCI 308, carrying the other half of the Commando, put in alongside 281 and was also found to be suffering from ramp trouble. One was totally jammed, the other partially so. The second one was coerced down after a twenty-minute delay. 'Disembarkation was extremely slow.' The single narrow path from the cove up the hillside further slowed the initial progress of the column. In addition to his normal full complement of equipment and ammunition, each man carried a 3-inch mortar bomb, weight ten pounds, in his pack. The heavy weapons, mortars and medium machine-guns, were broken down into loads carried on the backs of their teams. It would have been hard work for everybody in the best of circumstances.

The circumstances became steadily worse. The gradients of the hills on Mljet are possibly the steepest in the whole Dalmatian group of islands. The paths were rough and indistinct, sometimes petering out altogether. The advice from the Partisan guide at the head of the column was that if the Commando continued along the track, or what there was of it, the whole long snake would at sun-up be in clear view of the highest of the German positions, thus both forfeiting surprise and offering an invitation for the calling down of artillery fire from German gun emplacements on the mainland. The advice, later found to be wrong, was taken. Also accepted was an offer by the guide to lead the procession along another track that followed the north shore of Mljet. There was no track. The column had to hack its way for two miles through dense, tangled scrub.

Wireless silence, an important adjunct to surprise, was the rule of the day. It did nothing for co-ordination. Simonds, back at 43 Commando Headquarters, and with nothing to suggest to him that the planned timetable was by now an illusion, reported to Brigadier Tom Churchill that his Commando was where it should have been at the time. The Commando was in two separate groups, Neilforce led by Major Neil Munro, and Blakeforce led by Captain John Blake. They should have been on two separate start lines, on the lower slopes of two separate hills, at the top of which were two separate German positions, both forces ready to go in shortly after dawn. Tom Churchill called for his air support. Twelve Spitfires roared in at 6.15 a.m., and bombed spectacularly. At this time Neilforce and Blakeforce were miles away, still chopping a path blasphemously through the resistant thickets of the north-coast route.

The undergrowth was at last penetrated. The steep paths continued as sharp and as ill defined as before. Munro reached his start line at 11 a.m., five hours late. Blake reached his at 1.30 p.m., seven-and-a-half hours late. From shortly after the dawn airstrike there had been a certain amount of desultory two-way, long-range shooting, by the heavy weapons of both sides, the British ones positioned on a hill well behind the bush-whacking assault troops. The four German-held hills were mortared, machine-gunned and shelled. The Germans reciprocated both from their local resources and by calling down shoots from their mainland guns. Remarkably little damage was done to the British side. Probably much the same applied at the German end of the exchanges. The Germans were well protected in rock and log shelters. Some of the zeal with which the British mortar and machine-gun crews discharged their weapons was not attributable to a devoted enthusiasm to engaging the enemy. They were moved by the reflection that the more ammunition they fired, the less of the bloody stuff there would be to carry back over those bloody hills again.

By 2.30 p.m., 'C' Troop of 43 Commando, led by Captain Bob Loudoun, and part of Neilforce, was on top of the first objective. The Germans, it seemed, had abandoned the hill some time previously. No. 2 Commando had also taken the first of their two assigned hilltops. For the remainder of the afternoon there were further fire-fights with the two outstanding strongpoints, more oath-ridden manoeuvring up and down rock faces, and fairly persistent but totally ineffectual German mortaring. It all lasted much longer than it should have. The naval force commander, Morgan Giles, had earlier in the afternoon told Tom Churchill that for naval reasons he wanted the time of re-embarkation of the troops to be brought forward. Churchill called the operation off. Both Commandos were ordered to disengage at 4.30 p.m., march back to the beach, and get aboard the LCIs by 6 p.m. Wireless conditions were bad. Blakeforce got the signal through its chance interception on a short-range 38 set, and tramped off over the mountains again on the first leg of their journey home. Neilforce, whose 18 set was out of order, missed the message altogether. Munro continued to struggle on the heights among intermittent mortaring and shelling for a while longer, until the withdrawal signal at last reached him. By then one of his troops, 'E' commanded by Captain Lee, was enmeshed in a local small-arms battle with two Spandaus, and Munro had some difficulty in extricating it.

Most troops were embarked by 8 p.m. Two LCIs sailed for Vis at once. Another waited for Neilforce, the advanced element of which reached the beach at 1 a.m. 'C' Troop, who acted as rearguard and who were encumbered by having to carry a wounded marine all the way, did not get in until 2.30 a.m. Four marines had fainted from exhaustion on this march.

Almost everyone on the Mljet operation found himself involved in a lot of toilsome clambering upwards, carrying something heavy on his back and shoulders. Newly issued felt-soled boots were stripped to ribbons on the sharp volcanic rocks of the tracks and hillsides. Denim trousers had suffered similarly from the spiky bushes. Neilforce were a ragged-looking company when they formed up on the jetty at Vis after disembarkation at nine o'clock on the following morning. Their drill movements were as polished as ever, but the condition of their clothing would not have escaped notice on the parade ground of the Royal Marine depot at Deal. They had marched a total of eighteen miles across the most unpleasant country that any of them had ever encountered, had climbed, and descended from, several mountains of over 1000 feet, and had been shot at spasmodically.

The casualties to the raiding force in Operation Foothound were one killed, one wounded and seven missing. Of the missing, it was later discovered, a small party with Colour-Sergeant Stevens had been caught in a minefield. One man was killed. The others, with Stevens, became prisoners-of-war. A few days after the disembarkation at Vis, Captain Bob Loudoun and a small support party went back to Mljet in a motor launch. They recovered two brigade signallers who had fallen out on the march, and also Marine Skinner of Loudoun's troop. Skinner had mislaid himself during a halt. He had subsequently had a lively time, dodging German search parties. His account of his sojourn at the bottom of a well, in which he sat while his searchers chattered away at the top of it, provided much entertainment in the months ahead.

PART THREE

Taking the Heat off Tito

FOURTEEN

The German Attack on Tito's Headquarters at Drvar

In the latter half of May 1944, Fitzroy Maclean was in London, accompanied by Vlatko Velebit of the Partisan Supreme Staff. They were engaged in delicate discussions with, among others, the Prime Minister on matters of high policy, partly to do with strategy and supply, partly with an attempt somehow to reconcile British military support of the Partisans with British political and diplomatic recognition of the Royalist government-in-exile. On 26 May Brigadier Tom Churchill also left for London. For some time Combined Operations Headquarters had been urging him to come home for discussions, always more fruitful and less open to misunderstanding than the exchange of views by signal and letter. They wanted to hear his personal account of lessons learnt in Commando operations in Italy and the islands that might profitably be applied to other ventures elsewhere. They also wanted his assessment of the performance of the relatively new Royal Marine Commandos.

On his own list of matters to be raised was a recommendation that the commanding officer of No. 40 Royal Marine Commando, Lieutenant-Colonel J.C. Manners, should be relieved of his command. Pops Manners was, in the considered Churchill opinion, the best Commando leader in the brigade. He had been involved in hard fighting in Italy at Termoli, Anzio and on the River Garigliano. He had done outstandingly well. He was now very tired and badly in need of a rest. He was not the sort of man to ask for one. Tom Churchill was determined to ensure that Manners was ordered to take it. The decision was reached over a luncheon in the Senior Service Club. Lieutenant-General Sir Thomas Hunton, the Adjutant-General, Royal Marines, was Churchill's host and he endorsed the recommendation at once. Manners would be replaced as soon as was possible.

On the day that Tom Churchill left Vis, after handing over command of the island's British force to his brother Jack, confident that with the completion of the unsuccessful Mljet operation and with no plans for major offensive activity on the stocks a quiet Dalmatian period lay ahead, the first reports began to come in of a German airborne attack on Tito's headquarters at Drvar in Bosnia. The attack had come dangerously close to success. Parachutist and glider-borne Germans had sprung an efficiently conducted surprise. They had missed Tito, just, but Tito was now on the run. So was the main headquarters of the British Military Mission, led by Maclean's second-in-command, Vivian Street.

Tito had been supervising the Partisan war from Drvar for several months. He himself lived and worked in a cave in a cliff-face that overlooked a broad, fertile valley, through which ran a river. The little town of Drvar, by now mostly incinerated ruins, lay in the valley. Hills, some gently rising, some precipitous, surrounded it. There were expanses of cultivated land, patches of forest and several farmhouses. The British Mission had set themselves up in one of these. It was surrounded by orchards of plum trees.

There was no doubt in any minds, Partisan or British Mission, that the Germans had accurate information about who was in Drvar and about the significance of what was being controlled from there. German aircraft had for some time assiduously bombed and machine-gunned the town and its neighbouring buildings. On an early morning in early May a light aircraft behaved uncharacteristically. Instead of trying to kill and destroy it flew peacefully up and down at a consistent height of about 2000 feet. It passed over the British Mission's house with regularity. Street concluded that it was taking photographs. He assumed that these would identify targets for an airstrike of an intensity beyond anything that the Partisan General Staff had so far experienced.

Street went to see Tito in his cave and gave his interpretation of the unusual behaviour of the German aircraft, suggesting that the Partisans should be prepared for something out of the ordinary, and adding that he intended to move the mission from its house in the plum orchard to somewhere less conspicuous a mile or so away in the foothills. Street, with his liaison team, signallers and Partisan escort, made the move that same afternoon.

After two uneventful days Street began to wonder whether he had been unnecessarily fussy. On the third morning, shortly after first light, there were shouts of '*Avioni!*' from the Partisan sentries. An exceptionally large number of small German aircraft were dropping bombs on the village of Drvar. The small ones were soon supplemented by six large Junkers 52s. The Junkers seemed to presage an aerial bombardment of a quality rare in Bosnia. Instead of bombs they dropped parachute troops. Further instalments of parachutists reinforced the initial drop. The parachutists headed for the village and made a lodgement. The Partisans recovered from their surprise and forced the parachutists out. German gliders, bearing light artillery and further supporting troops, hissed in sibilantly through the air and crash-landed noisily in the valley. One glider, its crew killed, came to rest in destruction on the valley floor below the entrance to Tito's cave. Partisans continued to hold out in the village, but the steady accretion of Germans soon dominated the lower slopes of the hills. One group were installed in a position from which they put an unremitting fire upon the entrance to Tito's cave.

Tito and his immediate staff were unable to get down. They went up. Using a rope, they scaled a fissure in the cliff, broke free from the engagement and, true to the established principles of guerrilla warfare, sought survival. Vivian Street and the British Mission were in similar case. Their routine job of organising the delivery of supplies by the RAF, and of evacuating Partisan wounded from improvised airstrips, was in temporary abeyance. Street, too, concentrated upon the survival of his team. They took up their wireless sets and as much else as they could carry on their backs and moved rapidly into the hills. Their planned destination was a Partisan corps headquarters higher up in the valley. It was a cross-country march that lasted for ten hours. When they arrived Tito and his people were already there.

In the village of Drvar the Partisans fought on bitterly for several hours. When the survivors withdrew the Germans instituted a general massacre of civilians and of captured wounded prisoners. A carefully prepared operation had gone wrong, and there was much German frustration. Tito, and the main Allied missions attached to him, were still loose. The only tangible capture of propaganda value was Tito's ceremonial uniform of a marshal of Yugoslavia, soon to be displayed in a glass case in Vienna.

But the Drvar assault had been only the centre-piece of a much more elaborate and wider plot for the elimination of the Partisan leadership. There were integrated German interventions from many directions. Tito, his staff, his bodyguard and the Allied missions were kept constantly on the move, wriggling and feinting their way through one enemy threat after another. Effective co-ordination of Partisan activity was, in the circumstances, impossible. Tito ordered that all Partisan formations and units, everywhere, should take early positive action to divert German attentions from himself and from his immediate companions, between them the brain and nerve-centres of the entire Yugoslav liberation movement.

The Partisan response to this instruction was of necessity *ad hoc*, but it was on the whole widespread, violent and effective. The British, to whom it was an appeal rather than a directive, also reacted promptly. In the seven days after the Drvar assault, the Royal Air Force flew one thousand or so sorties in attacks on targets in Yugoslavia with the aim of interfering with the German hunt. There were, too, some brisk arrangements for a major involvement in an amphibious operation of the British troops on the island of Vis. The preliminary order, of which a badly blurred copy is preserved in the Public Record Office at Kew, was wirelessed by Brigadier Miles, who commanded Force 266 from his headquarters in Bari, to Colonel Jack Churchill. This signal was to instigate an operation that in terms of

British manpower was the largest undertaken in Yugoslavia during the Second World War, and that in terms of blood and talent lost was the most expensive. It reads in full:

TO JACK FROM BONZO. TITO HAS ORDERED PARTISANS TO CARRY OUT DIVERSION BY ATTACKING HVAR, BRAC, PODGORA, TO EASE HIS SITUATION AND ASK OUR SUPPORT. CONSIDER THAT NOT MORE THAN 2,000 PARTISANS SHOULD BE USED. WE MUST BE PREPARED UP TO ONE COMMANDO, ONE TWENTY FIVE POUNDER BATTERY, ONE TROOP 75 MM, RSR, ONE HEAVY WEAPON TROOP, COMMANDOS. MY SUGGESTED PLAN, 500 PARTISANS HVAR, OBJECTIVE JELSA: 1,500 PARTISANS PLUS COMMANDO AND SUPPORTING ARMS, BRAC, TO LAND SOUTH WEST ISLAND AND ADVANCE ON NEREZISCE. FOTALI PREPARED TO PRODUCE FIVE(5) LCI'S. PROBABLE DATE OPERATION NIGHT 30/31st. OR 31st/1st. PEARSON ARRIVING BY AIR 29 MAY TO DISCUSS PLAN YOU AND CERNEY. WILL ARRANGE RAF AND RN SUPPORT ON RETURN TO TARANTO, PM 29 MAY. WILL PROCEED VIS WITH SASO, COS FOTALI 30 MAY IF NECESSARY.

The RSR were the Raiding Support Regiment. FOTALI was not, as it sounds, an Italian fishing port, but was short for Flag Officer Taranto and Liaison Italy, the full title of Admiral Morgan of the Royal Navy. SASO was the Senior Air Staff Officer. COS FOTALI was Admiral Morgan's Chief of Staff. Cerney was an anglicisation of Crni, the Partisan commander on Vis.

Although Miles described his scheme as a 'suggested plan', and although some later modifications were made to the original concept, no senior Commando officer seems to have queried, or pressed for an alternative to, its central element, the advance upon Nerežišće of whatever Commando was chosen. This was the upland village in which Barton had three months previously shot the German Commandant. That excitement, and the raids by 2 Commando on Šolta and by 43 Commando on Hvar, had persuaded the Germans of the unwisdom of taking their opponents too lightly on the islands. There had been a radical reshuffling of German dispositions. German soldiers were no longer billeted in relative comfort, and with relative vulnerability, in requisitioned school buildings and the larger houses. They had been withdrawn to the heights of commanding hills, upon which they had blasted prepared defensive positions of stone and concrete linked by trenches and surrounded by belts of mines protected by barbed wire. From each of these fastnesses there was only one way out, a narrow track. The stronghold of the former Nerežišće garrison, reinforced, was on a hilltop described in the operation orders of the attackers as Point 622. The figure was taken from the map and expressed the elevation of the position in metres. In British usage it was about 2000 feet high. The position's physical approaches and its artificial defences combined to make it formidable. Miles's signal had mentioned no more than an advance towards it. It was inevitable, if a satisfactory diversion were to be made to ease Tito's difficulties, that an assault would have to be made upon it.

There were some complications to be disposed of before serious planning could get under way. Tom Churchill was not the only officer in his brigade to have assumed that there would be an operational lull after Mljet and that he could reasonably take advantage of it in absenting himself from Vis. Colonel Simonds of 43 Commando had gone to Italy. So had eight officers of 2 Commando, who had volunteered for a course in parachuting. A number of other officers and men of all three Commandos had also been sent to Italy on a variety of courses or on useful errands of one sort or another. It would take time before these people, even a proportion of them, could be gathered back. It was clear that Miles's proposed timings were too optimistic. The job would have to be deferred until 1 June at the earliest.

When he received the warning order from Brigadier Miles, Jack Churchill's immediate feeling was that the job should be done by the unit that he himself had trained, led and best understood, his own No. 2 Commando. Churchill recommended that the parachute course in Taranto should be brought to a premature and logical end by the dropping of the students upon Vis that evening, thus demonstrating the usefulness of the training and simultaneously bringing No. 2 Commando's officer strength back to normal. Miles ignored the request. He said that the thing should be done by the largest intact Commando on the island, No. 43. This could, if necessary, be reinforced by No. 40.

Churchill thus found himself commanding a force of marines in a marine battle. He was unused to their ways. Simonds, of 43, had, as Churchill remembers it, asked to be transferred from Commandos and was in Italy awaiting a posting to the United Kingdom. He was recalled by Miles, and sent straight back to Vis. Jack Churchill was there to meet him, and was careful to explain that the twin embarrassments of the situation, one lieutenant-colonel giving orders to another, and an army officer controlling marines, were not of his making. He was doing what he was told to do from above.

Colonel Pearson, the General Staff Officer 1 (G1 for short) of Force 266, flew to Vis from Bari for the planning conference on the morning of 29 May. The conference, attended by all the commanders of the troops who would take part in the raid, was first briefed by the Brigade Intelligence Officer on what was known of German strengths and locations on Brač. Pearson then gave the outline plan. Commander Crni and the commander of the Partisan XXVI Division joined the discussion. No. 2 Special Service Brigade's report on Operation Flounced, the code-name for the undertaking, records:

> The discussion was long and many proposals and counter-proposals were made. It is never easy to plan in conjunction with the Partisan authorities, not only because of the language difficulty, but more particularly because their whole system of planning and their ideas on military tactics, whilst very successful when conducted by them alone, are so different from ours that it is difficult to arrange a properly co-ordinated detailed plan of attack.

Forty-one years later Tom Churchill, who was not present, but who for both professional and personal reasons made it his business to enquire into every aspect of the Brač battle, was more succinct: 'this conference was a most woolly affair, with the commandos asking stupid questions and making promises which they couldn't carry out.' The conference finally came up with firm conclusions. Pearson flew back to Italy during the evening with an agreed provisional plan and with specific requests for the kind of support that the ground force needed from the other two services. Colonel Jack Churchill was insistent upon elaborate air backing.

In Taranto there were consultations at a rung or two higher up in the hierarchy. Admiral Morgan (FOTALI), the Air Officer Commanding 242 Group and Brigadier Miles of Force 266 agreed the contributions to be made by their respective commands. Miles, on behalf of all three, signalled an outline of the plan to Allied Forces Headquarters at Caserta. The date of the landing was put back until the night of 1/2 June so that detailed planning could be further refined and to allow time for the assembly of all the necessary naval craft. Some last-minute adjustments were made to the plan. Operation Flounced was on.

FIFTEEN

The Launching of the Brač Raid

Viewed from the air, or on the map, Brač is a rather plump-looking island, much more so than its skinny neighbours, an attenuated oval with its edges fuzzed by coves, bays and headlands. The longer sides of the oval curve gently, approximately from east to west. The shorter ends, both irregular, run roughly from north to south. The island's maximum width is about twenty miles. Its maximum depth is about ten. A quarter of the way along the coast from the western end of the northern shore is the small port of Supetar. At the southern tip of the eastern end is another small port, Sumartin. Almost exactly in the centre of the south coast is an even smaller fishing port, Bol.

The interior of Brač is hilly and stony. In the nineteenth century Brač stone was famous, and Dalmatian sea captains carried it to the United States – St Patrick's Cathedral in New York is built from it. Among the limestone rocks are vincyards, vegetable gardens and scattered patches of grazing for mountain sheep. There are stunted trees and much scrubby undergrowth. Movement on foot through the intricate hills and valleys of this pile of stone is hard work, particularly when the movers are encumbered by up to sixty pounds of weapons, equipment, food, water and ammunition.

There were several independently conducted but inter-related components of the plan. The main task of the Partisans, 2500 in all, was to seal off the German garrisons in the northern port of Supetar and in the eastern port of Sumartin. The eastern Partisan force, which was supported by a troop of mountain guns of the Raiding Support

Regiment, would have to start by dealing with an outlying German position at Humac, a village about ten miles to the west of Sumartin, and then drive the Germans progressively eastward. No. 43 Commando, whose objective was the German strongpoint system on the heights of Point 622, south-east of Nerežišće, was given additional fire support in the shape of the Heavy Weapons Troop of 40 Commando and extra help for shifting stores and ammunition from a rifle troop of 40 Commando acting as porters. The Commandos were to land at Blaca Cove, on the south-west coast of the island. Jack Churchill, the British ground force commander, was to go with them, accompanied by a skeleton staff from 2 Special Service Brigade Headquarters. To inhibit German reinforcement of Brač from the mainland, the RAF had agreed to undertake an intensive bombing programme of the mainland harbours of Split, Omiš and Makarska. Artillery support for the Commando assault upon the Nerežišće position would be provided by a battery of 25-pounders, eight guns, later supplemented by two more, of 111 Field Regiment, Royal Artillery. The chosen gun position was at Bol, in the centre of the south coast. The Battery Commander was Major Pat Turner.

Before all this could be put properly into motion there was a potentially threatening obstacle to be disposed of. Some two miles to the north-west of Bol is the highest peak on the island, Nidova Gora, approximately 2400 feet high. From its summit there was a clear view of most of Brač, including the approaches to the Commando objective above Nerežišće. Nidova Gora was known to be manned by a German artillery observation post. Unless the post, thought to be guarded by about thirty soldiers with two machine-guns, could be taken out right at the start of the operation, it would be able to direct accurate shell and mortar fire from German emplacements upon the island and the nearby mainland on to both Commandos and Partisans, on the march or forming up for their various attacks. The job of eliminating the Nidova Gora post was given to 'B' Company of the 2nd Battalion, the Highland Light Infantry. The company was led by Major R.S.H. Brotherhood.

The Jocks were no ordinary infantry battalion. They were trained specialists in mountain warfare. They had

mountaineering equipment. They wore cross-country ski
boots, not the ammunition boots of normal infantry or the
experimental (failed) felt-soled footwear tried for a short,
uncomfortable time in the islands by the Commandos. The
lowest rank in 2HLI was not private, or fusilier, or
rifleman. It was mountaineer. The Jocks opened the
proceedings on Brač.

Brotherhood was given little time to work out his options.
At half past three on the afternoon of Wednesday, 31 May,
he was summoned to the Special Service Brigade Headquarters in Komiža and told what was wanted of him and
his company on Nidova Gora. At a quarter to five he gave
his orders to his company officers. At half past nine that
night he, with three weak platoons of his company,
embarked at Vis harbour in a convoy of four Partisan
schooners. With him were his company second-in-
command, Captain Howell, and a total company headquarters of thirteen other ranks; Lieutenant Galbreath's
platoon of twenty-one other ranks; Lieutenant Brooke's
platoon of twenty-one other ranks; and Lieutenant
Campbell's platoon of eighteen other ranks. They were
dressed in ski boots, gaiters, khaki drill slacks, khaki drill
shirts, jerseys and assault jerkins. In their packs were spare
socks, spare jerseys, steel helmets, water bottles and forty-
eight-hour ration packs. Between the 'Marching-Out
Strength' of five officers and seventy-three other ranks,
they carried nine Bren guns, with twelve magazines to each
gun; eleven Thompson sub-machine-guns with ten magazines per gun; and each mountaineer without automatic
weapons bore one hundred rounds of 0.303 rifle ammunition and either three or four grenades.

On the four Partisan schooners, they were joined by a
Gunner officer, six gunners with a wireless set, and an
American radio operator with the type of long-range
apparatus that was the envy of every British unit upon Vis.
The schooners were also boarded by sixty Partisans, whose
purpose was different from that of Brotherhood.

Brotherhood's company should have been landed at
Planica, a short, three-mile but (given the topography of
Brač) exhausting cross-country march from their objective

of Nidova Gora. The Partisan schooner skippers, understandably giving priority to the sixty of their fellow countrymen whose mission was different from that of Brotherhood, were adamant in disembarking the whole lot, Partisan and HLI, at Blaca, the cove at which the Commandos were to land later. Blaca was four miles west of Planica. Four miles added to an approach march to an attack sounds superficially trivial. Four miles over the limestone ridges of Brač is significant to the physical condition of those, carrying heavy loads, who are to fight a battle at the end of it. Tom Churchill, who years later studied the ground closely, was to remark, 'It's bloody awful country. It goes up and down all the time.'

The party reached Blaca at 2 a.m. on Thursday, 1 June, and after a fifteen-minute delay were joined by Partisan guides. These led them on a three-hour march to a lying-up position hidden in dense scrub. Sentries were placed, off-duty men rested or ate. It was a hot, dry day. Partisans replenished the company's water supplies three times. Brotherhood spent most of the day in an attempt to get up-dated information about the defences and strength of the target. He was given a mass of well-meant, mostly conflicting data of little help, but at last learnt something from the Partisan Brigade Intelligence Officer that at least seemed to be unambiguous. This was that the German garrison on Nidova Gora had had its numbers increased from thirty men to forty. Their two machine-guns, sited in sangars (low protective surrounds of rocks), had been supplemented by an 81-mm mortar. There were neither mines nor wire around the position. It could, if necessary, be reinforced within half an hour's travelling time from adjacent German posts near Gazu and Korita. The configuration of the ground was such that a pre-attack visual reconnaissance in daylight would be impossible. And, when the attack went in, the Partisans had no heavy supporting weapons with which to give it a hand. These details gave Brotherhood a rough and ready basis upon which to make his preparations. His company left again at 5.15 p.m. in a long, laden, single file, through thick scrub, using tracks unmarked on the map but known to the Partisan guides.

At 11.30 p.m. they halted for half an hour in the hamlet

of Prajca, where they were to be joined by fifteen extra Partisans. These failed to put in an appearance. Instead, three strangers arrived, saw the Jocks at rest in the scrub, dropped what they were carrying and ran away shouting. Some of the Jocks opened fire on the three men, but were soon stopped. The men were thought to be Partisans who had mistaken the Highlanders for Germans. But whoever they were, there was concern that the shooting might have been heard by the Germans on Nidova Gora. The company resumed its journey at midnight. At five minutes past one on the morning of 2 June the guide halted and told Brotherhood that they were close to the German position. They had indeed crossed some 'bloody awful country'. It had taken them a few minutes short of six hours to make a seven-mile approach march.

A short look at the North star confirmed Brotherhood's suspicion that the guide had not led them to where they wanted to be led, the assembly areas that he had chosen for the support team and for the storming party. Brotherhood was giving brief consideration to the implications of this misplacement, when the guide offered some new information. A telephone line ran alongside the road from Nidova Gora to Korita. The Germans could clearly use this to summon help. Their observation post was in a house surrounded by a stone wall built in a shallow rectangle, about 300 yards long at its wider sides. Near the house was a wireless station. The German machine-guns were grouped in a position in the wall on the north side of the house, sited to cover the ground on that side. A sentry was posted on the north-east corner of the same wall. And, repeated the guide, so far as he knew there were no mines or wire protecting the position.

Brotherhood rapidly readjusted his plan and issued new orders. Brooke's platoon was to move to the east, cut the telephone wire, cover the road from Korita, kill the sentry, and from 1.45 until 1.55 a.m. fire all its weapons hard at the house. Brotherhood, with the other two platoons, would go towards the west side and stay poised to move in as soon as Brooke's people had ceased fire.

Brooke moved off, disconnected the telephone, left a section as a block on the road, had no time left to deal with the sentry, and, exactly on time, opened up on the house with everything he had at a range of 350 yards. Again exactly on time, he stopped shooting. Brotherhood's group came in fast over the west wall, killed the luckless sentry spared by Brooke, and headed for the house. They immediately met very heavy fire. Three Highlanders went down wounded. Brotherhood shifted to the right, to the south-west corner of the house, where there was an area of ground out of sight of the Germans. From here the attackers started another rush. The German machine-gun fire was thickened up by flurries of grenades, which wounded four more Highlanders. Lieutenant Campbell was killed by a mine. Brotherhood, Captain Howell and Lieutenant Galbreath were wounded on other mines.

With all the assault-party officers now casualties, the attack faltered. Brotherhood was badly hit and unable to move, but he rallied the survivors, who went in again led by the injured but still mobile Howell. This time, in addition to the heavy machine-gun fire and the grenades, Howell's party ran into thick barbed-wire entanglements. His attack was beaten off with further losses.

Three sergeants and several more mountaineers were by now also seriously wounded. The incapacitating of the sergeants, along with all of the officers, removed the company's familiar and accepted leadership. Control slipped. Confusion developed. The unhit, by now under heavy mortar fire, removed themselves and such wounded as they could help, over the lower part of the western wall to a point well beyond it. Stragglers and further wounded joined them there. The mortaring continued. At 2.30 a.m., thirty-five minutes after the assault party had first run at the house, separated groups of varying size, unwounded, wounded and mixed, began to make their way down to the southern shore of Brač, over steep rock faces and through the abundant scree. Brotherhood, Galbreath and Mountaineer White, all difficult to move, stayed at the top of the hill. They reached Vis two days later. Partisans helped them to get out, after a gruelling march of seven miles across Brač.

Brooke, whose platoon had shot the attack in with its ten-minute rapid-fire extravaganza, was left on Nidova Gora in something of a dilemma. He had seen clearly that Brotherhood's attack had failed. Brooke's own much fewer numbers were correspondingly unlikely to be able to do any better if he decided to have a go on his own. He had fired off nearly all his ammunition. The Germans had put up red Very lights, and guns from well inland had begun to shell an area 500 yards to the west of the encircling wall, presumably in an attempt to interfere with the withdrawal of the remnants of Brotherhood's party. Brooke continued to keep an eye on the German house, and to keep a block on the Korita road, until 2.40 a.m. Then he too decided to pull out.

His platoon was mortared and machine-gunned as it moved down the rough going of steeply falling tracks and heavy scree. At 5.45 in the morning Brooke caught up with some of the early arrivals from the Jocks' assault party. These were on a narrow, steep track, and were joined at intervals by further groups, the unwounded helping along – in some cases carrying – those who had been hit. Some of Brooke's people climbed upwards again in a search for other wounded stragglers. They found and recovered some. They also found a handy well on the mountainside. The water bottles of the wounded, and then of everyone else, were refilled.

The final extrication of the company from Brač was a rather haphazard, improvised affair. A few small clusters simply walked to the coast, attracted the attentions of passing assault landing craft and hitched lifts. Captain Woodward of Turner's battery of 25-pounders, now ensconced in Bol, lent a jeep which carried four of the seriously wounded to the monastery in Bol. Brooke sent the rest to the beach at Dračeva. At 12.45 two LCAs arrived, the first at Bol, the second at Dračeva with a Commando doctor aboard. The craft cruised slowly along the coast, putting in from time to time to pick up groups of hitch-hikers. By 1.30 they were in Blaca, where the wounded were given hot tea. The American signaller, still with them, used his superior set to send a message to HLI Battalion Headquarters in Vis to arrange for two ambulances and transport to be standing by at the disembarkation point in Vis harbour. The craft tied up in Vis at 4.25. At five o'clock the men received a hot meal.

Lieutenant Brooke, the only officer in the company alive and unwounded, completed the operational report on this action within forty-eight hours of his return to Vis. Of the total strength of seventy-eight led by Brotherhood to Nidova Gora, three were killed, one was missing believed killed, and fourteen were wounded – about one casualty for every fourth man. Among the officers and senior NCOs the proportion was much higher – four out of five officers, three out of four sergeants.

Brooke was commendatory about some Partisan characteristics – their knowledge of the ground, their familiarity with unmapped tracks, the ease with which they provided water, their helpfulness in getting the wounded back, their skill at landing troops from their schooners ('even though at the wrong place'). He was more acerbic about Partisans who 'try to enforce their own ideas about the conduct of operations regardless of what a British officer's view may be', and curt about the inaccuracy of the information provided by them. But he felt that the Jocks had responded well to the circumstances. 'Throughout the entire operation the fortitude and morale of all ranks was at its highest peak; the leadership displayed by Major Brotherhood, Captain Howell, Lieutenant Campbell, and Lieutenant Galbreath, while under intense enemy fire, was of the highest order. The courage of the wounded during a difficult withdrawal was magnificent.'

Brooke made no attempt to conceal his opinion that the attack had been a failure. This, he wrote, was because of the impossibility of making a proper reconnaissance, being landed at the wrong place, the over-long approach march, the over-late arrival at the objective, the guide's taking of the company to the wrong assembly area, and, of course, the wrong information about how many defenders held the house with what and where.

But Tom Churchill's retrospective judgement upon the Highland Light Infantry action at Nidova Gora was that while it was plainly not a win, it was far from a complete failure. No. 43 Commando, when moving towards Nerežišće during the following day across ground in clear sight of Nidova Gora, were not interfered with by observed gunfire directed from the observation post. The HLI 'hadn't actually taken it out, but they'd knocked it about quite a lot'. This softening up had made its contribution to the success of a Partisan attack on the house while Brooke was shepherding his weary followers back to Vis. Later, and until the end of the raid, the observation post became the property, highly valued and in constant use, of 111 Field Regiment, Royal Artillery.

Tom Churchill preserved a warm admiration for Brotherhood. The two of them stayed in sporadic touch until Brotherhood's death in the early 1980s. Brotherhood's leg wound was severe and 'gave him terrible trouble every year' for the rest of his life.

An indication of the haste with which the operation was mounted, or possibly a product of the length, and what Tom Churchill called the woolliness, of the planning conference held on Vis on 29 May, was that the 'Object' defined by Colonel Bonzo Simonds in his orders to his subordinate commanders was different from that laid down by Force 266, accepted by Colonel Jack Churchill and transmitted to the leaders of every element in the force.

The 'Object' of 2 Special Service Brigade Headquarters, as recorded in their report on the operation, began with a preamble about the German attack on Tito's headquarters at Drvar, and quoted his orders to the Partisans to initiate diversions. The Partisans on Vis were to carry out one of these 'in order to prevent the enemy from moving further formations from the coast against his [Tito's] HQ, and if possible, to make him [the enemy] pull back to the coast certain formations about to be committed. This was the primary object of the operation. . . . The secondary object was the destruction of the enemy forces and material on the island of Brač.'

The Simonds orders to 43 Commando put all this the other way round. 'OBJECT: 1. To destroy the enemy garrison of BRAČ ISLAND. 2. It was hoped that this would cause the enemy to move strong formations from the mainland interior to the coast, thus relieving pressure on Marshal Tito's H.Q.' In practice this switch probably had no effect on the course of the battle; had the operation lasted longer than it did, some reconciliation of aims might have become necessary.

*

During the night of 1/2 June landing craft of the Royal Navy and Partisan schooners brought to Brač the varied components of the raiding force, the Partisans who were to mask Supetar and Sumartin, the RSR mountain guns who were to support the latter, and the battery of eight 25-pounders of 111 Field Regiment whose priority task was to support 43 Commando's attack on the Nerežišće defended complex, but which could also be turned on to targets elsewhere. Forty-five craft in all sailed from Vis harbour and Komiža between 8.30 p.m. and 10 p.m. Most carried troops – 2500 Partisans, 900 British and about 100 Americans of the Operations Group. There were escorts of motor gun boats and motor launches. The armada travelled by night because most of its various routes would by day have been in full view of German positions on Šolta, Brač and Hvar, and from a number of places on the mainland. German observers, aside from alerting the Brač garrison to the sheer size – unprecedented – of what was heading its way, would also have alerted the Luftwaffe, still very much alive and formidable. There were major Luftwaffe bases at Mostar and Zagreb, both within easy range, and several satellite airfields elsewhere, also within range.

At half past midnight on the morning of Friday, 2 June, 43 Commando, augmented by 40 Commando's Heavy Weapon Troop of four 3-inch mortars and four Vickers belt-fed medium machine-guns, accompanied by the 40 Commando troop allocated as porters plus a force of Partisans, pulled in to Blaca Cove on the south-west of Brač. The Commandos made the journey in a Landing Craft, Infantry, LCI 260, crewed by experienced and trusted friends. Their voyage had been unimpeded. 'The landing and re-embarkation arrangements for the Commando', reported 43 afterwards, 'were excellent. The beaching and handling of LCI 260 was again beyond reproach.' The absence of reproach was generated by more than admiration for the seamanship demonstrated by the LCI's captain. He had put the troops ashore dry-shod, a consideration highly valued by people faced with hard cross-country marching who did not want inevitable ardours to be amplified by wet feet, socks, boots and trousers. The landing was unopposed as well as dry. In a long snake of a single-file column, the marines marched off towards Nerežišće, about four miles to the north-east in a straight line, nearer to nine by narrow, winding, stony tracks that crossed a seemingly endless succession of ridges, valleys and gullys.

In addition to the weight of their equipment and individual weapons – in the fighting troops these ranged from the heavier Brens and 2-inch mortars through rifles and Tommy guns to pistols – every man on this occasion was burdened with a 3-inch mortar bomb weighing ten pounds. There were no mules available. The ground was impassable even to so versatile a vehicle as a jeep. Everything had to be carried on the back, including the Vickers machine-guns and the 3-inch mortars of the two heavy weapons troops. The Vickers, broken down to their components of barrels and tripods, the mortars to base-plates, barrels and bipods, were, with one competitor in close unwonted rivalry, the heaviest loads of all. The competitor was the sum of the medical stores of the Regimental Aid Post, packed in ninety-pound loads on the backs of Captain Ralph Bazeley of the Royal Army Medical Corps, of his medical sergeant and of the two orderlies who made up his medical team. Between them they also had two heavy Airborne stretchers, of clumsy design, to manhandle wherever they went.

It was Bazeley's first operation, and it began unpromisingly. During one of the periodic halts on the march to Nerežišće, he and his team, who had been travelling with Colonel Simonds and Commando Headquarters, fell into what was intended to be a light doze. They awoke at dawn to find themselves alone. The Commando had moved on. Bazeley, who had not until now included navigation among his preoccupations, set out in a not very optimistic chase in what he assumed to be the direction of Nerežišće. His party was much impeded by the hellish Airborne stretchers. They were unsure of whom they would bump into first: Germans who would shoot at them on principle, Partisans who customarily shot first and asked questions afterwards, or Colonel Bonzo Simonds of 43 Commando, who was famously uninhibited in his expression of displeasure. Bazeley rated the Bonzo wrath as the least pernicious of these three unattractive options.

*

The landing at Bol of 111 Field Regiment's battery, also unopposed, took place at one o'clock in the morning, shortly after 43 Commando had left Blaca on its cross-country march. The eight 25-pounders, quickly put ashore from a Landing Craft, Tank, were soon positioned on a little plain to the east of the village. The Partisans, who had accompanied the LCT in their schooners, pushed inland at speed, and before long were fighting Germans at a number of different places. One of these was the observation post on Nidova Gora. It held out with diminishing resistance until noon, when Partisans finally overran it and took prisoner the survivors of its garrison. The Gunner Forward Observation Officer, with his accompanying signaller, at once took it over and began to register the range and bearing of targets that seemed likely to be in need of treatment later.

Farther to the east the Partisans, backed by the 75-mm mountain guns of the Raiding Support Regiment, were pressing the Germans satisfyingly back from Humac towards Sumartin. No. 111 Field Regiment's gun positions at Bol came under sporadic, and mostly ineffectual, shellfire as the morning wore on, from locations that were difficult to identify. On the north coast, the Partisans given the task of bottling up the German garrison of Supetar had reached the outskirts of the town, but were being heavily mortared by the defence and shot at by artillery from the mainland.

By 7.45 a.m. the leading troop of 43 Commando's five rifle troops, still on a mountain track but by now in daylight, was approaching from the west the German strongpoints on the hilltops behind Nerežišće. These strongpoints were on the summits of the metrically named adjacent peaks, Point 622 (the Commando's prime objective), Point 542 and Point 648, integral parts of an interlocked defensive system. Broadly speaking, and allowing for the mishaps inseparable from an operation of war carried out by night with little time for preparation and none for detailed reconnaissance, matters had so far gone well. There had been no losses on the sea-crossing. Every component of the ground force was more or less where it should have been, doing or ready to do what it was meant to do. Aircraft of the RAF flew

206

overhead in an abundance previously unwitnessed in the islands, bombing Sumartin and Supetar and machine-gunning throughout Brač anything that they identified as hostile. A feeling developed within 43 Commando during the day that the pilots were a touch too easy-going in their identification procedures. The marines were twice shot up by Spitfires.

When, at 7.30 on the morning of 2 June, 'A' Troop of 43 Commando, after an all-night march, was put in to a rather tentative attack upon a German entrenched position on Point 542, an encouraging artillery shoot from the 25-pounders at Bol was dropping upon that summit and upon Point 622. German soldiers were seen moving about freely on both these hills. 'A' Troop, led by Captain Jock Hudspith, ran into a minefield. The support available was judged by Simonds to be inadequate. Hudspith's attack was called off. 'A' Troop were to play little further part in the action.

Their attack was replaced, as the morning wore on, by Partisan attacks on the other, southern side of the feature. These were supported by continued accurate shelling by the 25-pounders in Bol and by mortar fire from the heavy weapons troops of 43 and 40 Commandos. The Partisan attacks did not succeed. By 1 p.m. they had petered out. Observers, both those professionally involved in directing the shell and mortar fire and a large number of self-interested spectators, noticed a disquieting effect of the fall of shot. To some extent it kept German heads down, but it did little physical damage to German defensive positions blasted into solid rock and as often as not roofed by tree trunks placed side by side.

During the early afternoon the Commando, resting in loosely dispersed troop positions on the hillsides and valleys, were extensively mortared and machine-gunned from Point 622 and were shelled by some distant guns. It was noisy, but largely harmless. At 3 p.m. three troops set out for a forming-up position prior to an attempt on Point 542. Their route took them through Nerežišće. The route of a passing patrol of four Spitfires of the Royal Air Force took them over Nerežišće. The marines laid out their silk identification panels. The airmen were indifferent or uninstructed and they fell into acute and foully expressed disfavour when they roared down in a spirited attack upon those whom they had come to help. By good fortune only two marines were wounded during this episode, but it was an unhappy opening of the Commando's Brač casualty list.

The agreed plan for the Point 542 attack was that 'B', 'D' and 'E' Troops of 43 Commando would come on to the objective from the north in concert with a similar Partisan assault from the south, the whole to be preceded by a half-hour concentration of shelling from the battery at Bol. The shelling was intense, accurate and precisely on time. The three troops of 43 left their start line on time. The Partisans did not conform. Their brigade commander sent his woman interpreter to Colonel Simonds's headquarters, fifteen minutes before the attack was due to begin and halfway through the supporting artillery programme, to say that his people would not, after all, be joining in. No. 43 Commando went ahead alone. They soon reached the outer minefield wire, which they cut or blew gaps in with Bangalore torpedoes (lengths of metal piping packed with explosive and designed specifically for gapping wire entanglements). Mines were lifted and some progress was made in the face of a growing volume of Spandau and mortar fire, doubly strong because the Partisans were not there to attract their share of it.

At 4.45 p.m. German reinforcements were seen to be moving up from the south-east. They were a threat to the exposed flank of the three troops. At five o'clock Simonds decided to break off the fight, which was becoming pointless. The battery at Bol, which in all accounts by the foot-soldiers of the Brač operation is mentioned with unreserved admiration, shelled the German holdings heavily to cover the withdrawal of the three troops. The RAF, who in the interim had had time to restock with fuel and ammunition, shot them up once again as they marched through Nerežišće, thereby knocking a further dent in the well-being of inter-service relations. Simonds concentrated his entire command for the night of 2/3 June in an all-round defensive position. They had had little sleep and had put in a lot of hard marching during the previous thirty-six hours. Sentries, signallers and orderly officers aside, they slumbered deeply.

Few of the Partisans had much sleep on that night. Different groups of them put in individual attacks on every German position to the south of Nerežišće. German heavy artillery from the mainland shelled the area around Humac continuously. The fighting lasted throughout the hours of darkness. None of the Partisan assaults was successful.

One small but essential entity belonging to the Commando also did badly for sleep. The abandoned Ralph Bazeley and the staff of his Regimental Aid Post had sat tight for most of the morning in the hope that a runner (or message-carrier) would be sent back to look for them with instructions about where they were to go. No British messenger put in an appearance, but Bazeley briefly acquired a hospitable Partisan who refreshed the party from a goatskin container filled with watered wine. More permanently Bazeley became the proprietor of two donkeys. The donkeys were loaded with the two awkward Airborne stretchers and with much of the weight of the medical stores. Homing on distant bangings and thumpings, Bazeley walked towards where battle seemed to be engaged. Corroborative visual indications that he was going the right way came from the sight of Spitfires shooting up what he assumed to be Germans, but which may well have been 43 Commando.

It was almost dusk when Bazeley led the way into Nerežišće. The donkeys at once disgraced themselves by breaking loose and bolting for a pond that was in the middle of the village. In this they stood hock-deep, slaking their thirsts and befouling the local water supply. There were no troops, Commando or Partisan, in the village, but friendly civilians showed Bazeley the track by which the Commando had left. The donkeys were enticed from the pond with difficulty. The party set off upon what it hoped, wrongly, was the last leg of its deferred journey. Night fell with Mediterranean haste. After an hour or two of tramping along in almost total darkness, illuminated from time to time by the gun flashes and flares of neighbouring Partisan attacks, Bazeley told his team to settle down, and went ahead on his own. In the middle of the night he found Commando Headquarters on a ridge. Bazeley was by then very tired, and soon became very offended. Nobody, it seemed, had noticed his absence. He climbed into a handy sangar for a brief sleep.

A nearly full moon had arisen by the time he awoke. By the light of this he was shown a saddle, on the far side of a small valley. The saddle was occupied by Captain Gerry Schooley and 'B' Troop. Bazeley was instructed to instal his aid post next to 'B' Troop. He went back to collect the staff of his sick bay, pointed himself towards where he thought the saddle was, and soon discovered that in the intricate uplands of Brač one moonlit silhouette looks very like another. Once again he told his followers to settle down while he went ahead to get the route right. In the course of this search he was shot at by a Commando sentry, bumped into some Partisans who after a suspicious interrogation through their interpreter showed him where to go, was shot at again by the Commando sentry on his way back to collect the unit's medical resources, and finally reached 'B' Troop shortly before dawn.

Bazeley's welcome by 'B' Troop was less than whole-hearted. His donkeys were of different sexes, and fell in love as soon as they reached the end of their journey. They celebrated this event by a noisy consummation that disturbed those marines who were sleeping, and provoked austere comment from the wakeful ones about the military value of silence as an adjunct to concealment. Bazeley was too tired to pay serious attention to these complaints.

SIXTEEN

Brač: No. 43 Commando

Developments in the battle elsewhere on Brač were beginning to suggest that the raid's object, as defined by No. 2 Special Service Brigade, of drawing some of the heat from the hunted Tito in Bosnia, was at least in part being achieved. German resources committed to the frustration of the Brač attacks were increasing. Intelligence reports suggested that 2000 German reinforcements were expected to arrive on the island during the night of 2/3 June. German batteries on the mainland had been in almost incessant action against the Partisans in front of Supetar, who had withdrawn a short distance but were still in a position to block any German attempt at a breakout from the town. In the eastern end of the island the Partisans and their RSR collaborators pressed strongly towards Sumartin.

As a response to the warning about the 2000 additional Germans, Brigadier Miles (now at Force 266 Advanced Headquarters on Vis) decided to send over the three remaining troops of 40 Commando, led by Colonel Pops Manners. (One troop of 40 had remained in Italy. Two others, it will be recalled, the Heavy Weapon Troop and a fighting troop acting as porters, had been lent to 43.) Manners and his depleted unit embarked in an LCI at Vis harbour at 11.30 on the night of Friday, 2 June, put to sea at 1.30 in the morning, and were landed at Planica, near Bol, at 3.45 a.m. on the Saturday. They marched inland at four o'clock, travelled for two-and-a-half hours, and settled down in a lying-up area, where they passed the rest of the day. With 40 Commando came 300 extra Partisans. At eight o'clock in the morning two further 25-pounders were landed at Bol to strengthen Pat Turner's battery.

*

In the area of Nerežišće, the daylight hours of that Saturday were relatively peaceful, but there was much preparing, conferring and considering. The 43 Commando war diary records that from ten o'clock until noon Simonds was at Jack Churchill's tactical headquarters, sited some distance from that of 43 Commando, where he was told to mount a night attack that same night. He would be sent detailed orders later, after Churchill had completed a detailed reconnaissance. Simonds left for 43 Commando, and Churchill set off on his reconnaissance, which lasted for five hours. Meanwhile the Partisans asked for support from the two heavy weapons troops for an afternoon attack that they planned on Point 622. This they later cancelled – after the heavy weapons had given their supporting bombardment.

Jack Churchill's personal recollection, over forty years later, was that he himself walked the mile and a half to 43 Commando Headquarters and spoke to Simonds there. Wherever the meeting took place is of small consequence. Churchill had become increasingly impatient with what he saw as Simonds's reluctance to press his attacks home, and urged him forcefully to 'assault this bloody hill and knock the Germans off it', at the latest on that same night. No mention seems to have been made during this discussion of the possibility that 40 Commando might be put in simultaneously against the hill. Churchill returned to Brigade Headquarters. His brigade major, Alf Blake, framed detailed orders and wirelessed them to Simonds. These again seem not to have referred to an involvement of 40 Commando.

Simonds received his orders at a quarter past five: 43 Commando were to take Point 622. The start time was given at 9 p.m. The Partisans would put in simultaneous attacks on the adjacent peaks of Points 542 and 648. At 6.30 Simonds co-ordinated the details of his attack with those of the Partisan commander. Artillery support from Bol, already arranged, began to fall accurately, noisily and persistently on all three objectives from 8.30 onwards. The shoot was timed to end at nine o'clock.

'C' Troop, on the left of the attack, was commanded by

Captain Bob Loudoun. They had been lying up on a small escarpment, on which they were mortared occasionally, without hurt. During the evening, a runner from Commando Headquarters brought the order that the troop was to move. Led by Loudoun, guided by the runner, they went in single file over the shoulder of a hill. Major Neil Munro, the second-in-command, was waiting in the valley on the far side. Munro walked along with Loudoun, told him that the troop were going into the attack and ordered him to spread them out into an extended line. This often-rehearsed manoeuvre took little time. While it was being executed Munro, still walking with Loudoun, pointed out the objective. It was about a thousand yards ahead, a skyline of rocks and low scrub silhouetted in the light of a full moon. The German positions, invisible, were some-where on either side of the skyline, which sloped down-wards from right to left as Loudoun looked at it. Munro said that it was a three-troop attack. Captain John Blake with 'D' Troop would be on Loudoun's right. Captain Gerry Schooley, 'B' Troop, would be on Blake's right. The attack would be shot in by a timed programme from the 25-pounders in Bol, and by the Commando's heavy weapons firing from behind the start line. The start time was at once.

'C' Troop set out towards the skyline, over broken country of scrub, rocks and stone walls. They kept their own formation, but early on lost touch with 'D' Troop on their right. Quite soon, a lot of German machine-gun tracer fire came in their direction, but it was all aimed high. Shortly afterwards, they walked into a fairly persistent mortar stonk, some of which, Loudoun suspected, came from the Commando's own mortars falling short. There was a tremendous amount of noise, but still no casualties. The noise was at a crescendo when Loudoun, in front, reached the German barbed wire, 'an extensive entangle-ment'. He could hear Germans talking and moving about beyond the wire, but he was unable to see whether there was a second line of wire at an interval behind the first, which would have suggested that the intervening space was mined.

Loudoun summoned Marine Charlie Nicholls,* the

*Charlie Nicholls was a character familiar to almost every fighting unit: a

213

Bangalore torpedo carrier, to breach the wire. Nicholls came up 'with great speed, delighted to get rid of the bloody thing', which he had been carrying around with him for days. It blew a gap, one-man wide. Loudoun ran for the gap, but he was beaten to it by two men, Nicholls and Corporal Royle. Both went down, almost at once, Nicholls badly wounded in the leg, Royle unconscious and dying. German small-arms fire was concentrated on the narrow gap. Loudoun turned Royle on to his back, decided that there was nothing that he could do for him and made a rapid assessment of the immediate prospects.

The alternatives that presented themselves were easily defined. The first was to lead his followers one by one through a yard-wide gap which was under close-range machine-gun fire and around which a lot of explosions were going off from what appeared to be electrically detonated mines. Those few who got through the gap would then probably, but not certainly, find themselves in a minefield with more wire at its rear and no more Bangalore torpedoes to cut it. The second option was to look for a more accessible part of the hilltop to attack. Loudoun picked the second alternative. His decision was warmly disputed by Marine Reg Skinner, the former Mljet well-dweller, who, close behind Loudoun, became very incensed. Loudoun shut Skinner up, and told the nearest Bren gunner, Marine Raven, to fire past the gap.

Marine Ernie Cox, Bob Loudoun's MOA (Marine, Officer's Attendant, or batman in army – and 40 Commando – parlance), went to see if he could do anything for Corporal Royle. Royle recovered consciousness for long enough to say, 'Don't bother with me, I've bloody well had it. Look after the next bloke.' Cox moved to the next bloke. This was Raven, the Bren gunner, by now badly hit. Loudoun, who had earlier shouted 'Come on,

---

model of enterprising reliability in action, the scourge of the Military Police when out of it. On Bob Loudoun's recommendation he was awarded the Military Medal for his courage on Brač. In January of the following year he was thrown out of 43 Commando, again on Bob Loudoun's recommendation, for becoming spectacularly drunk when the Commando was embarking for Italy at Dubrovnik. Nicholls's end was sad. He was one of the last men in Britain to be hanged for murder before the death penalty was abolished.

"C" Troop!', ordered a withdrawal. From the German side of the wire somebody else also shouted 'Come on, "C" Troop!', a call that has puzzled Loudoun to the present day. Was it by somebody from the 40 Commando attack which he did not yet know had gone in? Was it by a German pulling Loudoun's leg? Or was it, as suggested by Marine Harry Thirkell, who also heard it, a German NCO calling to his soldiers *'Kommen Sie hier!'*?

Casualties began to mount as 'C' Troop made its way back down the hill. Marine Snowden, seriously wounded, was carried down on a stretcher improvised from a groundsheet by Sergeant Bill Ash, Reg Skinner and two other marines. Skinner found an aid post manned by Americans from the Operations Group, and asked for morphia for Snowden. The Americans had none to spare. Snowden died a little while later. Bob Loudoun was hit in the ankle either by a mortar-bomb fragment or by a piece of mine (he has never determined which) and was unable to stand. Sergeant 'Bunny' Green gave him a pickaback. Lieutenant Gregory, with a painful wound in his foot, was helped down by Lance-Corporal Peak. When yet another mortar stonk came howling down, Peak lowered Gregory for safety to a shadowy patch of ground that turned out to be a thorn bush. Gregory thought little of this and told him so. Similar stories of the unwounded helping the wounded prevailed across the hillside.

Because of a shortage of numbers brought about by unreplaced casualties from earlier operations, 'C' Troop had before Brač been reorganised into three sub-sections instead of the standard two sections of two sub-sections each. As a consequence of this rearrangement, Loudoun's second subaltern, Lieutenant Jack Stevens, had been left with no one to command, and had been ordered by Loudoun to stay on the start line. Stevens, an Irish neutral of an independent cast of mind, had disliked this order and had decided to disobey. He had tracked the advance from close behind, and he now joined Loudoun, who had been put down with his back to a stone wall. Loudoun asked no questions about mutinous behaviour. There had been signs of a German counter-attack down the hill. Stevens, the only troop officer still on his feet (indeed the only officer of all three assaulting troops still on his feet), was at once put in charge of a covering screen to hold off any German interference.

At about this time, two strange marines arrived at Loudoun's wall. He asked them if they were from 'D' Troop or from 'B' Troop. They said that they were from neither, they belonged to 40 Commando. Loudoun was incredulous. It was news to him that 40 Commando were on Brač, let alone taking part in the assault. Sergeant Green resumed his lifting, and carried Loudoun along a path that led past Commando Headquarters. Loudoun reported to Simonds, and added that he had just met two marines from 40 Commando. Simonds refused to believe him.

Corporal Peak, the escorter of Lieutenant Gregory, met a tall, fair NCO from 'B' Troop later identified as Corporal Shearer, who fetched a stretcher and two Partisan girls. Gregory was loaded on to the stretcher and carried to Dr Bazeley's Regimental Aid Post.

Meanwhile, Marine Jeffs – Loudoun's troop signaller – had been wounded, not too badly, by grenade fragments in his back and shoulder. Every time he tried to move from his cover somebody either took a shot at him or threw something at him. The sound of bagpipes, moving from right to left across his front behind the ridge, suggested to him that an improvement was imminent. His assumption was that the Highland Light Infantry, the only pipers of whom he knew, had come to put things right. His confidence increased when German fire in his vicinity quietened, and when the Very lights of a success signal soared into the air above the main German position. Jeffs stood up, and looked around the silent, moonlit ridge. He saw some movement, started towards it, and was taken prisoner by four German soldiers.

'D' and 'B' Troops, to the right of 'C', found themselves in similar case, but with variations. Their approach was a climb over the same difficult, broken ground. There was Spandau tracer firing high, some through error, some in accordance with the standard German procedures for indicating the axis of advance of attackers so that they could be engaged by mortar and gunfire. Both troops suffered casualties on their way up from heavy mortaring, broke into the German forward positions, and with rapidly accumulating losses could make no further progress. There were small-arms and grenade exchanges amid the insistent din of the mortaring. Captain John Blake of 'D' Troop was killed. Both his subalterns were wounded. Over to the right, Captain Gerry Schooley of 'B' Troop used wire-cutters while being shot at to gap two successive barbed-wire entanglements, and ordered the wounded Troop Sergeant-Major Hugh Fuller to collect all casualties who could move and take them down the hill. Schooley set himself up with a small party in some overrun German trenches. His two subalterns were wounded. So were four sergeants of the two troops. The number of experienced leaders still on their feet was diminishing fast.

The holders of this precarious lodgement were puzzled after a while by a persistent and unexpected sound that penetrated the overall level of noise. From their right, and then growing louder as it moved steadily across their front behind the Germans they were facing, came the skirl of pipes.

The end of the involvement of the three troops of 43 Commando on the slopes of Point 622 is summarised in the unit's post-action report:

2215 hours	Enemy counter-attack in strength from left flank. Remnants of 'C' and 'D' Troops driven back to lower slopes of hill. 'E' Troop at bottom of hill heavily mortared.
2230	Ammunition exhausted and casualties heavy. Commanding Officer decided to break off fight.

Word of this decision of Simonds either did not reach Gerry Schooley and his 'B' Troop party or, if it did, was found by Schooley to be impossible to implement. He stayed where he was on the shoulder of the hill, defending the captured German trench position.

In the penultimate paragraph of his report Simonds listed his casualties: 'Captains JP Blake and RG Schooley missing. Reason to believe Captain Schooley killed assaulting the objective. 13 Other Ranks missing or killed. Captain Loudoun, Lieutenants Gregory, Nunns, Odendaal wounded. 47 Other Ranks wounded.'

No records survive of the precise starting strengths of the three troops who went in to this attack. Each was in theory sixty-five strong. Unreplaced casualties from previous operations, sickness and absences on courses and so on invariably meant that in the islands the full and theoretical totals were never met. At a reasonable guess the manpower committed by each troop was about forty-five, giving an overall total of 135, all ranks. In less than two hours, sixty-seven of these were to be put permanently or temporarily out of the war, more of them temporarily than permanently.

Simonds's headquarters were set up in a small coppice on a ridge to the west of Point 622, the peak which was the Commando objective. Captain Ralph Bazeley had initially sited his Regimental Aid Post beside Commando Headquarters, but once the attack began the ridge came under fire from German Spandaus, firing tracer on fixed lines. It was clearly no place for treating wounded. Bazeley shifted to a small house with an attached stable, in a sheltered gully. The occupants, an old woman, her daughter and a small child, gave Bazeley an hospitable welcome and incorporated themselves into his medical team.

The first casualties to come in were treated individually by Bazeley. The numbers soon became so great that he had to delegate the swabbing, cleaning, bandaging and injecting to his medical sergeant and his orderlies, who in the more complex cases worked on advice and instruction from him. He performed no surgery. That had to be deferred until the patients could reach the properly equipped hospital on Vis. The aid-post work was a patching-up process. The patched-up who could walk made their own way down to the beach, where an LCI awaited them. A shuttle of stretcher-bearers carried the more seriously hurt. The old woman took some down on a donkey. The leavers were replaced by a steady stream of new arrivals, Partisan as well as British, some carried in, some helped in, some walking or limping. The carriers and helpers were Commando stretcher-bearers and Partisan girls – the girls mostly in their teens or early twenties – who searched the hillside for wounded while under mortar and machine-gun fire.

Bazeley only discovered later that two other medical teams were working busily within a few hundred yards of his own, one from the American Operations Group, the other a temporary Partisan hospital established in Nerežišće. The flow of casualties to Bazeley diminished, and then stopped altogether. He saw his last patient off towards the beach and then turned his attentions to tidying up the house and the stable. He picked up used dressings, empty morphia syrettes, cigarette ends, sweet papers, and everything else that would indicate to German searchers the use to which the buildings had been put. He wanted no reprisals to fall upon the kindly old woman, her daughter and the child. They refused his offer of evacuation to Vis, and he said goodbye. He heard later that the house had been burned down. There were unconfirmed accounts of the shooting of the family.

SEVENTEEN

Brač: No. 40 Commando

At 6 p.m., three hours before the start time of 43 Commando, Pops Manners with 40 Commando, still in the lying-up position to which they had marched in the morning, was given orders to stand by to move. Word of these orders to Manners did not reach Simonds. Whether this was because of a corrupt signal, faulty cyphering or decyphering, bad radio reception conditions or for some other reason, the outcome was that the two Commandos were put in to attack different parts of the same objective without anyone in 43 knowing that 40 were to join in too: 40 knew that they were to help 43; 43 thought that they were to do the job alone.

Jack Churchill had earlier selected 40 Commando's start line, in the valley at the foot of the southern slope of Point 622. Manners was to be led to it by Captain Roger Wakefield of Brigade Headquarters. Since Wakefield did not know precisely where 40 Commando were, and Manners knew where Churchill was, the arrangement made was that Manners would send a guide to lead Wakefield to 40 Commando and that Wakefield would then take 40 Commando to the start line. The guide collected Wakefield in good time, but was then unable to find his way back to the Commando. He and Wakefield spent the best part of two hours marching exhaustingly through convoluted defiles and craggy hills, lost.

At 8 p.m., one hour before the attack was due to go in, 40 Commando had still not moved. Manners, in increasing puzzlement about the reason for the delay, lost patience and set out for Brigade Headquarters. On his way there he chanced upon Wakefield.

Churchill's early intention had been to go back to 43 to watch their start. The delay brought about by the lost guide from 40 Commando caused him to change his mind. He had in fact set out for 43 when he ran into Pops Manners and Wakefield. It was clear that if 40 Commando were to perform their role effectively in co-ordination with the 43 Commando assault, everyone would have to move fast and conventional procedures would have to be short-circuited. Manners was ordered to run back to his unit, tell them to bolt the meal they were eating and bring them along at speed. Manners did this. When he was back, Churchill walked with him towards the objective and told him what was required of him.

They crossed a low valley and came to the foot of the hill, upon which undergrowth had been set alight by the artillery shelling. The fires, and the full moon, gave a very clear view. The three troops – 'A', 'Y' and 'Q' – of 40 Commando were told to sit down. Jack Churchill harangued them. He said that 43 were attacking the hill from the left, and had probably already taken it, in which case there would be nothing much for 40 to do. They would now – one hour after their start time – climb up and see what had happened.

Churchill (playing his pipes) and Manners led. On the hillside they came upon a party from 43 Commando (this was Captain Gerry Schooley and some of 'B' Troop; Lieutenant Odendaal, who was lying wounded nearby, wrote years later to Churchill and related how he had seen him going up, playing his pipes). They incorporated the party in the advance. What appeared to be a wired-in minefield was crossed in four single files, to minimise the chances of anyone treading on a mine. Nobody did. On the far side of the minefield, if that is what it was, they spread out again, and continued on upwards, Churchill playing his pipes throughout.

'Y' Troop, on the left, ran into mines. They shifted over to their right. 'A' Troop, commanded by Captain Jimmy Wakeling, went straight. So far they were unimpeded by either wire or mines, but they came under a growing weight of mortar fire and suffered casualties. The leading platoon commander was Lieutenant David Copsey. (It should be noted that – as with 'batman' – 40 Commando had preserved an idiosyncratic terminology. It had platoons; the other Commandos had sections. They were of the same notional strength, seldom reached in practice, of one subaltern, two sergeants and thirty junior NCOs and marines.) Copsey took his platoon right over the top of the hill, clearing trenches as he went, killing Germans and capturing six of them. The second platoon of 'A' Troop, following close on Copsey's heels, cleaned up another German trench, and lost heavily from mortar, machine-gun and small-arms fire. Only five men were able to join up with Wakeling and Copsey. Lieutenant Lew Cross, the commander of this platoon, was last seen charging a German machine-gun position. Copsey consolidated his position (that is, he put his remnants into a formation covering all sides, prepared to deal with a counter-attack) on the far slope of the hill. Wakeling passed a message to Manners indicating where 'A' Troop were. Manners ordered that the success signal of two green Very lights should be put up. This was done by Marine Marshall, Copsey's batman.

'Y' Troop, who had been slowed down by their change of direction, fought their way towards the left of the objective. Their troop commander, Captain Ian Laidlaw, was killed during this attack. So was one of his two subalterns, Lieutenant Lyn Dutton. The other, Lieutenant Jeff Beadle, was badly wounded and later taken prisoner. Troop Sergeant-Major Gordon took over command. He was unable to get as far forward as 'A' Troop, but consolidated to their left rear, leaving a gap between the two troops.

The Force Headquarters group of Churchill, Manners, Wakefield and Pirie, the Brigade Royal Engineers officer, joined 'A' Troop on the objective. Two more Germans were shot in their trenches, and four more prisoners, escorted by a marine, were sent back down the hill. It was not long before heavy concentrations of mortar fire came down on both troops. The mortaring lifted, to be followed by infantry counter-attacks, one along the far slope against 'A' Troop, one from the left against 'Y' Troop. 'A' Troop repelled theirs, killing six Germans in the process. The German attack from the left developed more dangerously. It was aimed not only at Sergeant-Major Gordon's 'Y'

Troop position, but took in, slightly farther back, 40 Commando Headquarters, commanded by Major Neil Maude, and the survivors from 'B' Troop of 43 Commando. Maude decided that his signallers were a liability and told them to make their way to the rear. Then, with the 43 Commando party, he started shooting at Germans. After a brief interval he joined Gerry Schooley, the commander of 'B' Troop. Schooley, who had eight of his men with him, was firing from a captured German trench. Maude brought with him two marines from 40 Commando Headquarters.

He was then joined by Lieutenant Thomson with 'Q' Troop, the second wave of the attack, who had had several losses from mortar fire on their way up. Thomson took 'Q' Troop in against the German counter-attackers, came under heavy fire from the left, lost further casualties, reached the first line of German dug-outs and paused there to re-form. Meanwhile, higher up and to the right, Sergeant-Major Gordon's diminishing party from 'Y' Troop were in danger of being overrun. He extricated them under the cover of his 2-inch mortar, which fired off all its bombs into the advancing Germans at point-blank range. Gordon moved over to the 'A' Troop position and placed his group under their command. His 2-inch mortar was not the only weapon on the hill to have fired off all, or most, of its ammunition. Schooley's party from 'B' Troop of 43 Commando had been in action for over an hour longer than had the three troops of 40 Commando, and he reported to Maude that he had little left to shoot with.

The German pattern of concentrated mortaring followed by infantry assaults continued unabated. Casualties were mounting. Churchill sent Manners to check precisely where each of his three troops were. Manners had covered about twenty yards when he called out that he had been hit. Churchill ran across and found him bleeding badly from a wound high up on his arm and shoulder. Churchill dragged him back and knelt beside him, trying to staunch the flow of blood. A growing mixed fire from German Spandaus, mortars and rifles developed. Roger Wakefield, also kneeling beside the wounded Manners and helping to check his loss of blood, was the next to be hit. Wakefield said only two more things. The first was: 'Help me, Colonel.' The second, a little while later was: 'Has anybody got any morphia?' Churchill gave him an injection. Wakefield died shortly afterwards.*

Jack Churchill was soon joined by 'a very splendid marine from 43 Commando', who came forward and asked what he could do to help. It was becoming increasingly clear that nobody was in a position to do much to help. The German counter-attack seemed to have cleared the position of most of 40 Commando. Churchill had eleven other people with him, some already wounded, some who became so as the mortar fire intensified. Jack Churchill, lying on his back, played 'Will Ye No' Come Back Again', on the pipes. A mortar-bomb fragment dented his steel helmet, cut his scalp and knocked him unconscious. When he came to, he found that he, and those of his party still alive, were prisoners.

The area of the hill and of its surrounding valleys in which all this concentrated fighting took place was remarkably small. Nobody was more than two or three hundred yards away from anybody else. Jack Churchill's pipes were clearly heard on all sides. Many people, like Ron Jeffs, and including Colonel Simonds, assumed that the Highland Light Infantry had joined in the action. Only old Admiral Cowan, back at Brigade Headquarters, recognised the tune, and understood the significance of 'Will Ye No' Come Back Again'.

'That', said the Admiral, 'sounds a bit sinister.'

The inevitability of withdrawal had become clear to Major Neil Maude, over on the left. He told Schooley to take his men from 43 Commando, with what ammunition they had left, to a point about fifty yards to the rear down the hill, and there to establish a firm base upon which 40 Commando could re-form. Schooley was killed almost immediately. The order was carried out by one of his wounded subalterns, Lieutenant Odendaal. Maude managed to make contact with elements of all three 40

---

*Tom Churchill had been a close friend of Wakefield, and went to see his sister when he heard that Wakefield was dead. Wakefield, in one of his last letters to his sister, had told her of a recurrent dream in which he was killed on a hillside.

Commando troops, brought them back downhill, collected Odendaal's party and set them all up in a defensive position, facing the Germans, about midway between the summit and the valley. Maude's description of the end of the action, written three days after it, reads:

> Apart from the fact that the Germans had reoccupied the top of the hill I had no information as to what was going on, and had no idea where Force Headquarters was. I therefore determined to hold on to our position in case 43 Commando should still be attacking as, apart from B Troop, I had seen none of them. However, after some minutes the battle seemed to be dying down and ammunition was very low. I therefore ordered [40 Commando's] A and Y Troops to re-form on the Start Line. Q Troop I ordered to remain with me to cover the withdrawal.

Once he was satisfied that 'A' and 'Y' Troops were safely down, Maude took 'Q' Troop on a search for wounded in the area. They found none. They did meet the unit's padre, the Reverend Ross Hook, who had already been dealing with the wounded. They then came across a badly hit man who had to be carried down. All three troops were reunited on the start line at about 2 a.m., four hours after they had left it.

The German commander of the hill's defence was a major named Thorner. Jack Churchill soon acquired a high respect for Thorner, both as a soldier and as a humane and considerate opponent. The prisoners, fourteen in all, were treated with complete correctness. Colonel Pops Manners and the more seriously wounded were cared for in the German aid post. Manners died there about twenty-four hours after he had been hit. A marine had been allowed in to visit him. Churchill, when he recovered consciousness, had removed the rank badges from the shoulder straps of his shirt, and the medal ribbons that had been attached by press-studs above his left breast pocket. He already had escape in mind and thought that his chances would be improved if he could pass himself off as 'Marine

Higginbotham or Hickenlooper or something'. Marine Jeffs, who did not know Churchill, recalls seeing what he assumed to be a spare marine sitting in the corner of the small stone hut in which the prisoners were held, cutting a loaf of bread provided by the Germans into fourteen exactly equal slices. A German came in, and asked which of the captives was Colonel Churchill. Jeffs was amused. He was surprised when the anonymous bread-slicer rose to his feet and identified himself as the Colonel.

The prisoners were held on the hilltop for two-and-a-half days. At first they were kept at the back of the hill in a hole in the ground. They shared the hole with a petrol-fuelled battery charger which put out an uncomfortable volume of exhaust fumes. Churchill watched German defensive arrangements with professional interest, and gave them full marks. There was a certain amount of moving about by night. Individual positions were recamouflaged, food, water and ammunition were distributed. By day, there was no movement at all.

Part of the pre-dawn movement on the second morning was the burial of the fourteen British dead left on the crest. The bodies of Manners, Wakefield, Laidlaw, Blake, Schooley, Royle and the others were laid by the prisoners side by side in a long common grave. For the simple ceremony that followed, Thorner returned Churchill's pipes. The prisoners paraded formally outside their stone hut in the hollow and marched the hundred yards to the grave. Jack Churchill said a little prayer and then played a lament on the pipes. The grave was partially filled in, but filling had to be discontinued because it was growing light and Thorner would allow no activity that might attract the attention of the RAF, still flying sorties over Brač. The grave was completed early the next morning.

Later they were all moved down the hill under close guard. Before long they were joined by twenty new prisoners from No. 2 Commando. Two troops of 2 Commando had been sent for by Jack Churchill on the morning before the attack on Point 622, and had arrived to find that their colonel was missing and that there were 130 other Commando casualties. These two troops mounted valiant attempts to rescue their commanding officer and the other prisoners ('a bloody silly idea', said Tom Churchill when looking back on it), only for they themselves to lose twenty captured.

The Germans were delighted to find that they had in their hands the redoubtable Jack Churchill, though they were confused about which particular Churchill he was. Within a day or two their radio propaganda was claiming that Brigadier Tom Churchill had been captured, and there were suggestions that the son of the British Prime Minister was the captive. Jack Churchill was separated from his fellow-prisoners, sent down to the coast in the side-car of a motor-cycle combination – escorted strongly by, among other things, a tank – and was taken across the southern reaches of the Brač Channel to a German divisional headquarters on the Yugoslav mainland at Makarska. Before he left, he was permitted a final military courtesy. He took the salute as the thirty-odd prisoners marched past ceremonially and gave him the 'eyes right'.

His subsequent career as a notably obstreperous prisoner-of-war is really beyond the scope of this account. It is, however, relevant to an appraisal of the spirit in which he had always conducted his operations, and which he engendered in his subordinates. Faced with unusually rigorous treatment, he responded with unusually effective and spectacular panache. He was not put into a standard prisoner-of-war camp. He was sent to four separate concentration camps, ending in Sachsenhausen, a murderously run institution supervised by the Nazi SS. Here he found himself in the company of Wing Commander 'Wings' Day, Flight Lieutenant Dowse and similar RAF incorrigibles. Towards the end of the war they escaped, headed for Austria and were recovered by Allied troops. It was one of the very few escapes, ever, from a concentration camp. In the 1960s, Jack Churchill was foremost among a litigious group of these British officers who wanted the Foreign Office to compensate them with a fair share of the government funds allocated for concentration-camp victims. He was unsuccessful.

There was a post-war postscript to Jack Churchill's capture in the Brač battle. The Yugoslav government asked for the return to Yugoslavia for trial as war criminals of a number of named German officers and soldiers held as prisoners by the British and the Americans. Most were handed over, including General Kuebler of 118 Jaeger Division, the formation with which the Commando Brigade had clashed most frequently in the Dalmatian islands. Kuebler was hanged. Churchill heard that his chivalrous captor, Major Thorner, was also on the list but had not yet been sent back. Churchill intervened forcefully with the British and American authorities on Thorner's behalf. The plea from a man who had himself recently emerged from nearly a year in Nazi concentration camps was given the weight that it deserved. Thorner stayed in the West.

Later, Jack Churchill was a guest at Thorner's wedding. Later still, he was invited to become an honorary member of the 118 Jaeger Division Old Comrades Association. He still attends their reunions from time to time.

As with 43 Commando, there is no extant, publicly available record which cites the total strength of the attacking force. Using the same rough and ready calculation to allow for depletions through various causes, it seems probable that each of the three 40 Commando troops numbered about forty-five, giving a total of 135. In addition there was the unit's headquarters of, say, twenty, and the Force Headquarters of Jack Churchill and three officers. Overall total: 165. Of these, five officers of 40 Commando, including its colonel, Pops Manners, were killed. One officer was lightly wounded. Of the three Force Head-quarters officers, two were killed and one, Jack Churchill, was missing. Fourteen other ranks of 'A', 'Y' and 'Q' Troops were killed, twenty were wounded sufficiently badly to be sent to hospital, and twenty others were 'lightly wounded'. Total casualties: sixty – slightly less than 43 Commando's sixty-seven.

On the morning of 4 June, when the attacks of both 43 and 40 Commandos upon the hill feature dominated by Point 622 had failed, Bonzo Simonds, now the Senior British Officer on Brač, summoned a conference. What was to be done next? The consensus favoured disengagement. One provisional dissident was Colonel Elliott of 111 Field Regiment, Royal Artillery. He had plenty of 25-pounder ammunition ashore on Brač, he said. He would gladly stay and fire it off. Old Admiral Cowan expressed admiration. 'There speaks a *soldier*,' he said. The advocates of extended belligerence were overruled. Simonds ordered the evacuation of the island. It was, in Tom Churchill's retrospective view, probably the right decision. The Brač raid had made its strategic point. Numbers of German soldiers who might have been committed to the chasing of Tito had been diverted to Brač. There was, indeed, a chance that too many might come and put the continued existence of the raiding force at risk. The Germans could reinforce much more quickly from the mainland than the British could from relatively distant Vis. The available pool of German manpower was also immeasurably bigger.

On Sunday, 4 June, both Commandos re-embarked on LCIs, 40 in the morning, 43 in the evening, and set course for the island base of Vis. The RAF regained some of its dented popularity shortly before embarkation. Two Spitfires shot down two Messerschmitts which tried to strafe the beaches. 111 Field Regiment and the Raiding Support Regiment came back in their various craft on the same day. Most of the Partisans remained on Brač. So did the two troops of No. 2 Commando, who were to launch their abortive attempt to rescue Jack Churchill, before the survivors, after several days, also returned to Vis. They reported that the hilltop, when seen by them on the first day of their expedition, had been littered with large numbers of German dead.

Afterwards Major Neil Maude, now the acting Commanding Officer of 40 Commando, wrote a brief, chronological account of his unit's part in the battle, upon which I have relied heavily in the narrative above. Maude added no comments or suggestions. The first part of Colonel Bonzo Simonds's report on 43 Commando's experiences was also terse and chronological, but he had quite a few things to say underneath the heading 'Remarks'. He was in no sense critical of Partisan courage or military ability when left to themselves to fight their own war, but he was outspoken about the difficulties that arose when acting in concert with them as mutually dependent components of the same enterprise.

The differences of language, temperament and military training of the two nationalities make the co-ordination of offensive operations in the same area impossible. . . . On no occasion of a joint attack during this operation did the Partisans conform to what was understood to be their plans. . . . An unnecessary number of casualties were caused by cross-fire from enemy positions which should have been neutralised by Partisan attack. It is considered that the Partisans did not in fact close with these positions, but merely attempted to neutralise them by fire.

Simonds had this to say about the type of objective selected for the attack.

The objectives . . . consisted of prominent hill features devoid of cover on the lower slopes. The enemy were strongly entrenched in holes blasted in the ground, with camouflaged stone roofs, minefields of irregular pattern, to a depth of fifty yards, and single apron wire fences on one or both sides of the mines. . . . These obstacles were covered by machine-gun fire not only from the position itself, but also from neighbouring positions on flanks or in rear. . . .

Against this sort of opposition, wrote Simonds, what was needed was not the artillery support of ten 25-pounders and four 75-mm mountain guns (to which elsewhere he gave praise) but heavy air bombardment and heavy artillery support on the objective, adjacent strongpoints and rear areas. There should also be special mine- and wire-clearing parties, separate from the assaulting troops.

One sentence, which looks like the final product of a great deal of drafting and redrafting to get it within the acceptable conventions of military discipline, reads simply: 'Unknown to 43 Royal Marine Commando, 40 Royal Marine Commando were brought into the attack but arrived too late to influence the enemy counter-attack on 43 Commando, and were themselves in turn counter-attacked.'

*

Was it all worth it? On 13 June 1944, Force 266 produced an 'Appreciation of Effects on the Enemy of Operation Flounced'. Its findings were that Brač had been reinforced from the mainland by 1900 Germans, 'clearly a direct result of the attack'. There had also been much German nervousness about the possibility that there might be further landings along the Dalmatian coast. Some formations had been moved to counter this threat. Others had been frozen where they were. To the extent that none of these troops could be made available to harass Tito in Bosnia, Tito's predicament had been eased. At the same time no Germans had been sent from Bosnia to strengthen the coast. The pressure on Tito had not been increased, but neither had it diminished. It had stayed constant, at a level of intensity that hamstrung his ability to influence and control Partisan operations. He had lost touch with nearly all his subordinate headquarters.

In the first week of June, Tito summoned Vivian Street and asked to be flown out of mainland Yugoslavia, to a new base from which he could reimpose his grip upon events without the distraction of being hounded through the forests and mountains. Street at once signalled to the RAF in Bari. Bari agreed to send in a Dakota that night to a landing strip which was temporarily in secure Partisan possession. The Dakota, when it arrived, was found to be manned by a Russian crew, controlled operationally by the RAF, a fact that was to be made much of later in Soviet propaganda. Tito and the Allied missions spent a few days in Bari, where they were joined by Fitzroy Maclean, and then sailed in a British destroyer, HMS *Blackmore*, to the logical secure base on offshore Yugoslav territory. After a convivial voyage, promoted by the traditional hospitality of the Royal Navy, and during which Tito stimulated warm admiration over dinner by a spirited recitation of 'The Owl and the Pussy-Cat', *Blackmore* tied up in Komiža harbour early on the following morning. Marshal Tito established his new headquarters in a cave on the side of Mount Hum, the highest peak on Vis.

Tom Churchill was in London when he learned of the consequences to his brigade of the Brač operation. On the previous day he had secured agreement to the relief of Pops Manners. Now he heard that Manners was dead, his brother Jack was missing and 'some bloody brave troop leaders' were dead too. Total casualties, in both absolute and proportionate terms, were the highest in any one British operation undertaken in Yugoslavia. Junior officers and senior NCOs, the kernel of any fighting unit, were particularly hard hit. Forty-one years later he put to himself the question: Was it a success? It was, he said, a tactical failure, compounded by the loss of so many people of outstanding quality. But on balance, he thought that it had made a worthwhile contribution to the achievement of the overall strategic object. A short time after it was over Tito, alive and unhurt, was once more functioning effectively as the directing force of the Partisan movement.

PART FOUR

From the Islands to the Mainland

EIGHTEEN

Tito and Politics

Three days after the night attack on Brač, and one thousand miles away, British and American troops went ashore on the Normandy beaches in the largest amphibious military operation in history. On the eastern front, the Red Army in its summer campaign was rolling the Wehrmacht inexorably backwards. For the first time during the five years of the war the territory of metropolitan Germany was under threat of attack by land. It was still a distant threat, and there was to be much shedding of blood and enormous destruction before it was realised, but its strategic consequences affected every German-occupied country in Europe. German military planners, unlike their Führer, were realists. One of their realistic assessments was to do with the Balkans. Continued embroilment in Greece, Albania and southern Yugoslavia no longer made sense. Too many German troops, badly needed elsewhere, were tied up to too small purpose. If the Russians continued to progress westwards at their present rate, and if the British Eighth Army in northern Italy broke through and moved north-east, or if there were a major British seaborne intervention in mainland Yugoslavia, the exits to the Balkan appendage could be sealed, and the German Army Group E locked in, to be destroyed piecemeal. Starting with Greece, the Germans began to thin out their garrisons. As the summer of 1944 moved on, the process developed into total evacuation. German columns, some with tanks and motor vehicles, some on foot with horse-drawn transport and mule trains, moved up slowly from the south, gathering more northerly garrisons as they went.

In Greece, and later in Albania, there was some guerrilla

harassment of this disengagement, but it was not nearly as whole-hearted as it might have been. Rival groupings of guerrillas in both countries were more interested in repaying old scores and in trying to establish the post-war dominance of their particular brand of domestic politics. They were less concerned to kill off a few members of a departing occupation force that however much it had been detested was for its own reasons on its way out. Internecine fighting developed in both countries. The Communists lost in Greece, and won in Albania. In Yugoslavia, too, there was a rearrangement by the Communist leadership of political priorities. There was still some way to go before the realisation of the prime objective, the removal of the Germans. They would clearly linger in Yugoslavia for longer than they intended to in Greece and in Albania. The timing of their final departure would depend upon military developments far to the north-east and the north-west.

But an end was at last in sight, even if the precise form that it would take was so far unforeseeable. Fierce fighting against the Germans must remain at the top of the list of what had to be done, but attention must now be paid to the achievement of what so far had been a distant aim, obscured by more pressing realities – the setting up of a Communist state. One prerequisite was the destruction of internal enemies – Chetnik, Ustashi, capitalist, bourgeois or those otherwise unsympathetic to Communism. Also required was a precautionary wariness about the motives of capitalist Western Allies who, however militarily co-operative they were at present, could be assumed to want to bring influences and pressures to bear upon future events in a manner that would not accord with Communist ambitions. The destruction of Chetniks and Ustashi had of course been in progress for years. It was stepped up. Paranoia about Western intentions had been latent for years. Its manifestations grew, at first subtly, into an obstructive suspiciousness.

The shift in the strategic emphasis was reflected by some changes in the composition of the British force on Vis. Tom Churchill with his Brigade Headquarters, No. 2 Commando, who had been the first to arrive, and No. 40

Commando left for Italy prior to their commitment to operations in Albania and Corfu. No. 43 Commando stayed, and were to become the British unit with the longest service in wartime Yugoslavia. The routine of training, planning and the despatch of reconnaissance parties by schooner and motor launch continued as before. Recovered Brač casualties slowly rejoined from hospitals in Italy. In early July, Captain Jock Hudspith, with Lieutenant Odendaal, ten men and an exceptionally powerful wireless set provided by Special Operations Executive, landed on Hvar to look into some information provided by the Partisans. A German patrol with regular habits was reported to make a visit to the village of Bogomilje at intervals of six to ten days. Outside the village the patrol always split into two parties. One picqueted the high ground on either side of the road. The other went into the village in search of loot.

On 5 July the patrol duly put in an appearance, and did exactly what the Partisans had said that it always did. This time it did it under the close observation of Hudspith and his party, well concealed. Hudspith wirelessed back to Vis that there was a ready-made ambush target on offer. Colonel Simonds came over five days later to look at the ground, and was followed on the next day by three troops of his Commando, totalling one hundred men. (The total is an indication of the damage done in the Brač battle. At full strengths the number would have been 195.) These landed soon after midnight and were installed in their respective ambush positions shortly before dawn. It was an unusual dawn for an Adriatic summer. It was raining hard, and low cloud drifted about on the hills and in the valleys.

The mist and cloud brought about an unplanned start to the operation. The German patrol, thirty men, arrived on time, walked unseen through the murk past the observation post that was to report its approach, walked unseen right through the ambush and arrived in Bogomilje, where it at once captured a surprised and resentful Captain Ralph Bazeley, who had laid out the apparatus of his aid post in one of the village houses. Bazeley had been a prisoner for a quarter of an hour before a break in the cloud cover made it evident to the ambushers that the sequence had not developed as forecast. Simonds put all three troops into a simultaneous attack on the village. They went in making a great deal of noise, later referred to disparagingly by Bazeley, at the receiving end, as 'banshee and bayonet methods'. The Germans fought back well, from inside the houses. Captain Mark Nunns was wounded after silencing with a grenade a Spandau firing from a cottage window. Captain Nobby Clark was also wounded in another shoot-out with a Spandau. Sergeant French chased one German for a hundred yards before downing him with a Tommy gun. The affray lasted for fifteen minutes. At the end of it there were seventeen German prisoners, eight German dead (with perhaps five missing or escaped), and a liberated medical staff giving their professional services to the wounded of both sides – in the British case Nunns, Clark and three lightly hurt marines.

The troops, crammed tightly into motor gun boats, bringing their prisoners with them, were back on Vis before midnight, feeling rather pleased with themselves. The success had been small in scale. It was some compensation for Brač.

From the middle of 1944 a tiny, adaptable and elite unit of specialists in navigation, signalling and deep reconnaissance began to operate on the Yugoslav Adriatic coast, pre-dominantly among the northern reaches, sometimes in the south. Its name, the Long Range Desert Group, had a ring of incongruity in a campaign conducted on offshore Mediterranean islands and mainland coasts. Its achievements represented possibly the best return for Allied manpower investment in the entire Yugoslav enterprise. Its chief function was to observe German coastal shipping and to report on its movements by wireless to the Royal Navy and to the Royal Air Force, who, circumstances of availability and weather being favourable, would then interdict the shipping. The cumulative results were impressive. The impressiveness was a product of the quality of the people in the LRDG, who, when engaged in deep reconnaissance, 'shone with truly unrivalled brilliance'. That was the opinion of General Sir John Hacket, who as a brigadier in Cairo had been responsible for allocating their desert tasks, hundreds of miles behind the Afrika Korps.

The LRDG had been formed in Egypt in mid-1940,

immediately after Italy had entered the war. A large Italian army in the then Italian colony of Libya threatened, or seemed to threaten, Egypt and the Nile. One possible line of approach from which much harm could be done to British communications was through a few desert oases far to the south near the junction of the frontiers of Libya, Egypt and the Sudan. There was no intelligence coverage of any sort for this huge area. Major Ralph Bagnold of the Royal Corps of Signals had before the war spent much of his spare time in studying, developing and experimenting with the techniques of desert travel by motor vehicle. He had invented a sun compass, devised metal sand channels for the unsticking of bogged-down vehicles, produced an improved condenser for the conservation of water in radiators, and had confirmed by trial and error his already deeply held conviction that success, and indeed survival, for desert journeyers depended upon far-sighted detailed planning, painstaking precision and the highest standard of mechanical maintenance. Bagnold suggested to General Headquarters, Middle East, that a small mobile unit carried in light trucks, issued with equipment of the kind that he had used in the past, and recruited from volunteers with the skills and characteristics that he considered to be essential for the work, should be raised to provide surveillance of the desert hinterland. Approval was given.

The force was recruited, equipped and its aptitudes polished within six weeks. Until the end of the North African campaign, its patrols, British, New Zealand and Rhodesian, ranged far behind the German and Italian forward positions, navigating by the sun and the stars, preparing 'going' maps of usable desert routes, lying up patiently in concealment for days on end to assemble and wireless back information on enemy movements and strengths. Its role was to gather intelligence, not primarily to fight. But when fighting became necessary, it fought, dangerously.

It is unlikely that anyone serving in the LRDG during its desert existence considered the possibility that a year later he would be delivered to his observation hideout by boat instead of by jeep or truck, that he would be in for a great deal of hard marching over coastal mountains and that the reports that he would wireless back would be to do with enemy shipping instead of enemy vehicles. But it was in essence a variant of the original job, requiring the same patience, precision and stamina.

Colonel David Lloyd Owen, who commanded the Long Range Desert Group in 1944, flew to Vis in June for discussions about where he could most usefully operate. He soon set up a clandestine advance base on Dugi Otok (Long Island), sixty-odd miles to the north-west of Vis, and from there his first coast-watching team were put ashore on the mainland at the end of the month. Captain Stokes and four men were in continuous business for almost five months, signalling back details of the movements of coastal shipping, sometimes in conditions of relative peace, sometimes on the run from searching Germans. On the small island of Ist, to the north of Dugi Otok, Lieutenant Gatchell spent two months observing and reporting. He had some distractions not available to Stokes. His party rescued the aircrew of an American Flying Fortress which had force-landed on an adjacent island. Later, they joined with Partisans in the attack and boarding of a German schooner. There was a rich haul of loot. The schooner carried a cargo of canteen stores. It also carried two concert party artistes – an embarrassment.

Lieutenant Gibson's party were the first of the LRDG to have practical experience of Partisan reservations about the real intentions of their British allies. Gibson was landed on the mainland from Vis with orders to make his way to Mostar, lie up in the hills above the aerodrome and report back on Luftwaffe traffic, with a view to the planning of aerial ambushes by RAF fighters of German aircraft at their most vulnerable, soon after take-off. Gibson's first stay on the mainland was brief. After one day the Partisans sent him back to Vis. A few days later he had another try, and was received more hospitably. Germans, presumably using radio direction-finding sets, were soon in pursuit, tracked him and attacked him and his Partisan hosts. The attack was beaten off, in a fight in which the LRDG fired off most of its ammunition. The Partisans warmed to Gibson after this shared defensive action, and he became the godfather of a Partisan officer's newly born child.*

*The Partisan code of celibacy (see p. 136) seems to have been enforced

Gibson never did get within range of the Mostar aerodrome. The German ground defences were too active. He was harried continually, but was able to send back a steady flow of useful information about the area in which he was then hiding. One Partisan ukase – emanating, he was told by the local Partisan commander, from 'above' – puzzled both Gibson and Lloyd Owen. No British troops were to take part in offensive operations against the Germans. The reason for this ban was to become clear to many other British troops a short time later. The Communist Party legend under construction demanded that military victory should be seen to be the product of the undiluted efforts of the National Liberation Movement, orchestrated by its Communist leadership. It was not until the 1970s that a more mature and relaxed Yugoslav government information machine was prepared to acknowledge publicly, and generously, that British sailors, soldiers and airmen had made a substantial contribution to Partisan wartime success.

Working closely with the Long Range Desert Group was another small volunteer unit, the Special Boat Section, the seaborne equivalent, as we have seen, of the Special Air Service. The SBS, like the SAS, had for three years specialised in the destruction with explosive charges, manually applied, of enemy aircraft on enemy airfields. The SBS's arena of operations had largely been islands – Crete, Corsica, the Dodecanese – in the last of which they had gone in for extensive privateering in caiques, illegally based in Turkish creeks, courtesy of the blind eye of the neutral Turkish government. The SBS were raiders, not information collectors, and did not aspire to the technical expertise of the LRDG. The two complemented each other comfortably. The commanding officer of the SBS was Lieutenant-Colonel Lord Jellicoe.

---

less rigorously in an isolated part of Hercegovina than it was in Dalmatia. But since there was also a christening ceremony and a feast, the Partisan was presumably a Christian enlisted under the umbrella of the Popular Front, and was perhaps exempt from the proscription.

In August two LRDG patrols, one led by Captain Skipwith and the other by Lieutenant Shute, were run ashore in southern Dalmatia near Dubrovnik. They were looking for something for the SBS to blow up. Skipwith recommended a suitable railway bridge. Towards the end of the month, Captain Anders Lassen and an SBS party came to deal with it.*

Lassen and Skipwith severed two long spans of the bridge. A retributory force of 300 Ustashi chased them for three days, caught up with them, and started a running engagement which lasted all morning. Skipwith, Sergeant Leach and an SBS soldier were captured while throwing grenades in a rearguard holding-off action. Lassen and the rest got away, and were collected from a beach three nights later, to fight again.

Shute's patrol, carried in a motor launch of the Royal Navy, overloaded the dinghy in which they were ferrying themselves to the beach in a choppy sea. It went down a quarter of a mile offshore. The party lost most of their stores and for a time were separated. The signaller salvaged his set, less batteries. They all met up again, borrowed a car battery from the Partisans and found that they could send signals but not receive them. They sent word of a railway tunnel ripe for demolition. An SBS party was shipped in to deal with the tunnel, asked for more explosive to be parachuted in after they had examined its stone construction, did not get the explosive in time and did their best with the 100 pounds of ammonal that they had brought with them. It did little damage. Before leaving they wrecked the points on the railway line and cut the telephone wires. It was more than a month before the party, short of food and with their boots in ribbons, were brought out from a Partisan airstrip in a Dakota aircraft of the RAF.

*

*Lassen was a Danish merchant marine officer, at sea when Germany invaded Denmark in 1940. As soon as his ship reached a British port he joined the British army. He went to the Commandos, and then to the SBS. By the time of the Dubrovnik bridge blow, he held the Military Cross with two bars. In 1945 he was killed in action in Italy. He was awarded a posthumous Victoria Cross, the only foreign VC winner ever.

Partisan co-operation, offered in Hercegovina to Gibson with one qualification after a reluctant start, and freely given in southern Dalmatia to Skipwith, Shute and Lassen, was barely available at all in Istria, the triangular peninsula, apex pointing downward, at the northern end of the Adriatic. To the LRDG, and to their British naval and air force customers, Istria was the best location of all for a prosperous coastal watch. German shipping moved constantly in and out of the major ports of Trieste and Fiume (now Rijeka). Its monitoring from hides in the mountains presented the usual difficulties of harassment and possible detection, but they were acceptable risks. To the Partisans, the benefit to them of sunken German tonnage deriving from the LRDG watch was outweighed by a political consideration. The Communist leadership was intent upon the incorporation into the new, post-war Yugoslav republic of the Italian city of Trieste, urban population largely Italian, population in the rural hinterland largely Slovene. British soldiers with wireless sets moving around Istria might have devious purposes more to do with the frustration of Yugoslav territorial expansion than with the sinking of German ships. The early welcome to the LRDG was cold. It later became actively hostile.

Two early Istrian examples of the frustration by Partisans of promising LRDG undertakings, in both cases after the patrols had made wearying approach marches hampered by German interference, came in September. Lieutenant Reynolds, with three other Rhodesians, was stopped by bad weather from parachuting in east of Rijeka towards the end of August. Two days later all four were landed by the RAF on a Partisan strip in the same area, charged with reporting upon sea traffic between Rijeka and Pula. The airstrip Partisans were not unhelpful and saw the four off on their way. The Germans, taking cross-bearings on Reynold's wireless transmissions, were extremely unhelpful and gave chase, as well as blocking likely routes to mountain observation posts. The Reynolds team tramped through the hills, evading pursuers, wriggling around blocks, on occasion going back to try something different, once after a German attack having to withdraw for fifteen miles at the end of a twenty-mile march on the previous night.

It took the party a month of hard dodging, side-stepping and marching before they were through the German screen and established in a suitable eyrie overlooking the inshore sea lanes. They were at once ordered out by the Partisans. Reynolds managed to stall for nearly three weeks, during which he transmitted valuable summaries of German sea movements, and killed three Germans from a searching group who came too close for comfort to the LRDG viewing point in the rocks. But the Partisans were increasingly insistent that he must go, and underlined their insistence by refusing him any help with food, information or protection. Without Partisan co-operation he was hamstrung. The navy evacuated his patrol to Italy in the middle of October.

Lieutenant Pitt took only one signaller with him when he left to learn all that he could about the harbours, and their users, of Trieste and Monfalcone. Pitt had a complicated and strenuous journey that took in delivery from Italy by an American torpedo boat to a small island, an onward stretch with a Partisan in a rowing boat to the mainland east of the island of Krk, and a long march north through the mountains of Slovenia. It rained almost ceaselessly. At an isolated spot in the hills during a rare patch of sunshine the two of them stripped off their sodden clothes and spread them on bushes to dry. The bushes soon disclosed themselves to be unhappily situated. They were in the centre of the target area of a German artillery range. A three-hour German field-firing exercise began at once. Pitt and the signaller, both totally nude, withdrew themselves from the beaten zone, and watched the shelling from a prudent distance, wondering what state their clothing would be in when the noise died down. When at last it did, they found that all was untouched. They re-dressed, and marched for a further nineteen hours.

The next obstacle was from Partisan obduracy, expressed bureaucratically. The Political Commissar at Partisan IX Corps headquarters wanted to see written evidence that Pitt was authorised to be in the Corps area. Where was Pitt's pass? Pitt had no pass. It had not before crossed his mind that operational soldiers risking their necks to help their allies should submit a formal application for permission to do so. The Commissar sent off to 'above' for a ruling. It came after several days of waiting. Permission to stay was refused for 'English Lieutenant Pitt', who was requested to return at once to Dugi Otok, amicably.

Like Reynolds, Pitt procrastinated, amicably. After an interval during which he met up with two British escaped prisoners-of-war and the crew of a downed American bomber, he slipped away towards his selected coast-watching site, doubled back and forth in the teeth of a German divisional search, and for two-and-a-half days was without food of any description. He reported on his movements regularly to Italy. He could not get through to where he wanted to go, and was pulled out in late October.

One LRDG four-man team, led by Lieutenant Rowbottom, inspected German shipping from a closer range than they had intended. They were in an E-boat, which had captured them when they were rowing between two islands. The E-boat made south to take up station as part of the escort of a convoy on its way to Split, where the prisoners were lodged in the civilian gaol. Under interrogation, Rowbottom claimed to be Private Rowbottom. All four held to their entitlement under the Geneva Conventions and refused to pass on more than their names, ranks (or what Rowbottom said was his rank) and numbers. Sergeant Morley, who had not demoted himself in time, was taken to be the commander of the party and on their behalf bore the brunt of the questioning, which he did with aplomb. Threats were uttered. Morley was told that unless something solid was offered in the way of information, there would be a firing squad for four on the following day. Morley suggested that, since none of them had more to say, the Germans would save themselves much trouble by advancing the time of the execution to that same afternoon.

After six days of this type of dialogue, the four of them were taken from their cells, marched to the centre of Split and put into the back of a truck, with an escort of five guards. The truck was one of a long road convoy, which ran into a Partisan ambush after dusk. Headlights were doused, there was a lot of wild two-way shooting, the five guards blazed away into the darkness, and Rowbottom loosened the fastenings of the truck's canvas canopy. The guards left the truck and took up fire positions in the cover of the roadside ditch. Rowbottom and Corporal Buss left the truck by way of the loosened canopy and the roof of the cab. Morley and Rifleman McConnell chose the tailgate. Both pairs lit out independently from the sound of battle and joined each other two days later. Partisans looked after them until they could be given a lift back to Italy.

On Vis, which a few months earlier was just a rocky little offshore island where farmers cultivated their vines and olives and vegetables, and from which fishermen fished in their schooners, and on which the Komiža anchovy-canning factory was the nearest thing to an industrial enterprise, and where nothing much else happened aside from the natural cycle of procreation, birth and death, the presence of Marshal Tito and the Partisan Supreme Staff added a new dimension to the changes already brought about by the conversion of the island to an advanced military base. This new dimension was not physically evident like the conspicuous red earth of the airstrip, or like the troops, Partisan and British, to be seen everywhere training or off duty, or like the stores dumps, gun lines, vehicle parks and arriving and departing aircraft, landing craft, motor launches, motor torpedo boats, motor gun boats. The fresh element was less tangible, an amalgam of power, influence, decision-making, politico-diplomatic negotiation and a strong spice of intrigue. For about three months Vis, in a heavily modified sort of way, was the *de facto* capital of the embryo government of Yugoslavia, an embryo by now unlikely to miscarry.

The modifications, at first glance almost impenetrably tangled, were on their way to becoming untied or cut through or partially replaced, by the end of the three months. Militarily the Partisans on the mainland, sustained by a growing volume of warlike stores delivered by the RAF, were hitting the Germans hard. The Germans would in any case leave Yugoslavia, whether the Partisans, Balkan Air Force and the British force on Vis hit them hard or not. Domestic opposition, military or political, to the Partisans was well within the capacity of the Partisans to deal with. Tito's constitutional status was still, to put it at its lowest, ambivalent, but some promising adjustments were soon in train. One adjustment, the British appointment of Fitzroy Maclean as the unofficial ambassador to a leader and an organisation regarded by their legitimate government as bandits, had been in efficient existence for several months. The Royal government-in-exile in London now showed, from their point of view too late and with too weak a hand, an anxiety to compromise. Dr Ivan Šubašić, the new Royalist Prime Minister, accompanied by the properly accredited Ambassador of His Britannic Majesty, Sir Ralph Stevenson, arrived on Vis for a preliminary exploration of the possibility of reaching some sort of acceptable accommodation with Marshal Tito. There was little doubt about which was Mahomed and which was the mountain.

This satisfying evidence of the willingness of the Partisans' major internal political enemy to give ground was followed by an invitation from the Partisans' major external military supporter to come and talk about the military and political future. On 6 August, Tito and his inner staff, accompanied by Maclean, were flown from Vis to Allied Forces Headquarters at Caserta in the personal aircraft of General Sir Henry Maitland Wilson, the Supreme Allied Commander. Useful staff talks, covering overall strategy but concentrating upon further arrangements for Partisan supply from British sources, were followed by a more elevated encounter still.

The British Prime Minister, invincibly peripatetic, had flown to Naples on the 11th. He questioned Tito at length about the Partisan fight, congratulated him on his achievements against the common enemy and discussed with him a forecast of what directions the war would move in next. To a guerrilla leader who three years earlier had been an underground Communist on the wanted list of the Yugoslav security police, who had subsequently fought a punishing three-year campaign in the forests and hills with little initial outside support and to constant vilification by the Yugoslav government recognised by the man he was talking to, and who a few weeks previously had been a hunted fugitive on the run after the Drvar attack – to such a man, this tête-à-tête with the leader of one of the Big Three world powers must have been sweet indeed. Churchill said carefully that

Britain would not be able to recognise formally the political paramountcy of the National Liberation Movement unless King Peter, to whom the British government held commitments that must be honoured, could be associated with it on terms acceptable to the King. Marshal Tito, an experienced Communist conspirator of nearly thirty years' standing, cannot have found this proviso too onerous. He had a renewed guarantee of practical support, and recognition in all but name.

Back on Vis, Tito renewed his discussions with Dr Šubašić. A formula was agreed. A provisional Royal government, joint Partisan and London exile, would rule until democratic elections could be held after Yugoslavia was freed of Germans. Šubašić flew to London to submit these proposals for King Peter's approval. In the latter part of September, a few weeks after Šubašić's departure, Tito also left Vis. He gave no advance warning to his British allies that he intended to go, and his remaining staff on the island claimed to be ignorant of where or how he had gone. An indication of the answer to these questions was that a Russian aircraft had landed on the Vis strip and had taken off again almost immediately, at the time of Tito's disappearance. Confirmation of the indication came in October from an entirely authoritative source. Churchill, in Moscow for a meeting with Stalin, asked the Soviet leader whether he knew where Tito had gone on his departure from Vis. Stalin did know. Moscow, he said.

This 'levanting' by Tito, as the Prime Minister crossly described it, provoked British irritability in other high places than No. 10 Downing Street. Allied Forces Headquarters at Caserta, who a few brief weeks previously had been impressed by Tito as a decisive and realistic leader with whom it would be possible to do constructive collaborative business, were outraged that he should choose to have himself spirited away without having the courtesy to tell them of his intentions or troubling to arrange with them adequate, or any, channels for future top-level consultation.

Added to the counts on the charge sheet of discourtesy and military administrative muddling was one of ingratitude. A major British effort, in the air and on Brač, had contributed to the lifting of the pressure on the Marshal after the German overrunning of his headquarters at Drvar. British casualties had been heavy. It would have been impossible for Tito to have been flown out of Bosnia without the liaison services provided to him by the British Military Mission. Vis would not have been available to him as a military and political headquarters had not first No. 2 Commando, and then its expanders and successors, secured the defence of the island. Marshal Tito was not behaving as an ally should. This last was entirely right. He was behaving as a Moscow-trained Communist, Stalinist division, would.

Tito spoke to no British representative until Fitzroy Maclean, who travelled as an observer and encourager of the Partisan advance through Serbia, met him in the newly recaptured Belgrade in the late autumn of 1944. Tito was blandly unrepentant, although he expressed regret when Maclean told him that in his absence his subordinates had been prickly, unreasonable and difficult to co-operate with. Tito would see to it that matters on this score improved immediately, he said. He had gone to Moscow to plan the co-ordination of Partisan operations with the Red Army's thrust at Belgrade. Since then he had been in the Vojvodina, controlling the fighting there. He had also, he told Maclean, reached agreement with Dr Šubašić for the setting up of a united Royalist/Partisan government. Tito was frank about his motives for entering into this accord. They were cosmetic. He wanted early formal recognition by the Allies.

By Balkan, or Communist, more especially by Balkan Communist, standards of judgement, these intricate, skilful, Machiavellian moves by Tito were justified by their success. He had secured for himself and for the Party the control of post-war Yugoslavia, and was ideologically convinced that that control would benefit both the country and the international Communist movement. To the policy-makers in London and Washington, committed to the principle in the Atlantic Charter which prescribed free, democratic elections as the vehicle by which the shape of the government of liberated countries should be determined, Tito's manoeuvrings, conducted in collusion with Stalin, were noted as one of a developing number of symptoms which suggested that the self-regulated ordering of the affairs of post-Nazi Europe would not be as straightforward as the devisers of the Atlantic Charter might have liked. The term Cold War had yet to be invented. For the percipient, the whiffs of the smoke from its first engagements were there for the smelling.

NINETEEN

Withdrawal from the Dalmatians

Few of the fighting men on Vis, British or Partisan, were among the percipient. They soldiered on as before. The summer became hotter. The rocks shimmered under a burning sun, and reflected a brilliant light and a burning heat. Daytime wear for most off-duty troops was a pair of shorts and a pair of PT shoes. Customarily pale northern European bodies were deep brown, in some cases almost black.

For some weeks after the successful Hvar raid in early July, Commando recce parties, still searching around as assiduously as ever, were less productive of exploitable results than they once had been. Targets were identified, but then moved elsewhere or changed in composition, or in some other manner became unsuitable material for the successive plans that were made for their discomfiture. The reason for this elusiveness slowly became apparent. The Germans were thinning out their island garrisons as part of their scheme for withdrawal from the Balkans. The islands were becoming irrelevant to them.

The process was gradual, and it still left opportunities for seaborne raiding by artillery, an unusual, possibly unique, form of warfare. Korčula, because a length of its coastline to the north-east ran close to, and parallel with, the Pelješac peninsula, was the chosen scene of the early Gunner enterprises. The first, on 18 July, carried a refinement devised by Commander Morgan Giles. Colonel Elliott of 111 Field Regiment landed by night on Korčula with a battery of his 25-pounders and set them up in a gun position from which they could engage German artillery at Orebić, on the mainland. There had been careful reconnaissance and preparation. In the hilly islands there was a limited number of combinations of accessible beach, negotiable approach and spread of reasonably flat ground, suitable for the movement and siting of the accumulated weight of the vehicles and guns of a battery of field artillery. The guns held their fire until daylight, when Morgan Giles's contributory diversion steamed into the view of the German defenders of Orebić.

With the creative use of canvas, timber and similar theatrical props, an LCI had been provided with an altered silhouette, a dummy funnel and a dummy gun. This strange, threatening warship manoeuvred about in the Korčula Channel, with its crew standing by for the next part of the act. Elliott's guns, behind a hill, opened. In synchronisation with their discharges, the dummy gun on the dummy warship emitted spectacular flashes and puffs of smoke. The flashes of the German counter-battery fire directed at the LCI were helpful to Elliott's Forward Observation Officer in the precise identification of the German gun positions, which were then shelled elaborately. The pantomime could not last. Any German artilleryman who could count must have soon calculated that there was something spurious about this remarkable ship's gun with the firepower of eight 25-pounders, but the ruse achieved its purpose. Elliott's gunsite remained undetected and unshelled. The LCI returned to Vis to shed its trimmings and to resume its more mundane job of ferrying troops.

Elliott led further amphibious artillery forays, the next one again to Korčula, this time without the benefit of the LCI in wolf's clothing. With a covering force of 170 Partisans, and a battery of the RSR with 0.5 Browning machine-guns on anti-aircraft mountings to deter the Luftwaffe, he brought a battery of his own guns ashore on the night of 31 July. Shortly after dawn, they began a concentrated shelling of German holdings in Korčula town, Orebić and Postrana. The Germans on the mainland located Elliott's position and put down some retaliatory fire, the nearest shot of which landed fifty yards behind the gunline. By seven o'clock the Orebić guns were silenced. They came back to brief life two hours later when the force was re-embarking, and dropped a few shells in the sea, but without causing casualties or damage.

On 25 August Elliott reversed his earlier procedure by landing his guns on the Pelješac peninsula to engage targets on Korčula. His chief target was the German garrison of Pupnat, a village in the central spine of the island. Elliott had with him four of his 25-pounders, four RSR 75-mm mountain pack howitzers, and RSR Browning machine-guns in their anti-aircraft role of protecting the gun positions and the anchored landing craft. The Pupnat Germans had 105s and 75s, already registered on selected landmarks on the peninsula. The operation was less of a walkover than previous ones had been. One asset was an airborne observation post, an Italian light aircraft flown by Captain Ross of the RSR.

The guns, from positions on three separate beaches, were in action shortly after first light. Accurate German counter-fire came down within a quarter of an hour and continued, initially causing surprisingly little harm. It became more dangerous later. In all, the force lost one man killed and five wounded. A naval officer brought in an LCA and evacuated the wounded. The whole force later re-embarked without further loss, leaving behind them a quantity of equipment shredded by German shelling, and artillery ammunition for later recovery.

By September there developed a change in the pattern of island operations. The original harassment for the sake of harassment, which had shifted into harassment for the sake of hampering the German thinning-out of numbers, reached its final phase of intervention to disrupt what had by now become a German implementation of their intention to evacuate the islands altogether. The aim was to prevent as many of them as was possible from getting away to fight elsewhere.

On 11 September, all the German garrisons of Brač had been withdrawn from their outlying positions and had been concentrated in two pockets around the ports of Supetar and Sumartin, clearly awaiting embarkation. Two brigades of Partisans, two batteries of 111 Field Regiment, a troop of RSR 75-mm mountain guns and 43 Royal Marine Commando sailed from Vis to make the German departure unpleasant. The Supetar group withstood the interference and extricated themselves by night to Split. The south-eastern group were held in. The navy sank every boat that tried to leave Sumartin and the adjacent coves. The Germans fought with courage and determination. For more than a week they held out against repeated Partisan attacks, supported by all the British guns and by medium bomber and fighter–bomber strikes by the RAF. Two hundred Germans at last surrendered to the Partisans. No. 43 Commando, who had been given what turned out to be the unexacting role of securing and patrolling the mountains in the north-west of the island, had one casualty, an illustration of the inconsequential nature of ill-luck among the by-ways of war. Lieutenant Odendaal, who had been wounded during the June assault on the hilltop above Nerežišće, went back to look at the old German positions to see what the battle must have looked like from the German end. He trod on a mine and lost a foot.

Šolta came next, and almost immediately. Since Jack Churchill's removal of the entire island garrison by No. 2 Commando and intimidatory use of the loud-hailer in March, Šolta had been reoccupied by two German companies of No. 892 Grenadier Regiment, who had set about the preparation of their defences in a more professional manner than had their predecessors. Grohote and Rogač, the scene of the 2 Commando exploit, were now protected by a wired-in minefield, fifty feet wide. Behind the minefield were four strongpoints, each further surrounded by wire and mines, and each consisting of clusters of concrete pill-boxes linked by trenches. One of the strongpoints held positions for a hundred men, one for sixty and two for forty. Outside the minefield, a large area to the south-east had been sown at random with *Schuh* mines, little wooden boxes easy to conceal, incapable, because there was no metal in them, of being identified by mine detectors, and designed to blow off the foot of anyone who trod on them. A German prisoner interrogated after the operation said that there were 32,000 mines around the positions. The defenders had the usual complement of Spandaus and small-arms, two Italian howitzers, four 81-mm mortars and, on call, the supporting services of

German coastal batteries behind Split, on Drvenik island and at Čiovo, south of Trogir. Šolta had formidable and tested defences. There had been two major Partisan attempts on them earlier in the summer. Both had been repulsed. The one in June, mounted by the 1st Dalmatian Brigade with air support by the RAF, had involved two days of bitter fighting.

No. 43 Commando returned in their LCIs from Brač to Vis shortly before midnight on Saturday, 16 September. Lieutenant-Colonel Ian MacAlpine of the Black Watch, who had replaced Simonds as the Commanding Officer of 43,* was at once told that tactical reconnaissance flown by the RAF 'seemed to indicate' that shipping seen in Drvenik harbour had evacuated part, possibly all, of the Šolta garrison. MacAlpine was ordered to take 43 to seize and hold the island, after first destroying what was left of the garrison, if anything. He would have the support of the mountain guns and heavy machine-guns of the RSR, three small teams of sappers to deal with mines, and a train of sixteen mules with handlers from the Royal Army Veterinary Corps.

MacAlpine was a wary and experienced soldier who had fought as a young man in the First World War and who had commanded No. 6 Commando in Tunisia in the Second. He was not altogether convinced by the RAF reconnaissance report, which seemed to him to owe as much to an assumption as to observation underpinned by firm evidence. His doubts grew when he heard that a recently returned patrol of the Highland Light Infantry confirmed that there were at least some Germans left on Šolta, although how many was unknown. One normally reliable source of intelligence was not on tap. The entire civilian population of Šolta had been evacuated by the Partisans. There were no longer any resident Partisans on the island either. MacAlpine declined to commit his Commando to what might be anything from a walkover to an under-supported assault on heavily defended prepared positions, until he had more information. He sent one of his troops to find it.

An LCI took Captain Ian Gourlay and 'D' Troop across

---

*MacAlpine was the only army officer to command a Royal Marine Commando during the Second World War.

during the late evening of Sunday, 17 September. Gourlay, who had recently joined the unit as a replacement for John Blake, killed on Brač, started his investigations as soon as it was light. The village of Gornje Selo proved to be German-free and without booby-traps. The hills around Grohote were occupied by Germans of aggressive habits who shot up Gourlay and his five-man patrol with Spandaus, rifles and mortars. That night, 43 Commando and its helpers came over, in an LCI that towed two ramped landing craft loaded with the mules and heavy stores, accompanied by two of the small Landing Craft, Personnel, and escorted by motor launches. Gourlay had guides waiting for them on the beach. The troops climbed up the narrow track of a rocky gully and deployed in a beach-head perimeter among the high ground.

Patrols sent out in the morning, one of them accompanied by MacAlpine, saw Germans moving about in Grohote itself and in outpost positions on the adjoining hills. Colonel Meynell, the commander of the Vis garrison, arrived in the evening with further news provided by RAF reconnaissance. Twelve ships loaded with German troops had been seen sailing from Šolta to the mainland. The RAF believed that there were none left on the island. MacAlpine, who had been looking at Germans a few hours before, was disinclined to share this belief. He put the matter to the test early on the next day. Different hills around Grohote were allocated to individual troops for seizure. If the hills were unoccupied, so much the better. If they were occupied, the occupants were to be thrown off and fire was to be drawn from the main position in Grohote, so that German positions could be located accurately and an assessment made of their strength.

The hills were occupied. The first on the list, Podvlake, was a not very strongly held observation post. 'C' Troop, led by Captain Bob Loudoun, advanced in a long extended line through the rocks and scrub under machine-gun and mortar fire. The observation post got out, leaving something of a mess of spent cartridge cases and half-eaten food, and taking with them a clear picture of the topography of the low hill that they had abandoned. Mortar fire came down on Loudoun's troop almost at once. Loudoun disposed his two sections in an all-round defensive position.

Digging in the stony ground here, as elsewhere in Dalmatia, was out of the question. The marines built sangars.

An hour after 'C' Troop had established themselves on Podvlake, 'D' Troop, Captain Ian Gourlay, and 'E' Troop, Captain Ralph Parkinson-Cumine, set out for their hills, two neighbouring bumps on Mala Staza, to the west of Podvlake. Both troops were mortared and shelled during their approach across the valley, were machine-gunned as they shot their way up the hill and were shelled heavily by guns from the mainland once they had taken their objectives. They too built sangars. Over on the right, Captain Jock Hudspith and 'A' Troop had reached Zukova. It was where they had been aiming for, but was found to be in the middle of an unmarked minefield.

MacAlpine sent Lieutenant Bolton with the 3-inch mortar section of the Heavy Weapon Troop to join Loudoun on Podvlake. Bolton mortared Grohote. The guns in Grohote, and in Split, Drvenik and Čiovo, shelled all the Commando's positions intermittently for the rest of the day and night. A 210-mm coastal defence gun in an emplacement behind Split was the biggest, noisiest and most distant. About the best that could be said for it was that it telegraphed its punches. There was an interval of fifty seconds between the bright flash of its discharge in front of the mountains and the arrival on the Šolta positions, with a sound like a railway train entering a tunnel, of projectiles that detonated mightily and made spectacular redistributions of rock and soil. MacAlpine, reflecting upon the proposition which he later summarised in his report, that 'it is manifest that valuable as may be the deductions made from [RAF] tactical reconnaissance, reconnaissances on the ground alone can establish the actual facts', signalled to Vis to ask for artillery and air support.

The next day was one of more shelling from the mainland, mortaring from Grohote, and further probing patrols. Bolton's 3-inch mortars firing from Podvlake and the RSR 4.2-inch mortars firing from the beach quietened things down in Grohote. The manhandling of the RSR's heavy Browning machine-guns across broken country was a slow and wearisome business, but they too were in action on Podvlake by the late afternoon, shooting up the German headquarters building in Grohote. Of the patrols, Parkinson-Cumine's, on the left, found one hill and two villages to be empty, but were heavily fired at by Spandaus in the main position. Of two patrols from 'A' Troop on the right, one was caught among the *Schuh* mines. A marine and a sapper each had one of his feet blown off, and despite a series of rescue attempts could not be brought back for another forty-eight hours.

The bura now intervened to complicate matters further. Violent, gusting winds, driving before them torrents of rain, drenched everybody. Gourlay's and Parkinson-Cumine's troops on the left underwent an additional deprivation. Mule trains carrying boxes of Compo rations intended for the two troops had earlier been forced back by concentrated shelling. Compo rations would get few marks in a Good Food Guide, but self-heating tins of soup, or mutton and vegetable stew warmed on Tommy cookers like modern fire-lighters, were more sustaining than the corned-beef sandwiches of haversack rations which, in most cases, had been finished in the first few hours. The two troops went hungry for two days. A naval LCP, with Captain George Frost, the Commando's administrative officer aboard, finally brought supplies through the storm. The LCP had nearly foundered several times during its voyage along the coast.

The storm also frustrated attempts to land the guns that MacAlpine had asked for. A battery of 25-pounders, embarked in an LCT with a squadron of the RAF Regiment, made the crossing in a high sea. The LCT's captain was unable to pick out through the spray and rain the recognition signal in the cove that he was heading for, missed it, nearly put in to the German harbour by mistake and returned through the wild night to Vis. After that, Commander Morgan Giles suspended until the weather abated any further attempts to reach Šolta by flat-bottomed landing craft, which were hard to handle in a heavy sea. The weather also ruled out the air support that MacAlpine wanted. The Vis strip was water-logged. Aircraft were unable to take off. MacAlpine continued to request both artillery and air support.

The storm was not a deterrent to German shelling. Their coastal guns were registered on all targets, and they banged away steadily. The Commando and RSR mortars and machine-guns banged back into Grohote. Hudspith's troop on the right suffered more casualties from the pernicious *Schuh* mines. One of the patrols sent out to rescue the two men who had lost feet earlier at last got through to them and pulled them back to cover, but were unable to get them back to the main body of the troop. Rescuers and rescued were caught by machine-gun fire from two German posts in the main position. To cover their extrication the 3-inch mortars put down smoke, the Vickers machine-guns engaged all nearby German positions, and a further rescue team of marines, sappers and Corporal Smith, the 'A' Troop medical orderly, who had been wounded on the previous day, inched forward searching for mines and defusing them as they went. Lieutenant Richards, of the Royal Engineer detachment who had accompanied the Commando on the operation, finally cleared a gap, and the earlier wounded were brought back. Three more had to be brought back with them: another sapper, another marine and Richards himself, all of whom had feet blown off. 'Great courage shown by Lt. Richards RE', reads MacAlpine's report.

The German shelling, the shooting by the heavy weapons of both sides and the only slightly diminished storm continued for the rest of the day and for the early part of the night. In the small hours of 23 September a series of flashes and heavy explosions came from the direction of Rogač cove. To many of the besiegers these seemed to be a further instalment of the thunder and lightning of the storm. The troops nearest to Rogač reported a different version. RN gunboats, they said, had come close inshore, opened fire and hit two German ammunition dumps.

At 6 a.m. Major Neil Munro took Major Pat Turner of 111 Field Regiment to watch a 3-inch mortar shoot into Grohote. The purpose of the shoot was to indicate German targets to Turner for future attentions by his guns. There was a puzzling absence of response from the garrison. At 8.30 an 'A' Troop patrol reported that it had reached the forward German wire, had fired into the harbour and had provoked no reply. MacAlpine at once ordered an advance into the town. It was a slow progress, much delayed by the need for the sappers to neutralise a profusion of booby traps and mines. Parkinson-Cumine and 'E' Troop were at last through to Rogač harbour by the early afternoon. Five German soldiers gave themselves up. The bodies of many more were floating in the water.

At 11.15 on the night of 22 September two motor torpedo boats, Nos 655 and 633, left Komiža harbour and set course for Šolta. No. 655 was commanded by Lieutenant MacLaughlen of the Royal Canadian Naval Volunteer Reserve, No. 633 by Lieutenant Rendell, also of the RCNVR. The Senior Officer of the MTB flotilla, Lieutenant Burke, another Canadian, was aboard 655. Burke had emergency instructions from Commander Morgan Giles. The two boats were to stop the evacuation of the German garrison of Šolta from Rogač cove, planned for that night. (No records survive to indicate the source of this information, which was not known by MacAlpine and 43 Commando. The most likely origin seems to have been a wireless intercept of German naval traffic.)

The two MTBs were off Rogač by shortly after 1.30 a.m. They immediately sighted three I-lighters, which had just left the beach, heading for the mouth of the bay. The MTBs ran in and attacked with their guns at 200 yards' range. All three lighters were hit by the guns of both boats. The lighters replied with sporadic 20-mm fire. This soon ceased. In a second run across the bay the MTBs closed the range to fifty yards and scored further hits. One lighter blew up with two violent explosions, showering the decks of the MTBs with debris. Burke then ordered 633 to stand off, and 655 went in to the bay alone to finish off the other two lighters. They were not needed. The craft had already gone down. No. 655 illuminated the shoreline by firing at the rocks with incendiary Oerlikon ammunition, which bounced upwards and gave a serviceable light, but nothing was seen. A limited amount of machine-gun and light mortar fire came from the shore. All missed. During the next hour or so, both MTBs made further searches of the bay, one with the help of star shell, but still no further boats could be seen.

They lay off the bay until 3.30 a.m., and then turned for

Komiža and home before they could be caught in daylight within the range of the German coastal batteries.

Some Germans did get away from Šolta. Two Poles, who survived the sinking of the lighters, and who had hidden in a slit-trench until they could surrender to the British, said that a party of about eighteen other survivors had signalled across to Split for help and had been taken off by E-boats soon after dawn. An earlier lift by lighter might also have been evacuated safely. Between 100 and 120 were killed in the explosions or drowned in Rogač cove.

MacAlpine, with a group of his own and Gunner officers, made a detailed inspection of the German defences. The consensus was that they were some of the strongest seen by anyone present. In MacAlpine's opinion they could not have been overrun without heavy air and artillery support on a scale not available in the Balkans. His message of thanks to the Royal Navy, in which he referred to 'a perfect combined operation', was more than a conventional piece of good manners.

There was one last casualty after the Germans had gone. Hudspith's minefield wounded, after being attended to by Dr Ralph Bazeley, were carried by Hudspith, Bazeley and six marines to a nearby beach, where an LCP was waiting. The wounded were loaded aboard. The doctor and the 'A' Troop party went back overland towards their positions. It was by now dark. They walked into another scattering of unmarked *Schuh* mines. A marine stepped on a mine, had his foot severed, and died later. The party waited until daylight and then cleared their way out.

Šolta was the last of the major British operations in the Dalmatian islands. It lasted for a week, and cost 43 Commando two killed and sixteen wounded. The sapper detachment had three wounded. Afterwards there were a few more reconnaissance patrols, some more provisional planning, and an abortive attempt by Lieutenant Preston, backed by 'B' Troop of 43 Commando, to talk the German garrison on Uljan island into surrendering. It all came to nothing. The Partisans were soon the sole owners of all the islands. A nine-month episode of spasmodically violent

Yugoslav history, with a relatively small number of British and a still smaller number of Americans contributing to the making of much of it, went out without any more bangs and with no whimpers. The war simply moved on. The sailors, soldiers and airmen followed it.

TWENTY

Balkan Air Force

The acquisition of bases in Italy, and the huge increases in the industrial production of war material that after a pause for planning and the equipping of plant had followed upon the entry of the United States into the war in December 1941, brought about a transformation in the intensity of Allied air operations over, and into, Yugoslavia from the end of 1943 onwards. In the very early days, such few airdrops as were made to Mihailović were from RAF aircraft diverted for the occasion, usually with reluctance, by air commanders with slim resources and a thick list of competing priorities. In May 1942, there was a small improvement. Four Liberators were assigned permanently to the sustenance of Balkan guerrilla movements. They were rarely all serviceable simultaneously, and they had to look after Greece and Albania as well as Yugoslavia. In March 1943, fourteen specially converted supply-dropping Halifaxes were added, and Special Operations Air Force, still working from North Africa, was formed. Its Yugoslav activities were concerned entirely with the Chetniks until the Canadian Croats were dropped in, in May 1943 (see p. 62), in the pioneer venture to the Partisans. The first Allied aircraft actually to land in Yugoslavia and take off again was the one which brought in Maclean and his reinforcements to Glamoč in December, and took out Maclean, Deakin, Velebit and Milojević to Brindisi and on to Alexandria.

The first offensive RAF operations, as distinct from supply, were on the Dalmatian coast in the latter half of October 1943. On the 20th, aircraft of the Mediterranean Tactical Air Force shot up and sank two coastal ships and damaged two more. In the ensuing week they sank a further six. On the 24th, a new precedent was set, the direct intervention of British aircraft in tactical support of Partisan ground operations. Fitzroy Maclean, on the island of Korčula, met up with one of the first Royal Navy craft to reach Dalmatia, a motor launch which delivered several tons of arms and ammunition and carried aboard Lieutenant-Commander Sandy Glen, an SOE operative who in pre-invasion days had been stationed in the legation in Belgrade under the guise of Assistant Naval Attaché. Maclean's wireless was on the blink at the time. The ML's was not. Maclean the soldier, using a naval set, signalled to the air force in Italy to ask for an airstrike on German troops who were pressing the Partisans hard on the Pelješac peninsula. Kittyhawk fighters flew over the Adriatic on two successive days, broke up the German attacks on land, set fire to a large motor vessel, barges and a schooner bearing Germans heading for a hook behind the Partisan line, and delayed the inevitable German advance by two weeks.

From these relatively small beginnings there grew a large, active, specialist air organisation that concentrated exclusively upon the support of resistance movements in Eastern Europe and the Balkans. The bulk of this backing went to the most effective resisters of all, the Yugoslav Partisans. Maclean, when in Cairo at the end of 1943, was authorised to enlarge the size and scope of his military mission to whatever extent was needed to bring it to a maximum of usefulness. Since airstrips were clearly an essential requirement, and their choice and preparation needed professional advice, Maclean recruited to his staff Wing-Commander John Selby. Selby landed at Glamoč in the first Dakota sortie. His pioneer work was expanded by the Balkan Air Terminal Service, which consisted of a number of four-man teams comprising an RAF officer, a sergeant, a corporal and a wireless operator. It was one of these teams, led by Flight Lieutenant McGrath, who inspected, and passed as fit for use, the strip at Kupreško Polje from which Tito, his staff, the Allied missions and 118 Partisan wounded were lifted out to Italy after the events that followed the German airborne attack on Tito's headquarters at Drvar. By then, May 1944, the Allied air effort had become international. A Russian crew flew the

Dakota that took Tito and some of his people. Americans took the rest.

In June 1944, Air Vice-Marshal W. Elliot was put in command of the newly named Balkan Air Force, with its headquarters in Bari. He had at his disposal eight squadrons and an additional flight, and the number and variety grew as the months went by. The squadrons were British, American, South African, Yugoslav, Italian, Polish, Greek and Russian. The Russians, in what seems to have been a unique episode in the Second World War, came under Elliot's command. They had twelve Dakotas and twelve Russian Yak fighters. Their job was to maintain communications with the belatedly arrived Soviet Mission to Tito and to help in supply drops.

The cumulative statistics of the administrative support side of Balkan Air Force's activities show just how much the Partisans benefited from them. During the eleven months between June 1944 and the end of the war in May 1945, BAF supply aircraft flew 11,600 sorties to Yugoslavia. They dropped, or landed on the thirty-six strips run by the Balkan Air Terminal Service, 16,400 tons of weapons, ammunition, clothing, boots, medicines, dressings and miscellaneous equipment. They delivered 2500 passengers of various sorts, British and American liaison teams, medical teams, returning Partisan emissaries and recovered wounded and sick. They evacuated about 11,000 Partisan casualties.

Of offensive air operations, the most significant strategic one was the sowing of mines in the Danube, which carried a vital barge traffic of oil and agricultural produce from Romania and Hungary to Germany. The first forty mines were dropped in the river near Belgrade in April 1944. The mining continued at intervals until the Partisans and the Red Army entered Belgrade six months later. The 1382 mines, sown in eighteen separate large-scale attacks, had by then sunk so many river boats and deterred so many others from risking movement that the Danube as a supply route was as good as paralysed. Storage depots were packed to their limits, more than a hundred large barges were moored, empty and unused, along the banks of the Sava and the Danube, and the tonnage carried had been reduced to between 30 and 40 per cent of the original totals: 'the enemy by the mining of the Danube harms us very considerably. . . . at present we are unable to cope with the situation,' noted a German officer responsible for coping with it.

German communications, in inland Yugoslavia and along the coast, were at constant risk from 1944 onwards. Strikes by Spitfires and Mustangs on the railway lines linking Zagreb through Belgrade and Skopje to Greece, and from Brod through Sarajevo to Mostar, destroyed 262 locomotives, about a third of them pulling troop trains, in a single month.

A notably successful application of air power in co-ordination with action on the ground came in September 1944, in Operation Ratweek, a codename allocated routinely as the next one to come up on the list prepared for such purposes, but which nonetheless carried apt connotations to do with swimmers from sinking ships. The aim of Ratweek was to refine, during a brief period when maximum air resources would be made available, processes that were already showing a military profit on a basis of opportunist exploitation. German troops evacuated from Greece by rail were being shot up from the air and held up by Partisan demolitions. Ratweek was designed to convert briefly these harassments from the *ad hoc* to the systematic.

The early outline planning developed from discussions on Vis between Fitzroy Maclean and Tito. Air Marshal Elliot was an enthusiastic collaborator. Tito, who could not have been criticised had he taken the line that from the Yugoslav point of view the sooner the German troop trains were out of the country the better, and good riddance, unhesitatingly gave orders for full Partisan participation. The essence of the scheme was that Partisan commanders in the section through which passed the south–north railway layout were, together with their British liaison officers, to make a detailed survey of bridges, viaducts, points, junctions, tunnels and anything else which if blown up would disrupt the German evacuation traffic. From these lists the chosen targets were sub-divided into two categories: the softer ones that could be dealt with by the Partisans, who would be specially supplied with elaborate quantities of explosive; and the more heavily defended ones which would be the responsibility of Balkan Air Force, supplemented where necessary by heavy bombers placed on call to Elliot by the United States army air force.

From the Greek border to northern Slovenia, from Montenegro to Croatia, those branches of the Maclean Mission with a stretch of railway in their areas did their reconnaissances, did their sums, did their target classifications in concert with the Partisan leaders, signalled their recommendations to Bari, and made reception arrangements for an enhanced weight of demolition stores. In Bari, Balkan Air Force, in consultation with the rear headquarters of the Maclean Mission and the Partisan liaison team, logged in the reports from the field, and fitted the pieces together into a detailed overall plan. The plan included provision for a simultaneous stepped-up onslaught by Royal Navy MTBs, MGBs and destroyers in the sea lanes of the Adriatic coast, now in extensive use by the Germans as an alternative way out of the southern Balkans.

Maclean left Vis and got himself flown to an airstrip in Serbia to watch the effects of Ratweek on the Salonika–Belgrade line. He did so with relief. The rarefied politicking on Vis was not to his taste. He had not previously been to Serbia, where the Partisan movement had been relatively slow to expand, where a persistent loyalty to the monarch prevailed, and where the acceptance of defecting Chetniks (influenced largely by the switch of Allied supplies from Mihailović to Tito) by the Serbian Partisan leadership was being transacted with an absence of bitterness that would have been unimaginable in Bosnia or Montenegro. Maclean discussed the Serbian contribution to Ratweek with Koča Popović, now commanding the Serbian Partisans, and with Major John Henniker-Major, the senior British Liaison Officer. Planning was complete by the last week of August.

On the first day of the operation, during which Partisans were to wreck two bridges and rip up the railway lines on either side of Laskovac, strongly garrisoned by Germans, Chetniks and Nedić quislings supported by armour, Balkan Air Force signalled that they would attack the town with fifty US Army Air Force Flying Fortresses at 1.30 a.m. Maclean was surprised at the size of the bombing force. Nothing like it had been used against targets in Yugoslavia

before. It arrived precisely on time, flying steadily in
formation at a great altitude, and bombed without altering
speed, course or height. Laskovac erupted in smoke, fire,
debris and dust. There were direct hits on German-
occupied buildings, on armour and on transport. The
survivors of the Chetnik garrison deserted in droves and
came over to join the Partisans. Sadly, civilian casualties
were high. The Partisans, who had never been deterred
operationally by the incidental risk to civilian lives, looked
subdued.

They did not stay so for long. That night they put in their
attacks on the railway line both north and south of the
town. Under cover of machine-gun and mortar fire directed
at the concrete pill-boxes guarding the line, Partisan
demolition parties planted charges under a series of
culverts and minor bridges. The charges were detonated,
the line was severed in a great many places, the rails were
torn loose manually, and the sleepers were lifted, piled and
fired. Fired too was a goods-wagon, given a push-start down
the slope towards Laskovac, where it arrived at speed to add
further to the confusion and devastation. One part of
Ratweek had got off to a start that would inhibit German
rail movement for some time to come.

Similar combined ventures were carried out from one
end of the country to the other: bridges blown, the
permanent way mangled, viaducts bombed from the air or
destroyed by demolition teams of Partisans and British
mission officers, on occasion supported by air strikes from
Balkan Air Force Mustangs, Hurricanes and Spitfires. The
doing of initial damage was followed by protracted
interference with German attempts to make it good.
Partisan observers reported the locations of repair gangs to
British missions. The missions signalled the co-ordinates
to Bari. Balkan Air Force sent fighters to shoot up the
restorers. The early phases of the departure of Army
Group E from the Balkans did not go smoothly.

Shipping strikes, on targets reported back from the
northern islands and the coast by the Long Range Desert
Group, complemented the attacks on German sea traffic
made by the motor torpedo boats and motor gun boats of
Coastal Forces, also largely homed in on their targets by
the LRDG. The spread of sub-missions now working under

270

Maclean, in addition to their primary task of keeping supplies flowing, were on occasion able to call for air support when the Partisan formations to which they were attached came up against more than normally stubborn resistance or were subjected to unusually strong pressures.

In July and August 1944, for example, the Germans mounted an elaborate operation against the Partisan II Corps in Montenegro. The Partisans were initially forced back. Mustangs and Spitfires from Italy came over on several consecutive days. They shot up concentrations of German troops in concert with a successful Partisan counter-attack. The Partisans counted 900 German dead, but had a great many casualties themselves. The need to look after 800 wounded hindered their mobility, and they were caught off balance by a renewed German attack in the middle of August. Humanity and military necessity joined to make evacuation of the casualties essential. The first strip prepared by the RAF ground team was heavily shelled by the Germans and was soon seen to be unusable. A second site was picked, two adjoining fields under ripening corn, out of range of the German guns. The 800 wounded marched or were helped to march or were carried for four days. When they reached the fields, the walking wounded cleared the corn and levelled the more obtrusive bumps.

On the following morning six Dakotas landed, protected overhead by eighteen Spitfires and Mustangs. The Dakotas were loaded with 200 wounded, and were airborne again in twenty minutes. A further twenty-four Dakotas continued the shuttle throughout the day, and the Russian Air Group finished it off with a final lift after night fell. The total number flown out was 1078 – the wounded, medical attendants, the escort, sixteen baled-out Allied aircrew and three members of the Maclean Mission. In similar circumstances a year earlier the Partisan II Corps would have been lucky not to suffer heavy casualties in the attempt to look after their wounded, and the wounded would have been lucky not to die of their wounds or to be slaughtered by the Germans. As it was, the Corps Commander, freed of his burden, was able to put in more counter-attacks. He was still in serious trouble when in the first week in September he was saved, and the war in the Balkans was transfigured, by events in Bulgaria and Romania. Both followed the Italian example and changed sides. The Red Army had a clear run through to the Romanian–Yugoslav border. On 20 October they were in Belgrade.

The size, versatility and flexibility of the Allied air effort in the Balkans had by June 1944 established the associated air forces as the dominant military arm in Yugoslavia. The dominance was recognised by a rearrangement of command responsibility. Air Marshal Elliot, from his Balkan Air Force Headquarters in Bari, took over the co-ordination and control of all Allied sea, land and air operations, in support of resistance movements on the eastern side of the Adriatic. Fitzroy Maclean retained his autonomy as the personal representative of the Prime Minister and of the Commander-in-Chief, his independence further strengthened by distance and by the nature of his work, but his mission too came under the Balkan Air Force umbrella for supply and support. FOTALI, the Flag Officer Taranto and Liaison Italy, continued with the detailed running of the naval force, but now worked to Elliot. SOE shed the control of ground operations which they had exercised since Colonel Jack Churchill and No. 2 Commando had first gone to Vis, and handed it over to Land Forces Adriatic. Commanded by Brigadier George Davy, this new organisation from its headquarters in Bari controlled all formal ground operations in the western and southern Balkans. Neither the organisation nor its commander were much liked by many of the commandos, the most notable disliker being Brigadier Tom Churchill. It was Land Forces Adriatic which was soon to assemble Floydforce from elements of former Vis raiders.

TWENTY-ONE

Floydforce at Risan

Strategically, the task facing Army Group E in late 1944 was to fight its way out of the Balkans before the Russians closed the northern exits. Tactically, its job was to push on north as hard as it could go, collecting its garrisons in Greece, Albania and Yugoslavia as it went. It was constrained geographically by the narrow, winding Balkan roads that in southern Yugoslavia provided only three possible routes through Montenegro. The westernmost was along the coast through Kotor and Risan; the middle one ran through Danilovgrad and Nikšić; and one farther inland ran through Kolašin. To a patriotic urge to return home to fight for the Reich was added a further, pressing incentive. With some creditable exceptions, German behaviour in occupied Yugoslavia had been abominable. The Southern Slavs were not by nature forgiving. German units or individuals who through incompetence, lethargy or ill-luck failed to conform to the role allotted to them in a mass military exodus would face a bloody vengeance if they fell into the hands of the Partisans.

When the advanced guards of Army Group E, found from the German XXI Mountain Corps, were emerging into Montenegro, Tito asked for British artillery support to help the Partisans to harry the German withdrawal. Land Forces Adriatic responded promptly. The dispersed batteries of 111 Field Regiment reassembled in the neighbourhood of Bari. No. 43 Commando was brought back from Vis, also to near Bari. A field unit of the Royal Engineers was acquired. And 'Floydforce', whose task was 'in general to give the greatest possible artillery support to the Yugoslav National Army of Liberation', sailed from Bari

273

for Dubrovnik on 27 October. Its commander was Brigadier J.P. O'Brien-Twohig, a flamboyantly moustachioed Irishman who had distinguished himself as a battalion commander in Sicily and Italy. The commandos had been given what was for them the uncustomary job of local protection of the artillery's gun-positions. The confusions and prejudices of the times had been illustrated by the reception given in Dubrovnik by the resident Partisan Command to Colonel Jago, the Gunner regimental commander, successor to Colonel Elliott, and Colonel MacNamara, the Chief of Staff of Land Forces Adriatic, who a week before had gone ahead to co-ordinate the operation with the Partisan staff. The two colonels were confined under armed guard in the Hotel Imperial, an aptly named and presumably comfortable establishment, until their credentials had been authenticated with the Partisan Supreme Staff.

The incarceration of the colonels, while providing much sardonic amusement to those in the force who were of an egalitarian cast of mind or who were relishers of military farce, was an earnest of much of what was to come. Politics was taking precedence over the requirements of joint participation in a fight against a common enemy. Partisan priorities were in the course of further, more radical readjustment. Getting rid of the invader was still important. He must be harassed and damaged while he went, which was why the guns of Floydforce had been asked for. Meanwhile everything must be done to ensure that once he was gone there would be total Communist control of the country. In the eyes of Marxist ideologues, Floydforce was militarily welcome and politically suspect. Technically it was highly qualified in the business of delivering shellfire accurately on to German columns, but it was manned by representatives of an imperialist, capitalist power that was a potential threat to the revolution.

There was thus a certain weird ambivalence about many of the operational proceedings of the next three months. The mistrusted agents of the capitalist system, whose uncomplicated collective ambition was to get the job done as quickly as possible and to go home to demobilisation, were occasionally annoyed and often puzzled. They would have been more puzzled, and rather flattered, had they known that their small contribution to the ending of the war attracted critical attention at the highest level in the Kremlin. The landing at Dubrovnik of a modest-sized force from four LCTs and three LCIs was described in a news agency report as a British invasion of Yugoslavia. Tito was in Moscow at the time, for discussions with Stalin. In the course of these, Molotov produced the news report. Tito was asked for an explanation. He said that it was no invasion. It was an artillery force sent at his request. If the British tried an invasion, he would fight them. It was perhaps as well that this unusual interpretation of the responsibilities of one ally to another was not known to Floydforce at the time. The guests might have felt out of place.

The seven landing craft carrying the force tied up in Gruz harbour, on the north side of Dubrovnik, in the mid-morning of 28 October. The Commando disembarked, marched to a large shed with a concrete floor in a nearby timber yard, and settled in, making philosophical assessments of the degree to which the unattractiveness of the concrete as a mattress was outbalanced by the evident fact that the roof kept out the rain. The gunners attended to the unloading of the guns, the quads that towed them, the ammunition limbers, the supply trucks, the jeeps and all the other expensive paraphernalia that stimulated envy among the marines, who carried almost the entire inventory of their possessions on their backs. Brigadier O'Brien-Twohig summoned a conference of his commanders at five o'clock in the afternoon. The first part of Floydforce to take part in a form of warfare that blended some familiar elements with some entirely new modifications set out from Dubrovnik at seven o'clock on the following morning. This was Finney Force. It began its life under a different name, but for simplicity's sake it will be as well to give it the name that it later acquired. It consisted of 211 Field Battery, and 'C' Troop of 43 Commando. The Battery Commander, Major Pat Turner, was in overall command. 'C' Troop was led by Captain Bob Loudoun.

The task of Finney Force was to support the Primorska Group of the Partisans, who were trying to block the German breakout along the coastal route through Kotor and Risan. The Germans had been held temporarily at

Risan, a small coastal town on a narrow alluvial plain at the head of the northernmost inlet of the Gulf of Kotor. Turner and Loudoun went ahead in a jeep to consult with the Partisan commander and to prepare their dispositions before their followers arrived. The followers trundled along well behind, slowed by heavy vehicles, by the eight guns and by mountain roads in understandably indifferent condition, the widths of which were in many places only a few inches wider than the wheel-bases of the bigger vehicles. There was also an abundance of precipitous, rocky drops, several hundred feet deep, usually where the road was narrowest. For the touristically inclined, the landscape, the few small towns and villages, and their inhabitants, were something new. Vis and the other islands had had their social and domestic simplicities, but there had been an ancient Venetian elegance about the little towns. Limestone rock had been plentiful, but so had vineyards, olive groves and vegetable patches. There were none of those in these wild, bleak and lovely mountains.

The few inhabited places on the route – Trebinje, Bileča, Vilusi – were small, sad, unimpressive places, badly dilapidated and partially incinerated as a consequence of successive occupation and reprisal by Italians, Chetniks, Ustashi, Germans and Partisans. The convoy stopped in each of them. The troops clambered down from the vehicles to stretch their legs and gaze about them. Sentries were placed. Each town at first seemed eerie, silent and uninhabited. After a time people began to appear in the street. In their recent experience, the advent of strangers had invariably meant suffering, destruction and death for someone. The townspeople were sensibly wary and reserved. The troops stared censoriously at the burned and destroyed buildings, chatted unselfconsciously and largely unintelligibly in a jumbled amalgam of Croatian, Italian, English and mime to the children and then to a few of the bolder old-timers, and explained that they were Engleski, something of a diplomatic concession by those who were Škotski, Irski or Velski. A cheerful general accord soon prevailed. Orders were given, the troops climbed back into their vehicles and the convoy moved on to the sound of mutual shouted statements of goodwill, not intelligible in detail, but understood nonetheless as goodwill.

By late afternoon the force had reached its leaders, Turner and Loudoun, who had been hospitably received by the Partisan Brigade Commander. He had joined them in their jeep, taken them to a vantage point from which it was possible to point out most of his own positions and some of the Germans', and showed on the map where those not in view were sited. The map was spread out on the bonnet of the jeep. Bob Loudoun suggested tactfully that there seemed to be an error in the placing of one of the German posts. If it was where the Partisan said it was, it was about 200 yards away and they were standing in full view of it. The Partisan confirmed cheerfully that that was indeed the case. A German Spandau gunner chose that moment to confirm it further by letting loose a sustained burst at the three of them. He missed. They withdrew prudently, with competitive dignity. Those were the first shots of the first battle to have been fought by the only British body of formed troops to have soldiered alongside a Communist army on the European mainland during the Second World War.

The gun position chosen by Pat Turner was on a small, rock-bespattered upland plain behind the tiny hamlet of Podhan. The guns were in action at first light on 30 October, the morning after arrival. Their targets were Risan itself, down on the coast at the foot of a 1600-foot escarpment, with an estimated German strength in it of between 200 and 400 together with two guns; an old Austrian barracks at Ledenice, two-thirds of the way up the escarpment and occupied by about 200 more Germans; a defensive position, 'Midway Bunkers'; and a string of five old Imperial Austrian forts, sited in the previous century to protect the inland approaches to the fleet anchorage of the Gulf of Kotor. The forts were on commanding features, and had stone walls six feet thick, steel doors and windows, and steel-lined weapon slits. The Partisans had made repeated, bloodily repulsed attempts on the forts. They had also made a series of similarly gallant and unsuccessful assaults on the two main strongpoints in Risan town – the sawmill and the hospital. The latter was a large, modern three-storied white building with a red roof upon which a red cross on a white background had been conspicuously painted. Like the sawmill, it had been fortified and garrisoned by German troops.

In one major essential, topography was kind to the gunners. High on the escarpment, approachable by a track out of view of the Germans and protected by a scattering of Partisan posts, was a compact rock shelf littered with huge boulders from which, when the weather was amenable, there could be seen in detail the entire layout of Risan, 1600 feet below and laterally less than a mile away. The panorama extended to most of the Gulf of Kotor, the only true fjord in southern Europe, an expanse of twinkling turquoise water enclosed by white limestone hills, 3000 abrupt feet high, that in some places rose vertically from the shore and in others were separated from the sea by narrow stretches of rocky flat land, seldom more than a few hundred yards wide. Along the eastern side of the Gulf, threaded around the base of the cliffs, and following the intricate line of a multiplicity of inlets, was the road from Kotor and the south, the road now in use by the German XXI Mountain Corps. From the high rock shelf most of it was visible. The stretches of it that were not, those hidden by some obtruding promontory, were in a military sense known about, because vehicles that disappeared into them could be counted, and the same number could be confidently expected to come into view again further along the road. The Gunner observation post, established in the eyrie of the rock shelf, permanently guarded by a sub-section of marines, had all the qualities of an invisible, moored balloon. Almost every overt German movement by day could be seen through binoculars, reported by wireless to the battery two miles to the rear at Podhan, and interrupted by accurately delivered shellfire of an intensity commensurate with the size of the target. In between shoots, the Forward Observation Officer had one of the loveliest views in the world to admire.*

Warfare, joined in so briskly on the morning after Finney Force's arrival, came to a stop with equal briskness on the morning after that. It began to rain. It stayed raining in a relentless, drenching downpour that flooded the upland

---

*For tourists with a leaning towards aesthetics or with an interest in military history, or a combination of both, the map reference of this incomparable viewpoint is 846455 on the 1:100,000 map of Yugoslavia. At any rate, that's what it was in 1944.

plain, washed out the stone sangars put up as defensive positions by the marines, immobilised vehicles, obliterated all view of Risan and the Kotor road from the observation post, and, by virtue of a noisy, flashing background of thunder and lightning, made wireless communication impossible. Sodden, blaspheming gunners and marines paddled dourly about in their dripping gas capes and saturated berets, the marines commenting freely upon a much-reiterated statement by their leader, Bob Loudoun. 'It would cost you hundreds of pounds', went the wording of this morale-boosting message, 'to come here in peacetime.'

Torrential rain, although never again of the intensity of the initial experience, was to be a recurrent curse upon the operation. Militarily it led to uncertainties about what advantage the Germans had taken of its cover to move up more troops. Domestically, its effects were unevenly distributed. The nature of the gunners' trade required that every one of them should travel in a vehicle. These were crowded, but there was adequate room for spare personal kit, sleeping-bags, cooking equipment and the like. ('Some of the buggers sleep between *sheets*,' reported a marine incredulously.) The marines' scale of equipment, governed by a theory long since displaced by the realities of practice, was based on the assumption that a Commando operation would be a short, sharp raid lasting not more than forty-eight hours, after which the participants would return to a well-found firm base. The marines thus had with them a standardised set of items that could be carried in their back packs. It included spare socks, but no other change of clothing. Wet marines did their best to dry out their one suit of battle-dress in front of the log stoves of the impoverished but marvellously hospitable peasants of Podhan, but since working wear doubled as pyjamas a total dryness was dependent upon the luck of the weather, not upon a sensible rotation of garments.

The weather was better on the day following the deluge. The Observation Officer in the high OP brought down shellfire on every German position in sight and registered the main ones – that is, once he had by trial and error established the precise range and bearing of a target from the gun position, the figures were recorded at both ends on maps and given a coded designation. In future if, for example, there was a sighting of incautious German activity in the hospital or the sawmill, he simply said into his throat microphone, 'Blue 2 [or whatever the chosen description was], five rounds [or ten, or however many he considered to be appropriate].' Another OP, with less attractive scenic amenities, was set up to cover the enemy positions obscured from the vision of the eyrie. A single gun was detached to an exposed position in an experimental attempt on one of the old Austrian forts. It fired over open sights at a range of 4500 yards and scored over sixty direct hits with high-explosive shells. They all bounced off the solid walls without doing any discernible damage. They also provoked a German response, uncomfortable for the handlers of the isolated gun, but ultimately to the common good, a consideration not for the time being dominant in the minds of those at the receiving end of it. German guns from both Ledenice and Risan, their fire presumably directed from the fort, put down a howling, crashing concentration of accurate shot around the exposed 25-pounder. The eyrie OP observer noted the muzzle flashes of the Risan guns, called for counter-battery fire from the gun position in Podhan and put out of action all three German pieces in the town.

At about this point it began to be borne in upon the garrison of Risan that a major change had come into the ordering of their so far relatively unimpeded progress towards home. On their way through Greece and Albania they had had little difficulty in brushing aside attempted interference by lightly armed and politically divided guerrilla bands who were glad to see the last of them and whose harassment had been not much more than token. The Montenegrin Partisans had been a much tougher proposition. They fought with unmatchable courage. But they were under-equipped in knowledge, experience and material to stop a German army that, although it was heavily reliant upon horse-drawn transport and mule trains, had with it armour, artillery and plenty of trucks, and was manned by seasoned troops firmly determined to fight their way home. Their unexpected confrontation with scientifically directed modern artillery dented German determination and confidence.

It also raised in some German minds the possibility of an

option that had not previously been open to them: surrender to the British, who would treat them honourably as prisoners-of-war in accordance with the specifications of the Geneva Convention. The option, in fact, was illusory. Under the agreement with the Partisan Supreme Staff that brought Floydforce to the Yugoslav mainland, all prisoners were to be handed over to the Partisans. But the option seemed attractive enough for some German soldiers to adopt it unilaterally; a number deserted and told the Partisan commanders that the whole German garrison might surrender if they knew that British troops were operating in the area.

Pat Turner spoke fluent German, which indeed was the language through which he conducted most of his negotiations and operational dealings with the Partisans. They asked him to write a letter to the German commander, Captain Brandstadter, suggesting that Brandstadter should raise a white flag and send out a parliamentaire. The Turner letter was delivered by a Partisan, watched carefully from the high OP, at eight o'clock on the morning of 4 November. A German lieutenant, also under close observation from the high OP, came out in response to the letter. He was at once taken away by Partisans of the 2nd Dalmatian Brigade. Captain Earle from the British Military Mission was sent to the Dalmatian Brigade Headquarters to collect the lieutenant. He was no longer available. He had, Earle was told, 'committed suicide'. The Partisan who had delivered the letter was never seen again either.

The Turner letter had included an undertaking that the guns would withhold their fire until three o'clock in the afternoon to allow the Germans to give themselves up unharmed. Unsurprisingly, Brandstadter, with his emissary still unreturned, made no move to surrender. Turner honoured his undertaking, and shortly after three o'clock turned his entire battery once more, devastatingly, upon the sawmill and the hospital in Risan. It was at about this time that what in retrospect seems to some survivors of the battle to be a symbolic illustration of the lunacy of war first made its appearance, and remained on permanent view to those looking down from the escarpment into the little town: the Red Cross painted on the hospital roof had a large, jagged hole blown into it.

Pat Turner's plan was now to keep German movement in Risan and along the coast road tightly under control, while at the same time giving priority to the destruction of the upland forts and the barracks at Ledenice. The reduction of the flank guard provided by the forts would clearly hamper seriously, if not frustrate entirely, any German attempt to move further forward. A second, equally urgent need was to keep down the growing number of Partisan casualties incurred daily in gallant, doomed assaults on the forts. The courage shown in these repetitive attacks was superb. The tactics used were those of mediaeval siege warfare. Variously trying scaling ladders, the ignition against the walls of bundles of brushwood soaked with petrol, a battering-ram improvised from a tree trunk mounted on a farm-cart and pushed by a foot party, the Partisans advanced over open ground, armed only with their heterogeneous collection of small arms and grenades, and tried fiercely to close on regular infantry firing Spandaus and Schmeissers through steel-lined weapon slits in six-feet-thick stone walls. The consequences were inevitable. All attacks failed, with an appallingly high percentage of casualties among the attacking force.

Pat Turner put into practice a fresh gunnery experiment. The earlier shoot with high-explosive shells had achieved nothing. This time he thickened up the mixture with a proportion of armour-piercing shells, solid shot designed to penetrate the steel carapaces of tanks. A selected corner stone was battered by a repeated stream of solid shot fired from one gun, which – as in the earlier try – had been detached and exposed in the open. The other seven guns stood by to deal with any attempted interference. When, in its loosening, dislodging and cracking process, the solid shot had stirred up such a cloud of dust, chippings and general muck that the gun-layer was unable to see clearly through his telescopic sight, the gun switched to high explosive and blew all the cloud away. After a succession of these alternations, involving an expenditure of forty rounds of armour-piercing and eighty rounds of high-explosive shells, the first fort walls came tumbling down, breached in two places, on 7 November. The Commando Brens, posted behind the guns, fired into the breach. The Partisan cheer echoed among the hills. The fort's garrison, leaving several dead behind them, scurried off to Ledenice.

Mist and rain ruled out a repetition on the following day, but on the 9th a second fort went, with an interval of one hour between the firing of the first shot and the installation of the Partisan assault party in the ruins. The Commander of the Boka Brigade was delighted. 'The gun is the God of War,' he remarked with satisfaction. The Gods of War, all eight of the 25-pounders, now supplemented by a troop of 75-mm guns of the Raiding Support Regiment and the 3-inch mortars of 43 Commando, who had just arrived, soon had matters other than the broaching of forts to attend to. For the past three days Partisans of the 2nd Dalmatian Brigade had been holding up the Germans on the coastal road from Kotor. The Germans finally broke through and added another 200 men and two guns to their advanced guard in Risan. It was so far a small accretion of minor immediate significance. If it were to be followed up in strength it could become serious. Parties of marines were sent off to prepare demolitions on two rock faces overlooking the winding road which the Germans would have to use if they broke out from the town. Gun cotton was packed where it would do the most good. Detonators were inserted into primers. Cordtex was laid from the detonators back to ancient-looking plungers, T-bars on cubical wooden boxes, of the type familiar to watchers of 1930s Hollywood movies.* Defensive positions were sited to cover the blow. There were rehearsals of a projected sequence of notional events, conducted with some scepticism, which included the bringing down of the cliffs, a tidy little road ambush and the disengagement of the ambushers at the appropriate moment in a 15-hundredweight truck. The matter of accommodating about thirty people in, on and around a dilapidated vehicle designed to hold eight involved some interesting improvisation.

---

*Some weeks after these precautions were taken, and when they were no longer necessary, Bob Loudoun took a party back to recover the explosives. The cordtex – cutting explosive encased in what looked rather like insulated wire and capable of severing a tree – was in popular local use. Peasants had abstracted it. They found it convenient for lashing loads to donkeys.

While these precautionary preparations for the withdrawal of Finney Force were under way, the guns were
busily making them unnecessary. The newcomers to Risan
were either unwarned about, or failed to pay attention to
warnings of, the fact that they were conspicuous targets for
observed artillery fire, put down with lethal efficiency.
They had had things too much their own way for too long.
They wandered about the streets, sight-seeing. They placed
their guns artlessly. In a protracted and devastating shoot
the 25-pounders and the 75s destroyed two German guns,
forced the abandonment of the gun position of a third, and
brought all overt movement in the town and its approaches
to a halt. Local acoustic peculiarities amplified the din. The
bang of the guns' discharges, the sibilant whistlings,
developing into howlings, of shells in flight, the crashes of
their explosions on impact, thundered in the enclosed
amphitheatre of the Gulf, and echoed and re-echoed back
and forth between the limestone crags and precipices of the
looming mountains. On the profit-and-loss sheet of battle
the only realistic entry that the German commander could
have made was a loss, still retrievable. Probably it was not
retrievable without help from elsewhere, but that seemed
as if it might soon be available. Seventy-five miles to the
north-west, a German force assembled at Mostar was trying
to fight its way south to loosen the grip held on the exit
routes by the guns of Finney Force at Risan, by the guns of
the rest of Floydforce further inland around Nikšić, and by
the courage and endurance of the Partisans in both areas.
For the time being, the same Partisan qualities were
containing the Mostar expedition. But the threat of a
concerted German try at a breakout remained a consideration for some time to come. Meanwhile Pat Turner shifted
his attentions once more to the forts.

It was not an exclusive attention. Any movement in
Risan still attracted a prompt flurry of whining, crashing
shells. The strongpoints in the sawmill and the hospital
were regular targets. A request to Balkan Air Force to put
in an airstrike on these was met by an apology. The BAF had
a long string of prior commitments elsewhere. Risan would
have to take its turn. Turner signalled back a sort of banker's
standing order: an airstrike as soon as possible on any
morning between ten and eleven o'clock would be helpful.

In consultation with Bob Loudoun he also gave consideration to the problem of how to give further discouragement to users of the Kotor road by night. Random shelling had forced German vehicles bringing up supplies and reinforcements to Risan to drive without lights, but there was no reason to believe that the night traffic was not still substantial. It was decided that Loudoun should blow a hole in the road. After a careful study through binoculars from the high OP of possible options, he selected a likely looking culvert near Perast, about two miles on the Kotor side of Risan. With 300 pounds of ammonal packed into sandbags and prepared for immediate detonation by the inclusion in each bag of a string of guncotton primers knotted together by cordtex, the load carried on donkeys, Loudoun, three marines, a Partisan guide and the donkey handlers set out from Podhan at dawn for a hard march through the mountains. The guide was good. He led them to the south-east, close to, but out of sight of, the German Ledenice defences, and round to the hamlet of Velenici, 2000 feet above the culvert.

They reached Velenici in the late afternoon. The Partisans had promised to provide a carrying party to help take the thirty bags of explosive down the steep, and in some places pathless, hillside. Loudoun had assumed that these porters would be Partisans. In fact, the Partisan guide had simply told the village headman of Velenici to provide a team. Since everyone of both sexes and of military age (as interpreted in Montenegro in 1944, everyone between about eleven and the early seventies) was already away fighting, Loudoun moved down the slope in the gathering darkness like the Pied Piper, surrounded by chattering children and a lacing of stout-hearted but equally noisy old-timers. These led the demolition party faultlessly to where they wanted to go, dumped their loads and disappeared up the hill into the night. A marine and two Partisans went a hundred yards up the road on the Risan side and laid a necklace of light anti-vehicle mines across it. A small group of Partisans did the same on the Kotor side. Loudoun and other Partisans stacked the bags in the culvert, got very cold in icy water and had just finished the attachment of the cordtex leads to the detonators when there was an interruption, in two instalments. Part One was the Risan roadblock team, sprinting. Part Two was a German truck that had driven over the necklace of mines without setting them off. Loudoun had intended to check each member of the party away in the prescribed manner before detonating the charges. There was no time for these niceties. There was also nowhere to go except down the road towards Kotor. The local cliff was vertical. Loudoun pulled the pins, and the demolishers headed south at speed, moving rather faster than the truck, which, lightless, was being driven with caution. Loudoun found a gap in the bank, saw his party up and scrambled after them. The truck trundled slowly by, its occupants apparently having noticed nothing unusual. The culvert blew up with a gratifying flash and bang. Loudoun's group was showered by flying bits of road. The lorry stopped, amid raised voices.

An over-long pause for self-satisfaction, followed by a still longer search for a couple of Partisans who were temporarily mislaid, delayed the departure for home. This was unfortunate, because the next item on the operational programme was an artillery shoot on to the blow, timed for half an hour after the bang. The timing was exact. The Loudoun party left through a shrieking, crashing, zinging delivery of shells by its own supporters. No one was hit. At dawn they looked down from the mountain at their handiwork: a nice big hole; a truck wrecked on the mine necklace; a foot patrol in single file approaching the hole from Perast. The same view, from a reciprocal bearing, was available to the high OP. Road repairs in daylight were made impossible by shelling. The damaged truck was pushed into the hole by night and bridged with planking. But from then on Risan was closed to heavy transport.

The third of the five forts was breached by the alternating solid-shot and high-explosive technique on 11 November. There was some inaccurate interference from the German guns in Ledenice, which were promptly wrecked by a massive concentration of over a hundred rounds from the other 25-pounders. The last two forts fell on the 17th. The survivors from their defenders fell back on the old Austrian barracks at Ledenice, now isolated by Partisans from the

Risan garrison. Unlike the forts, the Ledenice barracks had not been designed primarily for defence. They housed living accommodation and administrative offices. They were on a little upland plateau, overlooked by neighbouring high ground, now, with their protecting forts gone, in Partisan possession. During the late morning of the 17th, the eight 25-pounders, the two 75s, two 3-inch mortars of the Heavy Weapon Troop of 43 Commando and about 600 surrounding Partisans armed with a miscellany of rifles and captured Spandaus, poured a destructive, deafening and spectacular fire into a disintegrating collection of elderly buildings grouped together in a space about half the size of a soccer pitch.

The Germans held out until twenty minutes past one in the afternoon. They then showed a white flag, after which confusion ensued. Turner quietened his guns and the mortars. Partisan small-arms fire slowly dwindled and then stopped altogether. The Partisans understandably assumed that the white flag was a sign of surrender. They walked into the ruined barracks and helped themselves to German weapons, watches, rings and similar portable and useful items of loot. Pat Turner and Bob Loudoun, also under the impression that the white flag signified surrender, walked over together and met a very angry, very brave and very unrealistic German commander. This was an outrage, he complained, staring at the Partisans who were improving the size of their personal collections. All that he had wanted from the white flag was a truce during which his wounded could be evacuated. He had three proposals to make to put matters right immediately. His wounded should be taken to safety. Weapons and personal property sequestrated by the Partisans should be given back at once. The Partisans should return to their original starting points ('Get that rabble out of my position'), Turner and Loudoun should go back to theirs, and at an agreed signal the battle should recommence.

Turner pointed out succinctly the impossibility of enforcing these conditions, even had he wanted to, which he did not. The intended truce had already become a *de facto* surrender. The German commander at last reluctantly accepted it as such. The true depth of his gallantry in wanting to resume the fight was appreciated when his casualties were counted. In the shambles of his mountain barracks, on a grey November day, there were forty-three dead, seventy-odd wounded of whom six died later, and 197 unhurt. He had had a further seventeen killed during the shelling of the forts. They were from 334th Fusilier Regiment of 161st Infantry Division, and from 222nd Artillery Regiment. The unwounded prisoners were marched away by the Partisans. The wounded were taken in British transport for treatment at the Gunners' Regimental Aid Post. Captain Bernard Kieft of the Royal Army Medical Corps, helped by captured German medical orderlies and by gunner and marine volunteers, worked throughout the night in tending the patients.

A working party of marines, reflecting gloomily that the job was properly one for the uninjured prisoners who had been marched off by the Partisans, buried the forty-three dead in a mass grave. On a captured German cross,* Turner's battery craftsmen inscribed in German: 'In memory of forty-three German soldiers who fell in battle.' Turner planted the cross himself, stood back and saluted the grave. A Commando guard of honour presented arms. These formal decencies completed, Pat Turner returned to the supervision of his guns, still booming steadily away into Risan.

Materially the Partisans profited considerably from the action at Ledenice. They took two 105-mm guns of First World War vintage; several 81-mm mortars; a large haul of small arms of all kinds; and a great deal of useful equipment, clothing and food. From Ledenice onwards, Partisans with red stars on their forage caps and 'Gott Mit Uns' inscribed on the buckles of their belts became a common sight.

With the forts and Ledenice disposed of, Turner was able to concentrate his attentions upon Risan town and the Kotor road. The intensity of the shelling of the strongpoints in the town was increased. A sniping gun was sent down to the coast close to the little town of Hercegnovi on the shore at the entrance to the Gulf. From there Lieutenant Statham

---

*The Wehrmacht pressed detailed forward planning to ghoulish extremes. Units carried a stock of burial crosses with them as part of the inventory of the German equivalent of the Quartermaster's stores.

had a clear view across the waters of the Gulf to a stretch of road screened from the eyrie observation post. He saw a great deal of activity in progress at Tivat. He put a total of 240 shells into a transport park, a dock, a barracks, some gun positions and an ammunition dump. The dump was set on fire, and bits of it continued to explode for an hour. That same night, the 19/20 November, a German column either tried to retake Ledenice or possibly, in un-Germanic confusion about what had happened to it, tried to reinforce it. The column's composition – it included a mule train and horse-drawn carts – suggested the second. It was routed by Partisans. On the following morning the road was littered with dead German soldiers, dead mules and horses, and wrecked ammunition wagons.

The next day was the busiest yet. There were strong indications that the Germans were building up for a determined attempt at a breakthrough. During the night, the sound of much movement of vehicles had come from the Kotor road. Further movement, all into Risan, continued throughout the day, heavily harassed by gunfire. German artillery from the south and the east repeatedly shelled the escarpment. Two 25-pounders were moved to counter this fire. The shooting continued for the rest of the day, intermittently and irregularly reaching a series of crescendos. The marines of 'C' Troop set up a roadblock at the head of the zigzag road that climbed the escarpment. When dusk fell all sentries were doubled. A full stand-to was called before first light on 21 November. At the same time all guns fired an intensive defensive fire programme on to all likely forming-up positions for a German assault, and on to the routes leading to them and from them.

When it became light enough to see clearly, Lieutenant Owen looked through his binoculars from the high observation post into Risan and gazed at what at first sight seemed to be the finest target of his life. The streets and the waterfront were swarming with people. A more detailed inspection showed them to be Partisans and civilians. The Germans had abandoned their westernmost breakout route as too difficult and too expensive. They had withdrawn during the night, southwards through Kotor and beyond, to turn inland in the hope of getting out by one of the other two routes.

Pat Turner moved down into the town that he had done so much to disfigure. A party of marines set out after him a half hour or so later. They paused a third of the way down to look at what had once been a pretty, Adriatic coastal town in an unusually beautiful setting. Now the houses were battered and crumbled, and the neat gardens were pitted with the marks where shells and mortar bombs had exploded. From a distance there seemed not to be an intact pane of glass in the place. They were appraising all this destruction silently, when from out to sea they heard the distant sound of engines, growing noisier. Aircraft with Royal Air Force roundels swept into view, circled round the Gulf, formed up into line ahead and dived in succession to put in rousing rocket attacks on the sawmill and the hospital, targets suggested to them by Pat Turner in the long-forgotten banker's order. He was now sitting in one of them, wishing that the RAF would go away. Later in the day Balkan Air Force signalled a solicitous apology. The Turner reply was that the RAF couldn't hit a pussy-cat.

Risan was a mess of strewn rubble, broken glass, dead horses and mules, burnt-out German vehicles and two destroyed guns. There were many new graves and one more to be dug, for a German second lieutenant who had somehow been left behind at the time of the withdrawal had had his head beaten in by Partisans. Partisans clambered about the buildings, some of which were totally wrecked, all of them scarred by hits from shell and mortar fragments. The wards and corridors of the hospital were ankle-deep in rubbish, shattered glass, brickdust and piles of cartridge cases at abandoned fire positions. The Germans had left behind large stocks of small-arms ammunition and uniforms. Partisans helped themselves from an even bigger bonanza than that in Ledenice. Then they were fallen in, a ragged, ardent mixture of young and old, men and women, boys and girls, humping their miscellaneous armoury of captured Spandaus and Schmeissers and rifles over their shoulders, hung about with grenades. They left indomitably at the jog-trot which they favoured, heading towards Kotor along the road beside the lovely Gulf.

*

Finney Force was not invited to join in the Partisan follow-up after Risan. Instead the force withdrew to Bileča to refurbish itself, and to stay in readiness for intervention wherever else it might be required. In the three weeks between 30 October and 21 November its guns had fired a total of 12,000 rounds. It had done the job that it had been sent to do. One of the three German escape routes had been blocked, permanently. It is no denigration of Partisan courage and capacity to say that without the guns the Germans almost certainly would have broken through. The Partisans were the finest guerrilla force of the Second World War. But guerrillas are neither trained nor equipped to stop, as opposed to harass, a military machine of the size, and with the resources, of XXI Mountain Corps of the German Army Group E.

At Bileča, Pat Turner's battery craftsmen, mechanically versatile, rigged a complicated apparatus which provided hot water showers. When his battery had been suitably cleansed Turner offered the hospitality of the showers to Bob Loudoun for his troop of marines. Loudoun accepted with gratitude. The marines were hygienically in much worse condition than were the gunners. They had shaved daily, washed the grime from their faces and kept their weapons clean. They were otherwise deficient in personal daintiness. For three weeks they had sweated over hills, had been saturated by rain and had slept in their one set of clothes on the beaten-earth floors of peasant cottages and livestock sheds. Some had acquired that common passport of Partisan warfare, lice.

Loudoun was, and still is, immensely proud of 'C' Troop of 43 Royal Marine Commando. He had raised, trained, cherished and led them in action from Anzio onwards. He had been wounded at their head in the Brač battle. He would personally see to it that every one of them would wallow in the steam and soap, and wash away the muck of weeks. He decided that before doing so he would allow himself a little personal luxury. He would have a private bath, all to himself. He ordered one of his subalterns to take the troop out on a training exercise, telling the man*

*Me.

deceitfully that he himself was unable to accompany his followers because of urgent, unspecified military business. When they came back, dirtier and sweatier than ever, they would be met by a glowing, scrubbed Loudoun, who would tell them proudly of the marvellous surprise that he had for them.

He gave the troop ten minutes to get well clear of Bileča, rolled his towel neatly under his arm and walked happily to the Gunner headquarters. The sentry saluted. Loudoun returned the salute.

'Where's the shower?' asked Loudoun eagerly.

'They've just gone out on a training exercise,' said the sentry.

The Ledenice prisoners were kept by the Partisans in a wired-off cage on a hillside abutting a road which was in sporadic use by members of the force. As the weeks went by, the prisoners, greatcoat collars turned up, hands thrust deep into pockets, shoulders hunched against the wind and snow, looked progressively thinner, weaker, hungrier and more despairing. Turner and Loudoun visited them once. There was a great deal of disciplined heel-clicking and saluting. Turner, looking stern, addressed them in German. Was the man still alive, he asked grimly, who had fired that Spandau on the first day when Loudoun, the Partisan Brigade Commander and Turner himself had been studying the map spread on the bonnet of the jeep? A sheepish soldier, who seemed to fear instant reprisal, stepped forward and identified himself. Turner reproached him fluently for his inexcusably poor standard of marksmanship. 'You should have got the lot of us,' he said severely. There was a huge roar of relieved laughter.

Many years later, when Turner was stationed in Germany with the British Army of the Rhine, he was approached at a motor show by a prosperous-looking German. It was the Wehrmacht sergeant-major from the prison-cage. The prisoners had not all been shot after the departure of the British, as had been widely assumed by Finney Force. Their officers had been, but the rest were tried by a People's Court, sentenced to several years of manual labour during the post-war reconstruction of Yugoslavia, and repatriated – less those who had died – to Germany in the early 1950s.

TWENTY-TWO

Floydforce at Podgorica

The fight at Risan was essentially a straightforward affair, with a clear objective successfully achieved by a sensible use of adequate resources. With one major exception, and a few minor ones, the rest of Floydforce, the larger part of it, led a more complicated and more frustrating existence. There were several reasons for this. The first was the need to take seriously potential threats, notably the recurrent one from Mostar, that never materialised. Gun positions and observation posts were reconnoitred, Gunner batteries or individual troops were deployed to cover a range of eventualities from a variety of attempted German incursions from the north to cut a corridor for the use of Army Group E, to the fall-back of the entire force to concentrate in the defence of Dubrovnik. The guns could only travel by road. The Montenegrin road system of the time was sparse. The number of usable roads was sparser still, because of blown bridges, some demolished by the Partisans, some by the Germans. Observation-post parties in search of suitable viewpoints from which to control shoots marched for punishing miles over mountain tracks on a Balkan massif upon which the winter was beginning to set in in earnest. They, and their Commando escorts, carried heavy loads. Sometimes they used mules to take their equipment. But mules were advised against as bearers of wireless sets after an expedition led by Captain Pitt to observe the Podgorica–Bioče road. His mules collapsed from exhaustion when the journey was half completed, and the wireless mule destroyed the set. A replacement had to be sent up by a foot party.

Commando demolition parties also put in some extensive

mountain marching, most of it fruitless. Lieutenant Stevens walked sixty miles, across country and on hilly tracks, to blow the coast road at Budva. When he got there the cupboard was bare, and burning. The Germans had moved on, after firing part of the town. Farther to the east, in the Nikšić area, Captain Ralph Parkinson-Cumine did an even more arduous march to see about blowing the bridge at Bioče. This cupboard was crowded, by Germans, to whom the bridge's preservation was as essential as its destruction was desirable to their opponents. Parkinson-Cumine marched home again. The bridge was too hard a nut to be cracked by the unsupported troop attack for which he had been reconnoitring. The operation was abandoned.

The Forsyth Force flank guard, based on Bileća, in mid-November 1944 sent out two 25-pounders with Captain G.C. MacLeod-Carey to shell a German position at Nevesinje. They ran first into heavy snow and then into an impassable river. They returned to Bileća and tried again three days later. This time they got through. They fired off eighty-four rounds in twenty-five minutes, did a certain amount of damage and then were asked courteously by the Partisan commander to go away. The German counter-battery fire, he pointed out, was all landing on his troops. MacLeod-Carey conceded fair-mindedly that the complaint was reasonable, and returned to Bileća for the second time.

A second, and major, cause of frustration was political. There are few surviving old-timers from Floydforce who do not to this day retain an immense admiration and respect for Partisan courage and endurance. There are equally fervent recollections of tough, cheerful, hospitable peasants, who had endured three-and-a-half years of blood-soaked privation, who had had successive layers of ruin placed upon their already impoverished land, and who were still happily prepared to share what little they had left with strangers from overseas who had come to help them. But the chill wind of uncooperative suspicion, its point of origin the very top of the Partisan Command, was blowing chillier and more strongly. The locking up of the colonels had been symptomatic. The symptoms showed themselves further both in actual operations and in assorted incivilities in the Dubrovnik base. Operations were cancelled without notice, or delayed for referral to Belgrade, where Tito was now based, for a ruling on whether they should be allowed to proceed. Patently false information was supplied in some cases to divert Floydforce from areas where, for convoluted long-term revolutionary reasons, they were unwanted. In Dubrovnik there were curfews for British troops, wine bars were placed out of bounds, civilians were forbidden to speak to foreign troops. In January British troops were allowed into the town on three days a week only. They had to submit to the inspection of their papers by Partisan military police. There was a demand, which was accepted, that British provost patrols should cease to appear in the town.

It was all a long way from the old, easy, camaraderie of the islands. It was a long way, too, from what might reasonably be expected by a force doing its best to implement its charter 'to give the greatest possible artillery support to the Yugoslav National Army of Liberation', and doing it in conditions of harsh discomfort that was often prolonged into physical hardship. On the British side the matter was taken up at the very highest level, the Prime Minister. On 3 December Winston Churchill sent a personal message to Tito through the Maclean Mission:

> You seem to be treating us in an increasingly invidious fashion. It may be that you have fears that your ambitions about occupying Italian territories of the north Adriatic lead you to view with suspicion and dislike every military operation on your coast we make against the Germans. I have already assured you that all territorial questions will be reserved for the Peace Conference. And they will be judged irrespective of wartime occupation. And certainly such issues ought not to hamper military operations now.

There was no abatement of the suspicion and dislike. It continued to hamper military operations.

A major operation that went ahead only partially hampered was the block on the central German breakout route, on the road from the Albanian border through Podgorica, Danilovgrad and Nikšić. It had been clear from the outset that this would be one of the routes tried, and that if the stopper were to be screwed down effectively at Risan, the Nikšić road would attract an enhanced traffic. The road south from Nikšić ran through a deep, rocky valley, bounded on either side by precipitous mountains that were scenically magnificent but useless for 25-pounder gun positions. An advanced position in the grounds of a monastery was judged to be suitable for mountain guns, and to this on 13 November went a troop of the Raiding Support Regiment with four 75-mm guns and a troop of 43 Commando for local protection. The central element in the block was the bridge at Nikšić. It was about 150 yards long, stone-built and supported by fifteen piers. Some of the piers had already been prepared for demolition by the Partisans. No. 579 Field Company of the Royal Engineers took over the job, and took no chances. They put double charges on every pier.

It was evident that if the bridge had to be blown it would probably have to be blown in a hurry. The gun positions would have to be on the correct, north side of it so that they would not be marooned amid the angry hordes of the XXI Mountain Corps, more embittered than usual by the sight of the denial to them of yet another way home. A difficulty was that the land to the north flattened to an extensive plain. There was no ground of worth to an observation post. Brigadier O'Brien-Twohig solved this problem by ordering that one OP party should stay in the mountains to the south of the river after, or if, the bridge was demolished. This task fell to the lot of Captain J.S. Cuttress. It is recorded that 'he set about attempting to obtain folding-boat equipment for his escape'.

By the 22nd the Germans were still out of range of the Nikšić guns. Two 25-pounders were sent across the river to join the RSR's 75s at the monastery. They stayed there for two days and made something of a reputation for themselves as public performers. A large audience of Partisans attended the observation post, pointed out targets, applauded hits and expressed delighted amazement at the gunners' ability to land shot accurately upon places and things out of sight of the gun itself. On the second day, as the detachment were preparing to leave, they were engaged by a German 88. It wounded two of the crew and did some minor damage.

Pat Turner's battery, its job at Risan finished, came up to Nikšić later in the day. So did a troop of No. 64 Heavy Anti-Aircraft Regiment. The Nikšić artillery force was now formidably strong. The Partisans said that it was no longer needed. They had held the Germans at Danilovgrad. Nikšić was no longer at risk. The Germans were now relying solely upon their innermost route, through Kolašin to Sarajevo. A battery of 25-pounders and the RSR's 75s stayed in Nikšić in a defensive role, and, as noted in the records of 111 Field Regiment, 'occupied their time in training, football and bartering for chickens, turkeys, pigs, sheep and sheepskins with the locals in anticipation of Christmas and still colder weather.' The other guns, and parts of the Commando, dispersed variously to Dubrovnik, Bileča and Trebinje. British participation in the campaign came to a temporary halt.

One possible way in which the guns could interfere with the German withdrawal was for them to be taken down to the coast at Risan, along the road through the old Montenegrin capital of Cetinje, and on to the south-west approaches to Podgorica. From there the guns could shell the German flank. O'Brien-Twohig put this to the commander of the Partisan II Corps. He, as a soldier, was personally in favour. He was unable to commit himself until he could get authorisation from Belgrade. Belgrade took ten days to grant it. On 5 December a reconstituted Finney Force, commanded by Major W.H. Cheesman, the second-in-command of 111 Field Regiment, and consisting of a battery of 25-pounders, a section of 75s, 'C' Troop of 43 Commando, a detachment of the Long Range Desert Group and a detachment of sappers with a Bailey bridge, set out in convoy. To all but the organisers it was the most enjoyable excursion of the campaign – scenically beautiful, touristically interesting, touch of farce here and there, and not a drop of blood shed, except possibly internally from the hidden ulcers of senior commanders. The troops and the junior officers loved it.

Three bridges on the coast road between Dubrovnik and Risan were still down, blown by Partisans before Floydforce had landed. The column followed the narrow, by now familiar, inland road, through Vilusi and Grahovo, past the old gun positions at Podhan from which the attempted German breakout through Risan had been stopped, down the zigzag road of the escarpment, through Risan, over Bob Loudoun's by now repaired blow near Perast and on to another unrepaired blow shortly beyond it. At this obstacle there was a halt, and a long argument.

Sentries were posted as a matter of routine. The arguers argued. The temporarily unemployed majority gazed admiringly at their surroundings. Up on the high plateau, before the descent into Risan, the views had been beautiful but unremittingly bleak. Backdrops of snow-covered sharp mountains, sometimes gleaming in patchy sunshine, more often obscured by mist or showers of rain or hail or snow. An inconsistently changing sky, clouds being blown away, other clouds replacing them, pure, clean air, rocky outcrops variously grey, white, fawn, mauve, ochre, in the shifting light. Down here, at sea level, there was a different quality to the loveliness. The glinting, sapphire-blue waters of the Gulf of Kotor lapped gently against the shore. Enclosing, grey-white limestone mountains towered irregularly on every intricate side. There were enchanting glimpses across the water of little villages of white-walled houses with red-tiled roofs, of tiny chapels on domed hills, of olive groves, vineyards and vegetable gardens. The physical beauty aside, there was also the matter of physical warmth. It was a relative warmth. It was December. But December on the coast of an inlet of the Mediterranean was different from December in the Highlands of Montenegro.

The argument was about who should repair the blow: a bridge over a stream running high from winter rain and snow and flowing into the Gulf in a torrent. Bits of the bridge, demolished comprehensively by the retreating Germans, projected erratically from the surface of the stream, white water bubbling and gurgling about them. The sapper detachment had been sent on slightly ahead of the rest of the force to put up a Bailey bridge, a device with some similarities to a child's Meccano set. The metal part of it was broken down into standardised components of a size capable of carriage in a normal 3-ton truck. When needed, they were bolted together, pushed across the gap with the help of what to the laity seemed to be a complicated system of rollers and counter-weights, fitted with plank decking, and there was a bridge, usable by very heavy transport. The parts of this particular Bailey bridge were still stowed in their trucks. A Partisan engineer who for the previous week or so had been trying to put things right by more traditional methods, said repeatedly that he did not want them. He was a stone-bridge man himself.

This admirable perfectionism was offset by a clear weakness in his case. Every time that he assembled a promising-looking agglomeration of stones they were washed into the Gulf by sudden surges in the torrent. These setbacks had not disheartened him. They had made him more stubbornly determined to do the job, in his own way. His professional pride was deeply engaged. He was unmoved by all attempts at persuasion, cajolement and bullying. He was indifferent to the spectacle of the long column of guns and vehicles, immobilised in a snake that wound away out of sight behind a projecting cliff. He eventually conceded that he would give way if somebody would bring him a written authority from the Partisan II Corps Headquarters at Nikšić. This might have taken days. A more subtle approach was tried. A small section of the Bailey was assembled. He cast a professional eye upon it. He seemed to take a developing interest in it. The interest appeared to flower into secret admiration. At 3.30 p.m. he weakened. The sappers set to work.

The Bailey was completed and in working order by 2.30 in the morning. The column left at dawn, winding its way beside the alluring Gulf. There was a halt in the old Venetian town of Kotor, a place of great beauty, last visited by British troops in strength when it was captured during the Napoleonic wars in 1811 in a combined operation mounted by sailors and marines from the ships of Captain William Hoste. If anyone in the column had ever heard of this exploit, which is unlikely, they did not refer to it openly. There was a curious episode in Kotor. A message was given, furtively, to one of the Commando subalterns. A Miss Nellie O'Reilly would like to speak to him. Miss O'Reilly, it seemed, was an Irish girl who had been caught up by the war in Yugoslavia while working as a mother's help, or something similar, in the household of a wealthy Croatian family. Presumably she was now anxious to get out. The Partisans did not like rich Croatian households. The subaltern went in search of her. He was unable to find her, partly because of the obvious need to be discreet in making his enquiries, partly because the column was due to move on again. He had another try when the column returned. He was similarly unsuccessful. She remains a mystery, possibly a sad one.

Major Cheesman motored on ahead to make arrangements in Cetinje with the headquarters of the Partisan Primorska Group, and was at once cut off from the rest of the force by a landslide behind him on the road around Lovćen Mountain. The column leaguered for a second happy night on the coast. Two of the Commando officers were extravagantly welcomed in a hotel in Budva. They luxuriated in hot baths, climbed into beds with sheets and feather mattresses, and an hour or so later climbed out again. The switch to elegant comfort was too abrupt and they found themselves unable to sleep. They dossed down on the floor in the style to which they had become accustomed, using their packs as pillows. They slumbered soundly.

On the next morning, 9 December, developments were reported from several directions. Cheesman in Cetinje, once the capital of the old Kingdom of Montenegro, had been warmly and enthusiastically welcomed by Major Dalković, the Partisan commander. They had discussed the details of the operation. Dalković gave Cheesman dinner and a comfortable room for the night in what had once been the British Embassy. In Dubrovnik, Colonel T. de F. Jago had suggested to Brigadier O'Brien-Twohig that since something big was about to happen, he, Jago, should move up his Regimental Headquarters and additional signals equipment to join the force. O'Brien-Twohig agreed. Jago's party set forth. On Lovćen Mountain a Partisan working party cleared a path through the landslide. The column wound up into the mountains again, back to the hail and snow, and into Cetinje, a fascinating place where Rudolph Rassendyll and Rupert of Hentzau would have been in their element. A troop of 25-pounders went straight through the town and deployed on the Cetinje–

Danilovgrad road. They had arrived just too late. The Partisans were reported to have taken Danilovgrad.

Colonel Jago's party arrived that evening. He called an officers' conference at Force Headquarters in the Grand Hotel. A 25-pounder troop was detailed off to take up a position within range of Podgorica on the Podgorica road. A second troop was to join it at first light. A signal from Floydforce Advanced Headquarters in Nikšić came in to say that the Partisan Command had given specific approval for the guns to open up in the morning. The orders group completed, the conference adjourned for dinner in the hotel dining room, with Major Dalković as its guest of honour. Glasses were being charged with *rakija* prior to a toast to success on the morrow when a second signal from Floydforce was delivered to the head of the table. This one read: 'PREVIOUS SIGNAL CANCELLED. ALL FORWARD MOVEMENT STOPPED. CONCENTRATE ALL FORCES VILUSI 10 DEC.'

Jago called another officers' conference after dinner. Earlier arrangements were unscrambled. Fresh orders were given. At first light the vehicles and guns of the column took up their places once more, this time facing the direction from which they had recently arrived. It was a nice drive down to sea-level again, along the road beside the lovely Gulf, up once more, zigzag, across the Risan escarpment, through the hail and icy rain of the plateau, and back to the partially destroyed, dismal village at the road junction at Vilusi. It had been a round trip of 180 miles. To adapt the Loudoun manifesto about the cost of coming here in peacetime, the undertaking had cost the British taxpayer rather more than hundreds of pounds in wartime.

Jago reported to O'Brien-Twohig. O'Brien-Twohig said that Partisan II Corps had told him that Podgorica was on the verge of falling and had demanded the withdrawal of the guns to counter a new threat from Mostar. Jago went to see the Commander of the Partisan 29th Division at Trebinje. The Divisional Commander said that there was no threat from Mostar. The Germans had pushed a few strong patrols a little way south, presumably to help cover elements of Army Group E pulling out through Sarajevo. Jago went to Nikšić to see O'Brien-Twohig again, and returned with new orders. The travelling fiasco of the abortive ride to Cetinje was militarily irredeemable, but there was one superficially respectable option through which it could be made plain with an urbane bloody-mindedness that the leadership of Floydforce was unamused. The Bailey bridge outside Perast had by now become an integral and accepted part of the communications network of Montenegro. Jago had orders to repossess the bridge.

Three days after the return from Cetinje a little column once more went down to the coast. It comprised a detachment of the Field Company of the sappers, a Commando sub-section and Captain Peter Carey, a Croatian-speaking officer from the British Military Mission. Its instructions were enshrined in an impressive document shot through with bureaucratic verbiage and decorated with a seal embossed with the Royal Cypher of the United Kingdom of Great Britain and Northern Ireland, an effect achieved by pressing into the wax a General Service greatcoat button. For a number of essential reasons, proclaimed this mendacious piece of paper, it was important that the Bailey bridge should be held in reserve. The party's negotiators held obdurately to their brief. The Odbor in Kotor seemed to have no brief, but over the *rakija* became plaintive about the complexities ahead of them if the southern littoral of Montenegro were to be severed from the northern littoral of Montenegro. The Brits pointed out that the thing had only been installed in the first place after sustained opposition from the Partisans' stonework enthusiast, who would presumably be delighted at the chance to try his hand again. But that was a decision for the Partisans to take. The British decision had already been taken. The Bailey bridge was manifestly a British bridge, put up by British engineers. It was wanted elsewhere for British operations in support of Partisan operations. British engineers would now take it away.

The Partisan spokesmen said that they would have to seek instructions from their headquarters. The bridge collectors reported developments by wireless to theirs. There was further discussion, and more *rakija*, in the Odbor, the Communist Party Committee office. Telephoned assent finally came from an undisclosed level in the Partisan hierarchy. The bridge was efficiently dismantled. When, after mutual courtesies, the column left on the following morning the Partisans had already improvised a substitute for the Bailey. The new way of getting from southern Montenegro to northern Montenegro was by rowing boat.

While this rather ponderous farce was being acted out on the coast, more serious affairs were in progress on Army Group E's escape route through Podgorica. The Army Group numbered in all seven divisions. From the time of their first movement northwards in early October from Greece and Albania these divisions, and their communications, had been under incessant daylight, and some nighttime, attack by aircraft of Balkan Air Force operating from bases in southern Italy. The scale of this interdiction from the air was, by previous Balkan standards, immense. In about 3000 sorties Balkan Air Force had destroyed thirty-nine locomotives, twenty railway wagons, 129 motor trucks and twelve aircraft by cannon-fire and bombing. The cost had not been light. Forty-four BAF aircraft had been lost and a further forty-six damaged. The effect of this material destruction, and its accompanying loss of German lives, had been compounded by the danger, sometimes the impossibility, of using the roads by day. German troops, transport and equipment were building up into a congested mass in the area of Podgorica. Their rear and flank guards had to stay in place to cover this slowly moving concentration. One of the flank guards unable to disengage was at Spuž, and its adjoining high ground, about midway between Danilovgrad and Podgorica.

The only road between the battery of 25-pounders, and the Raiding Support Regiment's troop of 75s, who had stayed in defensive positions at Nikšić, and the German force at Spuž was breached by thirty-one separate demolitions, some made by Partisans to hinder a German advance from Spuž, some made by Germans to hinder a Partisan advance into Spuž. An earlier attempt to circumvent this handicap by flying a troop of the RSR with their mountain guns, and with a Commando troop as escort, by Dakota and Italian Savoias from Nikšić airfield to Berane to block the road there had been frustrated by the weather. The force had been loaded and ready for take-off when sheeting, icy rain reduced visibility to near nothing. The downpour lasted unbroken for eighty hours. The force unloaded their aeroplanes, waited for better days, found none and on 11 December were sent off over the mountains by Lieutenant-Colonel Ian Riches of 43 Commando, MacAlpine's successor, this time with mules. They were unhealthy mules, but they carried the guns and the ammunition to where they were wanted. The guns went straight into action in support of 10th Montenegrin Brigade. The Commando troop put out reconnaissance patrols.

Colonel Riches had meanwhile set about the problem of the thirty-one breaches in the road from Nikšić to Spuž. No. 579 Field Company of the Royal Engineers was called for, and bridged the more technically difficult gaps. Every otherwise uncommitted man from the Commando and from the various Gunner units, hundreds of Partisans and as many civilians as could be mustered fell to to fashion a negotiable, and partially precarious, track for the guns. The road was open to artillery traffic on 13 December. A battery of 25-pounders and a troop of RSR 75-mm mountain guns went through to Danilovgrad. Two days later they were joined by four 3.7-inch anti-aircraft guns, used to fire at ground targets, of No. 180 Heavy Anti-Aircraft Battery of the Royal Artillery. All guns put down observed and lethal fire upon the constricted German traffic-jam north of Podgorica.

O'Brien-Twohig ordered up another 25-pounder battery on the 16th. Since this was now a Gunner operation in strength, Jago took over command from Riches, and from then onward co-ordinated the artillery policy. Jago made liaison arrangements with the headquarters of the Boka Brigade, 10th Montenegrin Brigade and Primorska Group, all concerned in the assault upon Podgorica and upon the hills dominating it. The Partisan attacks were, as ever, mounted with a daunting courage, but they were products of individual brigade initiatives, not under a central control. Four hill peaks on a range to the north-west of the town were the prime objectives. They varied in height from 700 to 900 feet and were steep, rocky and contorted. Jago conducted his part of the battle from his headquarters in a half-wrecked building in Danilovgrad. His essential problems were to do with range and visibility. Further elaborate demolitions hampered the movement forward of his guns to positions from which they were close enough to engage German traffic on the road running north-east from Podgorica to Bioče. Observation-post parties had to plot likely looking sites for their work from the map, hope that neither rain and mist nor local irregularities unrecorded by the cartographers should impede vision, and march for hours with heavy loads and sickly mules over rough country before they could find out whether they had made the right choice.

On 17 December, while the sappers toiled at the construction of a Bailey bridge as a substitute for the stone one destroyed at Danilovgrad, six 25-pounders were ferried across the river and took up positions within range of the Bioče road. The Bailey was ready by the next morning. The other guns crossed. The Partisans captured one of the four peaks, from which there was a clear view of a crowded mass of German transport. Captain Cuttness set up his OP on this position and conducted a three-hour shoot into the traffic-jam. One hundred and fifty 25-pound shells were fired in all. They caused much observed death and destruction, and put out of action three German guns which had made an ineffectual attempt to interrupt the use of the Bailey bridge. These German guns lasted for eight minutes from the time of their first opening up.

One amenity to survive the mayhem was the civilian telephone system. At midday the Partisans announced their presence in Podgorica by telephoning from the town exchange. During the afternoon 10th Montenegrin Brigade, with supporting fire from a troop of 25-pounders, made considerable ground on a second of the four dominating peaks, but were unable to take the summit. An assortment of OPs was by now well placed on suitable mountain-sides, and the guns were registered upon nodal points, bridges, defiles and similar bottlenecks. They fired throughout the night. By nine o'clock on the morning of the 19th they had discharged 3200 rounds in twenty-four hours. This total, a weight of about forty tons, was more than equalled by the bombs and cannon-fire from the airstrikes of Balkan Air Force. Early in the morning Lieutenant Nick Demuth was sent into Podgorica with a reconnaissance patrol of 43

Commando to investigate the situation in the town. The Germans had moved out, but not as far or as fast as Demuth had thought. His patrol was heavily shot up by a stray German rearguard, disengaged itself circumspectly, had language difficulties with a body of Albanian guerrillas who had joined in the fight and wanted to put Demuth's patrol under arrest, talked themselves out of that, and went back to report to Colonel Riches.

It soon became evident that a great deal had happened in the course of the night. The Partisans had successfully assaulted all three of the peaks still in German hands, and now held all the high ground. The Germans, leaving a trail of bodies and abandoned wreckage of transport behind them, had exploited the darkness energetically. They had pulled out to beyond the Rivers Zeta and Morava, blowing all the bridges behind them. A great mass of them, moving doggedly northwards, was congregated in the neighbourhood of Bioče. The guns were moved forward as far as possible to engage this concentration. There was further difficulty, and further hard marching, in the search for mountain OPs, but Captain Hall, in a light aircraft, directed a series of accurate concentrations of shells on to the escape route. Captain Pitt found a suitable spot from which he arranged heavy supporting fire for a Partisan attack upon an isolated pocket of German resistance. The attack succeeded.

By the 21st the battle was as good as over. The Germans were straggling onwards towards Kolašin, harassed as they went by Balkan Air Force and by Partisans. Partisan wireless communications, improvised and understandably erratic, could not keep in reliable contact with their forward troops. The guns could only engage a diminishing number of targets that could be visually identified as enemy. There was a growing risk that Partisan units might be shelled in error. During the afternoon the last authenticated Germans had moved beyond the range of all but the anti-aircraft 3.7s, and these found less and less to do. Cease Firing was ordered. In driving snow on the next morning the force dispersed, some of it to Trebinje, some to Nikšić. A few reconnaissance parties left to cross the River Zeta to inspect the damage. They counted 400 destroyed trucks, one light tank and five 105-mm guns. In an intact and abandoned ammunition dump there were 700 automatic weapons and rifles, and a large amount of artillery ammunition of a variety of calibres up to 21 centimetre. All of this went to the Partisans.

In the eight days between 14 and 22 December British guns deployed against Army Group E fired 14,481 rounds. Of these, 7403 were from the 25-pounders of 111 Field Regiment; 4042 from the 3.7-inch guns of 180 Heavy Anti-Aircraft Battery; and 3036 from the 75s of 11/12 Troop of the Raiding Support Regiment. The guns were able to get to where they were needed because of the bridge-building skills of 579 Field Company of the Royal Engineers. No. 43 Royal Marine Commando provided security for both observation-post parties and gun positions, and carried out a succession of mountain reconnaissance patrols. The intensified shelling of the Bioče road on 22 December was the last British active intervention in the campaign. A month later, without firing another shot except in training exercises, Floydforce embarked at Dubrovnik on a shuttle of LCIs and LCGs (Landing Craft, Gun) to return to Bari, there to break up into its various components in preparation for the final phase of the Italian campaign.

The achievements of Floydforce were considerable, its casualties light. Its problems had been partly physical and partly political. The physical ones – wild, rough country, a scarcity of roads capable of taking artillery, the marines unprovided with adequate mountain clothing – were surmounted or disregarded. The political difficulties were not surmounted, could not be disregarded and were rarely understood. Floydforce and the Partisans shared one major aim, the destruction of as many Germans and of as much German military material as could be contrived. The Floydforce senior commanders, O'Brien-Twohig, Jago and Riches were professional soldiers trained in, and imbued with the ideas of, the British system by which the declaration of a war and its subsequent diplomatic and political conduct were the responsibilities of a demo-cratically elected government. The actual fighting was the duty of the soldiers, who, whatever were their personal views about the quality, or even the sanity, of the politicians, carried out their orders with a disciplined loyalty. It was hard for them, and for the officers and men commanded by them, to adjust mentally to a working co-operation with allies who did not share that approach, and who in addition to the common destructive aim had further aims, in their eyes of equal or greater importance.

The Partisans wanted, fervently, to throw the Germans out of Yugoslavia, and to that end they fought with a fierce courage. They wanted also to crush the Chetniks and the Ustashi, engineer a Communist hegemony in close league with the Soviet Union, prevent the return of King Peter, nullify post-war Western influence upon their country and retain the pre-war boundaries of Yugoslavia under a rewritten federal constitution and with a few bits of Italy added. Their leaders were hardline Communists who for years before the war had been hunted conspirators, who had survived because they had been efficient and successful conspirators. This necessary deviousness carried with it a consequential suspicion that their temporary allies were as devious as they were themselves. As they saw it, the British had for years been soft on the Chetniks, were solidly behind King Peter, would not take it amiss if Yugoslavia were to be dismantled as a state (with particular favour to be shown to Britain's old ally Serbia), and as experienced imperial manipulators would exploit ruthlessly any advantage that could be gained from the continued presence of British troops on Yugoslav soil. It flowed logically from this that the use of the guns of Floydforce was acceptable and profitable as an aid to the expulsion of German Army Group E in certain circumstances in selected localities. Once the Germans were clearly on their way out there was little merit in killing off a few more of them at the risk of leaving at large in the new state a sizeable armed force which might be used to hinder Communist Party ambitions. Balkan Air Force could continue to do the harassment on a non-residential basis.

Little of this was clear at the time to members of Floydforce. They saw, and resented, only its manifestations: the obstructionism, the suspicion, the unexplained delays and militarily inexplicable changes of plan, the restrictive boorishness of official attitudes to off-duty British troops in Dubrovnik. There was still a strong retained admiration for 'proper fighting Partisans'. There were instances, when the time came for the force to depart, of the old, cheerful courtesy that had prevailed in the islands. At Trebinje, for example, the officers of the Regimental Headquarters of 111 Field 'were invited to a farewell dinner party, and mutual speeches of genuine goodwill were exchanged'. But Trebinje was at some distance from the top Communist management. The feeling among Floydforce upon departure was of let-down, disillusionment and irritation.

TWENTY-THREE

The Last Operation

The withdrawal of Floydforce from Montenegro in January 1945 did not entirely mark the end of British land operations in wartime Yugoslavia. The widespread branches of the Maclean Mission continued to be busier than ever. In late January, at much the same time as Floydforce were embarking at Dubrovnik, the Partisans took the port of Zadar, which lies about midway between Split and Rijeka. The Partisan command agreed to a British suggestion that sea and air support for Partisan operations in north-west Yugoslavia could be knitted in more closely from a base on Yugoslav soil than from Bari. A related consideration was that German E-boats were proliferating in the northern Adriatic, and were becoming an increasing nuisance. Long Range Desert Group coast watchers were needed more than ever to call in sea and air attacks on these craft, and to help dispose of a growing volume of other German shipping. A combined British advanced headquarters was set up in Zadar under the command of Air Commodore Hallings-Pott. Naval, army and RAF officers worked together in the same building, and liaised efficiently and amicably with their Partisan opposite numbers. Balkan Air Force aircraft were based on a nearby strip. Colonel David Lloyd Owen brought over the Rhodesian squadron of the LRDG, with Captain David Sutherland's squadron of the Special Boat Service to back them. Later there were detachments of the Raiding Support Regiment and the RAF Regiment. The coast-watching undertaking began very well. It ended in a very strange manner, in the old bogey of a location – Istria.

*

Captain Mike Reynolds went by sea with a coast-watching team from Zara to the east coast of Zadar. He established his observation post on a hill overlooking the Arsa Channel in late February, and kept it in profitable being until 13 April. He also kept a diary.* It recorded an almost daily succession of sunken or burning German ships and the near destruction of a large coal jetty by fifty-six Liberator bombers. Rocket-firing Hurricanes and Mustangs, half an hour's flying time away at Zadar, were summoned by Reynolds to attend to targets that included coasters, lighters, tramps, barges and E-boats. Coastal Forces MTBs and MGBs, patrolling nearby, were given precisely described bearings, courses and speeds of passing shipping, and came streaming in at speed to add to the carnage. German sea movement in daylight became almost impossible. By night it was only safe after about 2.30 a.m., when the Royal Navy craft left to return to their bases. The Germans mounted a huge search for Reynolds. They used patrols, dogs, spies (one of whom reached his camp, only to be captured and handed over to the Partisans), concentrated mortaring and machine-gunning of areas where they thought he might be, and the burning off of undergrowth on an extensive scale. They came close several times, but they did not find him. He persisted with his messages, with friendly help from Partisans, his food, laundering and barbering catered for by friendly civilians.

Lloyd Owen sent three more coast-watching parties to Istria. Sutherland and fifty of the Special Boat Service were slipped in too, Sutherland taking overall command locally of all British groups in the peninsula. While they were operating there, there were significant happenings in northern Italy, where winter weather had for the most part bogged down the armies. On 1 April, the Allied spring offensive opened with a comprehensively successful attack north of Ravenna, on the eastern side of Lake Comacchio. The attackers were No. 2 Commando Brigade, three units of which, Nos 2, 40 and 43 Commandos, were old allies of the Yugoslav Partisans. The Comacchio action was followed by co-ordinated assaults by the British Eighth Army in the east and the United States Fifth Army in the west. It was

*It is quoted in David Lloyd Owen, *Providence Their Guide*.

clear that the Germans would be unable to hold for long. It was equally clear that soon after the Germans broke, the British Eighth Army would be in Trieste. The Yugoslav National Liberation Movement had its own ambitions about Trieste. The LRDG and the SBS in Istria were doing work that was invaluable to Partisan operations. The presence of British troops in a sensitive area close to Trieste was a potential embarrassment. The potential for embarrassment was given precedence over operational usefulness.

It was Reynolds's hospitable habit to serve tea to a small group of Partisan visitors who called upon him almost daily to discuss developments. On 13 April, eight of the usual callers appeared at his camp, sat down, drank their tea and entered into the customary exchange of views. Then they stood up, covered him and his party with sub-machine-guns, and told them that they were under arrest. Reynolds's signaller was not with the tea drinkers. He sent off a swift message to describe what was happening. He was soon interrupted, also at the point of a gun. Naturally enough, the signal generated mixed wrath and incredulity. Lloyd Owen, temporarily in Italy, hurried back to Zadar. Two further messages arrived. Captain Eastwood's LRDG team was also under Partisan arrest. So was Sutherland and his party of the Special Boat Service. Only Captain John Olivey's LRDG team was still at large, and it had to be assumed that they would not stay so for long.

It was, to put it at its lowest, an extraordinary situation. British aircraft were still flying regularly in support of Partisan operations. Allied ships and aircraft were still delivering supplies of all kinds to Yugoslavia, and were still evacuating Partisan wounded. The various sub-units of the Maclean Mission were still working away with their various Partisan headquarters. Maclean himself had left Belgrade a month previously, after receiving the personal thanks of Tito, the Partisan Star (First Class), and, from a guard of honour provided by the Yugoslav Army of National Liberation, a farewell salute as he climbed into his aeroplane. About sixty British soldiers, who had been engaged upon dangerous and militarily profitable work on behalf of the same Army of National Liberation, were now its prisoners, held under armed guard.

The prisoners were in no way physically ill-treated. They were allowed to use their sets to keep in touch with Lloyd Owen. His immediate worry was that their anger, expressed forcibly in their messages, might rise to breaking point and an attempted solution by violence. He ordered them to comply with all Partisan instructions, and in no circumstances to do anything that would put British lives at risk. Reynolds, whose look-out position had been compromised when he was escorted from it in daylight, signalled that he could no longer continue with his watch even if he were released. He had been given the alternative of being picked up by the Royal Navy or of forcible evacuation on a Partisan schooner. His preference was for a motor torpedo boat. 'I would prefer to be picked up by the Navy rather than be shanghai'd by these garlic-eating bandits.' The navy picked him up.

Olivey was still loose, and operating normally. The other parties were brought together with Sutherland's on 16 April. By that time Balkan Air Force had strongly urged that Allied Forces Headquarters should press for the personal intervention of Tito; the Partisan Fourth Army commander had told the Maclean Mission Liaison Officer attached to him of his regret about the arrests and that he did not know who had ordered them; and the Istrian Partisans had told Sutherland of their regret at having to carry out a disagreeable course of action ordered by the Partisan Fourth Army commander. Meanwhile, the duress continued.

Lloyd Owen saw no practical alternative to the removal of the prisoners by the navy. Air Marshal Mills of Balkan Air Force, who was visiting Zadar, agreed with Lloyd Owen in a telegram to Italy which owed something of its prose style to Reynolds, describing the Istrian Partisans as 'a gang of ghastly garlic-eaters'. Brigadier Davy of Land Forces Adriatic took an opposite view. Voluntary evacuation, he argued, would be interpreted by the Partisans as an acceptance of their authority to order British troops out of Istria. Allied Forces Headquarters, with an eye to the frustration of future Partisan claims to Trieste, agreed with Davy. The argument went on until 25 April, twelve days after the arrest of Reynolds. Minds were made up and then changed. Allied Forces Headquarters were sent an elaborate apology from Belgrade, accompanied by an assurance that Sutherland's party would be released at once. Sutherland's position stayed the same. On 24 April, when a final decision had been taken to bring the group out, and boats had been sent to collect them, Sutherland reported that the guard had been lifted and that he was free to resume operations. It was too late for further vacillation. The Sutherland party, conspicuously lacking in affection for their allies, were landed at Zadar by night on the 25th.

Throughout all this furore, Olivey was untouched. Lloyd Owen put down Olivey's immunity to his profound skill at pretending not to understand orders that he found distasteful. The Olivey technique in this specialised branch of soldiering was to put on a comic turn of such originality and verve that the orderer was soon lost in helpless laughter. However he did it, he kept his watch going until the war ended in May. He then closed down, drove through Trieste into Italy and rejoined the Long Range Desert Group at their headquarters.

The British Mission was rapidly dismantled. A few of its members stayed on, or returned, as diplomats. The Zadar based closed. The Royal Navy escorted to Italian ports a mass of surrendered German shipping. British and New Zealand troops were soon confronting the Partisans in front of Trieste in a prolonged demonstration that the future of the city would not be determined by the unilateral use of Yugoslav force. The shooting war was over. The Cold War between old allies had begun.

Postscript

There have since been critics, arguing from a variety of standpoints, of the British decision to support the Partisans. One view is that the British, with American backing, exploited the fighting qualities of the Partisans for the achievement of British and American ends. The real interests of the Yugoslavs, who were caught in a complex and volatile domestic dilemma, were ignored in favour of a mathematical calculation about which resistance movement was 'killing the most Germans'. The more Germans killed in Yugoslavia, or held there killing Yugoslavs, the fewer there would be available for the killing of British and American soldiers in Italy. The 'killing Germans' formula was given an addendum to solace those uneasy about the prospect of a Partisan victory leading inevitably to a Communist regime. Fitzroy Maclean put the question to Winston Churchill in Cairo in 1943, making it clear that it seemed to him that the Partisans would come out on top whether they were given British help or not. The Churchill reply was to ask Maclean if he intended to make Yugoslavia his home after the war. Maclean said not. Churchill said that he had no plans to live there either. The form that the government of post-war Yugoslavia took was a matter for Yugoslavs to decide. The 1943 priority was to find out which Yugoslavs were harming the Germans the most, and to help them.

By some, this approach is held to be simplistic and cynical. It certainly reduced a tangle of issues to an easily comprehensible working doctrine that covered almost all eventualities. It is also arguable that it was the only realistic and practical attitude that could be taken in the circumstances of the times. By tradition, shared First World War experience and outlook, the British were more in tune with the Mihailović philosophy than they were with that of Tito. But Mihailović, for his own defensible reasons, was doing next to nothing and meant to continue to do next to nothing until there was a major Allied landing in the Balkans. There were never any serious Allied plans for such a landing. The Partisans were doing all the fighting, and were doing it very well. There was no alternative to supporting them that made any kind of military sense. If the support were given on the self-interested premise that it would help to ease the pressure on the Western Allies in Italy and elsewhere, there was the corollary that the British and the Americans in Italy were simultaneously fighting a large number of German divisions that might otherwise have been put in against the Partisans. The cynicism, or realism, was mutually applied and was mutually beneficial.

Another argument put forward by anti-Partisan commentators is that the switch from Mihailović to Tito was the product of a plot engineered by Communist infiltrators within SOE. Certainly there were Communists within SOE; at different times Kim Philby and Guy Burgess were among them. One, Major James Klugmann, who before the war was the secretary of the Cambridge University Communist Party and who after it was on the Central Committee of the Communist Party of Great Britain, was in the Yugoslav Section of SOE in Cairo and later in Bari. Klugmann doubtless did what he could, overtly and covertly, to influence a change in policy to the support of Tito. But whatever efforts he made were unnecessary. The decision was taken on straightforward grounds of military expediency by a Conservative Prime Minister acting on the recommendations initially of a regular army officer, Brigadier Keble, supported later by evidence gathered at first hand by Sir Fitzroy Maclean, a temporary brigadier who was also a Conservative Member of Parliament.

One of the oddities of the pedigree of this true-blue decision to support a bright-red cause was that when decision became practice a remarkable number of its practitioners were dyed-in-the-wool right-wing capitalists. Lord Glenconner, the Head of SOE in Cairo when Keble gave his crucial memorandum to the Prime Minister, was a rich shipowner. The officers of one of the Maclean missions in Croatia, Major Randolph Churchill, Captain the Earl of Birkenhead and Captain Evelyn Waugh, were recruited in the bar of White's club by Randolph Churchill,* who stood as a Conservative candidate in the 1945 general election. Many of Maclean's officers were regular soldiers, at that time a caste that if not exclusively Tory held a strong inclination to be so. Brigadier O'Brien-Twohig, who commanded Floydforce in Montenegro, was a Southern Irish practising Roman Catholic. Commander Morgan Giles, the Senior Naval Officer, Vis, retired as a rear admiral and was elected to Parliament as a Conservative. Major Henniker-Major, of Maclean's headquarters staff, was the son of a peer. The list can be amplified almost indefinitely. What these people, and others like them, did was to recognise that the Partisans were a brave and effective fighting force, who could at times be exasperatingly demanding, devious and ungrateful, but who in terms of getting the war over were worth every ounce of logistic and tactical help that could be given to them. (E. Waugh dissenting.)

The deviousness and ingratitude, expressed in the incivilities experienced for some of the time by most of Floydforce, and reaching a climax with the indignities piled upon the Long Range Desert Group and the Special Boat Service in Istria, were extended into the peace, both politically and in the rearrangement of history to demonstrate that the liberation of Yugoslavia was an almost unaided achievement of the Partisan movement under the guidance of its Communist leadership. Vladimir Dedijer, a member of Tito's Supreme Staff who kept a daily diary regarded by Deakin the historian as 'the most valuable single record of those days', published in 1952 a book called *Tito Speaks*.† Some of the book describes the operations in the Dalmatian islands. The British and American contribution to these gets one sentence: 'A

---

*This mission suffered from severe internal turbulence. For a maliciously funny, one-sided view of its dissensions see *The Diaries of Evelyn Waugh*, ed. Michael Davie (London: Weidenfeld & Nicolson, 1976).

†Vladimir Dedijer, *Tito Speaks* (London: Weidenfeld & Nicolson, 1954).

group of British Commandos was stationed at Vis, chiefly to man the anti-aircraft artillery.'

As time went by, and the Socialist Federal Republic of Yugoslavia evolved into the most liberal and relaxed Communist society in existence (although still considerably short of Western democratic interpretations of these qualities), the sort of attitude exemplified by Dedijer in 1948 disappeared. Old memories of wartime comradeship and shared enterprises revived. On the Yugoslav side it became respectable to write and speak of them. They were written about and spoken of with a generous warmth. Some of the British participants might still nourish ancient resentments, but all those that I have met have long since forgotten them. The abiding recollection that has overlaid the irritations is of a marvellously brave, tough, enduring people of unbounded hospitality who made enormous sacrifices in a commonly fought war.

Old sailors, marines, soldiers and airmen have for years been returning to Yugoslavia, notably to Dalmatia, on nostalgic visits to old haunts and old friends. Some go individually, or with their families. The Churchill brothers and a group from No. 2 Commando, parties from the Royal Navy Coastal Forces Association, several parties from No. 43 Royal Marine Commando, have all been back. They are lavishly entertained by SUBNOR, the Partisan old comrades organisation, by local officials and by a younger generation for whom the war is something that happened in the remote past. The old songs are sung, the new wine is drunk, and old reminiscences, possibly embellished here and there, are exchanged. When a 43 Commando party visited Vis in 1984, they were greeted by children bearing flowers (beautifully dressed children, unlike their ragged predecessors); wined, feasted and taken to see their old troop positions; and finally played away in their hydrofoil from the jetty by the town band, supported by what seemed to be the entire population of the island, who had come to wave goodbye. By a happy coincidence, the same party, who were staying in a hotel on Korčula, were present when honour was done to one of the island's distinguished residents. Sir Fitzroy Maclean has bought a house there, and has for years stayed in it regularly. He was made an honorary citizen of Korčula in gratitude for his services in war and for his friendship in peace.

In Britain, the guest of honour at the annual 43 Commando reunion is invariably the Yugoslav Ambassador to London. Partisan guests are invited too. Partisan visitors come to stay in the houses of former British commandos. Nobody is getting any younger, and the number of survivors is diminishing. But while they last, they provide a constructive unofficial link between two countries with radically different social and political systems.

The link was underlined with unusual symbolism in the course of a British Royal visit to Yugoslavia in 1972, the first and, so far, only visit by a British monarch to a Communist country. It is customary on these occasions for the visiting Head of State to present the host Head of State with a high decoration. President Josip Broz Tito, one-time hunted subversive agitator, Commintern agent, Secretary General of the banned Communist Party of Yugoslavia and leader of his country's war of national liberation, was invested by Queen Elizabeth II with the Grand Cross of the Most Excellent Order of the British Empire.

Bibliography

Published Works

Auty, Phyllis and Clogg, Richard (eds), *British Policy Towards Wartime Resistance in Yugoslavia and Greece* (London: Macmillan, 1975).

Beevor, J.G., *SOE: Recollections and Reflections, 1940–45* (London: The Bodley Head, 1981).

Clissold, Stephen, *Whirlwind* (London: The Cresset Press, 1949).

Davie, Michael (ed.), *The Diaries of Evelyn Waugh* (London: Weidenfeld & Nicolson, 1976).

Deakin, F.W.D., *The Embattled Mountain* (Oxford: Oxford University Press, 1971).

Dedijer, Vladimir, *Tito Speaks* (London: Weidenfeld & Nicolson, 1954).

Djilas, Milovan, *Wartime* (London: Martin Secker & Warburg, 1977).

Foot, M.R.D., *SOE: The Special Operations Executive, 1940–46* (London: BBC, 1984).

Lloyd Owen, David, *Providence Their Guide* (London: Harrap, 1980).

Maclean, Fitzroy, *Eastern Approaches* (London: Jonathan Cape, 1949).

Saunders, Hilary St George, *The Green Beret* (London: Michael Joseph, 1949).

Saunders, Hilary St George, *Royal Air Force 1939–1945*, Vol. 3: *The Fight is Won* (London: HMSO, 1975).

Unpublished Papers

A History of The Period of Active Service of 43 Royal Marine Commando, in the Central Mediterranean Forces Until the End of the War in Italy (private circulation).

111 Field Regiment, Royal Artillery, Report on Operations with Floydforce in Yugoslavia

Papers Held by the Public Record Office, Kew

The war diaries of:
  No. 2 Commando
  No. 40 Royal Marine Commando
  No. 43 Royal Marine Commando
  The Raiding Support Regiment
  111 Field Regiment, Royal Artillery
  2nd Battalion, The Highland Light Infantry
(*Note*: In addition to an almost daily record of routine affairs, these diaries include detailed reports on all major operations, written within a few days of the events that they describe, and a broad selection of records of boarding parties, reconnaissances, patrols and minor actions.)
Action reports by the commanding officers of various motor torpedo boats and motor gun boats of the Royal Navy
Summaries of various operations by the Royal Air Force

Papers Held by the Naval Historical Branch,
Ministry of Defence

This is a miscellany of action reports, appreciations, summaries, recommendations, assessments and so on. Their authors remain anonymous. Most were unsigned. A few were initialled illegibly.

Index

Index

179–82; Brač raid, 193–4, 196, 202, 204–8, 212–19, 221–2, 224, 225; Bogomilje raid, 238–40; and German withdrawal from Brač, 255–6; in Floydforce, 273–92, 298, 299, 307–9; Commacchio assault, 314; return to Yugoslavia, 322; Heavy Weapon Troop, 157–8, 161, 164, 259, 287

Commando Basic Training Centre, Achnacarry, 114, 179

Communists: banned in Yugoslavia, 11; increase strength, 12; attitude to war, 26–8; preparations for revolt, 27–30; Tito nominated as Marshal of the Army, 144; and German withdrawal, 238; try to deny British role in German defeat, 243, 321–2; and Trieste, 245; improve political position, 249–52; attitude to Floydforce, 274; in SOE, 320; *see also* Partisans

Conservative Party (Britain), 320–1

Copsey, Lieutenant David, 222–3

Corfu, 239

coup d'état (1941), 14, 27

Cowan, Admiral Sir Walter, 146–7, 157, 225, 230

Cox, Corporal, 160

Cox, Marine Ernie, 216

Crete, 2, 81, 83, 112, 243

Crni, Commander, 121, 141–2, 143, 145, 191, 193

Crnjanski, Lieutenant, 41

Croat Peasant Party, 11

Croatia, 7–10; and the Constitution, 10–11; independence movement, 11–12; Communists, 12; Hungarian occupation, 19; Independent State of, 19–20; massacre of the Serbs, 20–1, 23; Partisan operations in, 59; German operations in, 61; British missions sent to, 93; Operation Ratweek, 269

Cross, Lieutenant Len, 223

Crozier, Sergeant, 69

Cuttness, Captain J.S., 298, 307

Dakić, Spasoje, 45, 46

Dalković, Major, 302–3

Dalmacija, 105–6

Dalmatia, 8–9, 19, 20, 43, 101

Dalmatian islands, 93; Germany and, 101–6; Partisans in, 128–34, 167; LRDG in, 241–5; German withdrawal from, 253–64; RAF operations, 265–6; *see also individual islands*

Danilovgrad, 273, 297, 299, 303, 306–7

Danube, river, 16, 55–6, 267–8

Davidson, Major Basil, 61

Davidson, Lieutenant, 105

Davy, Brigadier George, 272, 316

Day, Wing Commander 'Wings', 228

Deakin, Captain Bill, 72, 84, 88, 93n., 94, 95, 265, 321; support for Partisans, 61–2; goes to Yugoslavia, 62–5, 67–70; assessment of Tito, 70–1, 92; and the Italian capitulation, 79–81, 84; goes to Split, 89–91; meeting with King Peter, 97

Dedijer, Vladimir, 321–2

Demuth, Lieutenant Nick, 307–8

Derna airstrip, 64

Detained 1, 149

Dieppe, 113, 114

Dinaric Alps, 95, 173

Disclaim Mission, 39, 41, 46

Djilas, Milovan, 21, 32, 33–4, 40

Dnieper, river, 7

Dowse, Flight Lieutenant, 228

Dračeva, 201

Dragičević, 31n.

Drar, 143

Drina, river, 20, 44, 45

Drvar, 31n., 249, 266; Germans attack Tito's headquarters in, 188–90, 203

Drvenik, 104

Dubrovnik, 101, 244, 274–5, 295, 296–7, 309, 313

Dugi Otok, 242, 247

Duncan, Sergeant, 89

Dunkirk, 110, 111, 122, 158

Dunton, Lance-Bombadier C.J., 142

Durmitor, 62, 64–5, 66, 265

Dutton, Lieutenant Lyn, 223

Dvrenik, 257, 259

Earle, Captain, 281

Eastwood, Captain, 315

Eden, Anthony, 48, 94

Egypt, 1, 40, 69, 240–1

Eighth Army, 106, 174, 237, 315

Eisenhower, Dwight D., 138

Elizabeth II, Queen, 323

Elliott, Major Cavan, 41, 46

Elliott, Colonel J.S., 175, 178, 229–30, 253–5, 274

Elliot, Air Vice-Marshal W., 267, 268–9, 272

Farish, Major Linn 'Slim', 89, 95

Finney Force, 275–92, 299

First World War, 7–8, 23–4, 25, 76, 146, 320

Fiume (Rijeka), 245

Flounced, Operaton, 193–4, 195–233

Floydforce, 295–7, 321; formation of, 272, 273; operations in Risan, 275–91; at Nikšić, 297–9; at Podgorica, 299–309; achievements, 309–11; withdrawal, 313

Foča, 40, 41–2, 44, 45

Foothound, Operation, 179–83

Force 133, 117, 140

Force 266, 140, 159, 190, 193, 194, 203, 211, 232

Foreign Office (Britain), 15–16, 45, 50, 60, 61–2, 75, 82, 84, 85, 228

329

Index

Forsythe Force, 296
FOTALI (Flag Officer Taranto and Liaison Italy), 191, 272
France, 11, 12, 110, 111, 112, 121–2
Free Dalmatia, 91
French, Sergeant, 240
Frost, Captain George, 260
Frost, Lieutenant, 163
Fuller, Troop Sergeant-Major Hugh, 213
Fuller, Lieutenant-Commander T.G., 169–72
Fynn, Major Ted, 120–1, 160

Galbreath, Lieutenant, 197, 200, 202
Garbin, Yurko, 151, 153, 155
Garigliano river, 145, 174, 187
Gatchell, Lieutenant, 242
General Headquarters, Middle East, 60, 241
Geneva Conventions, 143, 247, 281
German Army, 237; 1st Alpine Division, 66, 68; 222nd Artillery Regiment, 288; Brandenburg Division, 66; 334th Fusilier Regiment of 161st Infantry Division, 288; No. 892 Grenadier Regiment, 256; 11th Jaeger Division, 101; 118th Jaeger Division, 229; XXI Mountain Corps, 273, 278, 291, 298
Germany, Germans: North African campaign, 1; Operation Barbarossa, 13, 19; pact with Yugoslavia, 13–14; attacks Yugoslavia, 14–15, 19; First World War, 23–4, 25; massacres in Yugoslavia, 24; Partisan operations against, 24; invasion of Russia, 28–9, 83, 113; Montenegrin revolt, 35–6; operations against Yugoslav resistance, 36–7, 61, 64, 66–8, 101; wireless codes broken, 59–60; intercepts Mihailović's signals, 50; Chetnik operations against, 73; and the fall of Italy, 79–80, 101; and the Dalmatian islands, 101–6; blitzkrieg, 110; Commando raids against, 110–13, 125; attacked in Dalmatian islands, 129–34; Nerežišće Commandant killed, 131–4; Partisan treatment of prisoners, 140–5; and the assaults on Šolta, 149–60, 166; and the assault on Hvar, 160–6; and the Mljet operation, 180–3; attacks Tito's headquarters, 188–90, 203; hunt for Tito, 190–1, 232; Brač raid, 195–233; evacuation from Yugoslavia, 237; Bogomilje raid, 239–40; LRDG operations against, 241–7; withdrawal from Dalmatian islands, 253–64; later attacks on Šolta, 256–63; Operation Ratweek, 268–70; withdrawal from Balkans, 273–92; Floydforce operations against, 275–92, 295–311

Gestapo, 57, 63
Gibson, Lieutenant, 242–3, 245
Giles, Lieutenant-Commander Morgan, 103, 126, 139, 159, 160, 182, 253–4, 260, 262, 321
Glamoč, 95, 96, 265, 266
Glen, Lieutenant-Commander Sandy, 266
Glenconner, Lord, 60, 61, 87, 320–1
Glina, 21
Gordon, Troop Sergeant-Major, 223–4
Gornje Lipovo, 49, 53, 54
Gornje Selo, 149, 150–1, 153, 258
Gourlay, Captain Ian, 257–60
Grahovo, 144, 300
Greece, 2, 13, 15, 74, 83, 237–8, 265, 268–9, 273
Green, Sergeant 'Bunny', 215
Greenlees, Major Kenneth, 54
Greenwood, Major Erik, 55–6
Gregory, Lieutenant, 162–3, 215, 216, 218
Grohote, 149, 150, 152–3, 154, 155–6, 157–60, 256, 258–9, 261–2
Gruz, 275
Gypsies, 20

Hackett, General Sir John, 240
Hagana, 63n.
Hall, Captain, 308
Hallings-Pott, Air Commodore, 313
Hallitsis, Corporal, 160
Hancock, Lieutenant, 176
Harding, General John, 109
Hardy, Flight Lieutenant, 157, 159
Hargreaves, Lieutenant, 55
Haussman, 129
Hawksworth, Captain, 57
Heller, Joseph, 176
Henna Mission, 39, 41, 45, 46–7
Henniker-Major, Major John, 89, 269, 321
Hercegnovi, 288
Hercegovina, 8, 50, 54, 64, 243n., 245
Highland Light Infantry, 175, 179–80, 196–203, 216, 225, 257
Hitler, Adolf, 11, 13–15, 124
Holland, 12, 110
Hook, Reverend Ross, 226
Horlock, Lieutenant, 169–70
Hoste, Captain William, 127, 301
Howell, Captain, 197, 200, 202
Hudson, Captain D.T., 15, 40, 49, 59, 76; first operations in Yugoslavia, 2–3, 16, 31–8; and the Chetnik-Partisan feud, 36; Germans attack, 37; and the Hydra Mission, 44–5; doubts about information from, 47–8, 50–1
Hudspith, Captain John (Jock), 164, 207, 239, 259, 261, 263
Hughes, Lieutenant, 104–5
Hum, Mount, 173, 232
Humac, 196, 206, 209

Index

Hungary, 13, 19, 267
Hunter, Captain Anthony, 62
Hunton, Lieutenant-General Sir
  Thomas, 188
Hvar, 94, 103, 118, 125, 173, 204;
  Coastal Forces operations, 104–6;
  reconnaissance of, 127; assault on,
  160–6, 177, 191; patrol reports,
  167–8; Bogomilje raid, 239–40
Hydra Mission, 39–46
Hyslop, Lieutenant, 106

Ibar river, 74
Infantry Replacement Depots, 123
Inter-Allied Commando, No. 10
  Troop, 124, 137
'International Soccer Match', 135
Islam, 9, 20, 53
Ist, 242
Istanbul, 1, 45, 47
Istria, 3, 102, 245–7, 313, 315–16, 321
Italian Army: 1st Alpine Division, 101;
  41st Firenze Division, 101; 19th
  Venezia Division, 101
Italy, 69, 192, 265; defeat in Egypt and
  Libya, 1; Croatian dissidents in, 10;
  invades Greece, 13; and evacuation
  of Allied diplomatic staff, 17;
  occupation of Montenegro, 19, 47,
  53–4; Mihailović, 50–1; Allied
  invasion, 72, 73, 92–3, 106;
  capitulation to Allies, 79–81, 84,
  101; LRDG operations against, 241;
  Allies push northwards, 314–15

Jack, Captain Archie, 56
Jago, Colonel T. de F., 274, 302–4,
  306–7, 309
Jajce, 71, 80, 89, 95, 143
Japan, 43
Jastrebac Mountain, 56
Jeffs, Marine, 216, 225, 227
Jellicoe, Lieutenant-Colonel Lord,
  243
Jelsa, 161–5
Jenkins, Captain S.I., 153–6, 160
Jerusalem, 33n.
Jewish Agency, 63n.
Jews, in Croatia, 20
Jones, Captain William, 62
Jovanović, Arso, 32–3, 34, 138
Juraj, 155

Karlo, 154
Kastella, 90
Keble, Colonel C.M., 60–2, 63, 84,
  85–8, 320
Keep, Captain Ray, 117, 118, 120–1,
  127
Keserović, 56
Kieft, Captain Bernard, 288
Kitchener, Lord, 146
Klugmann, Major James, 320
Knight, Captain Donald, 95, 96
Knight-Lacklan, Lieutenant, 171

Kolašin, 48, 273, 299, 308
Komiža, 107, 119, 138, 142, 145, 147,
  156–7, 169–72, 176, 180, 197, 204,
  232, 248, 262, 263
Kopaonik, 56
Korčula, 103, 108, 118, 140, 170,
  253–5, 266, 322–3
Korčula Channel, 163, 254
Korita, 198, 199
Kosivina Cove, 170–1
Kosovo, 19
Kotor, 273, 275, 283, 289, 301–2, 304
Kotor, Gulf of, 2, 15, 17, 276, 277–8,
  289, 300–1
Kragujevac, 24, 36
Kren, Captain Vladimir, 14, 15
Krstulović, 90–1
Kuebler, General, 229
Kuibschev, 46
Kulina, 57
Kupreško Polje, 266

Laidlaw, Captain Ian, 223, 227
Lalatović, 31n., 35, 49
Lancaster, Lieutenant, 105
Land Forces Adriatic, 272, 273–4, 316;
  see also Floydforce
Landing Craft, Assault (LCA), 177–8
Landing Craft, Infantry (LCI), 177–8
Landing Craft, Tanks (LCT), 178
Laskovac, 269–70
Lassen, Captain Anders, 244, 245
Laycock, Colonel Robert, 112
Layforce, 112
Leach, Sergeant, 244
League of Nations, 63n.
Ledenice, 277, 280, 282–3, 285, 286–9,
  292
Lee, Captain, 182
Leeper, Rex, 83
Lees, Captain Brian, 136
Libya, 1, 64, 241
Lloyd Owen, Colonel David, 242, 243,
  313–17
Lofoten islands, 112
Long Range Desert Group (LRDG),
  83, 317, 321; formation of, 240–1;
  functions, 240, 241–5, 270, 313; in
  Istria, 245–7; in Floydforce, 299;
  Partisans arrest members of, 315;
  withdrawal from Yugoslavia, 3–4,
  315–17
Loudoun, Captain Bob, 182, 183,
  212–16, 258–9, 275–7, 279, 283n.,
  285–6, 287, 291–2, 300, 303
Lovćen, 40, 302
Loviste, 104
Luftwaffe, 81, 110, 145, 176, 204, 242
Lüters, General, 66

MacAlpine, Lieutenant-Colonel Ian,
  257–63, 306
McCallum, Captain, 159
McCartney, Colour-Sergeant, 161–2

331

Index

Index

Nicholls, Marine Charlie, 213–14
Nidova Gora, 196–203, 206
Nikšić, 40, 273, 284, 296, 297–9, 301, 303, 305–6, 308
Normandy landings, 107, 177–8, 237
North Africa, 1, 52, 72, 123, 265
Norway, 12, 112, 122
Novaković, General, 42, 44, 45, 46
Nunns, Lieutenant, 218
Nunns, Captain Mark, 240

O'Brien-Twohig, Brigadier J.P., 274, 275, 298, 299, 302–4, 306, 309, 321
Odendaal, Lieutenant, 162, 163, 218, 222, 225–6, 239, 256
O'Donovan, Sergeant, 39, 44–6
Olivey, Captain John, 3–4, 315, 316, 317
Operation Barbarossa, 2, 13
Operations Group *see* United States Special Operations Group
Orebić, 253–4
O'Reilly, Nellie, 301–2
Orthodox Church, 9, 20, 21
Ostojić, Major, 31n., 35, 44
Ottoman Empire, 9
Owen, Lieutenant, 289
OZNA (Communist Secret Police), 76

Paget, General, 75
Palestine, 63n., 81
Pannonian Plain, 7
Parker, Major Michael, 88–9
Parkinson-Cumine, Captain Ralph, 259, 260, 262, 296
Parnell, Lieutenant, 160
Parsons, Lieutenant, 127
Partisans: feud with Chetniks, 3, 24–5, 36, 42, 43, 47, 51, 54; and the massacre of the Serbs, 21; operations against Germans, 24–5; attitude to war, 27; Montenegrin rebellion, 31–3, 35–6; and Hudson's mission, 32, 33–4; Germans attack, 37, 66–8, 101; and the Hydra Mission, 40–6; SOE information on, 59–62, 70; Brtish co-operation with, 62–5, 69–74, 92–4; Bosnian base, 69, 71; and the Italian capitulation, 80–1, 101; go to Split, 89–91; Churchill's support for, 97; in the Dalmatian islands, 101–6, 118, 128–34, 167; establish base on Vis, 106–10, 119–21; Hvar raid, 125, 161–6; and the attack on Nerežišće, 132–4; relations with No. 2 Commando, 135–9; treatment of prisoners, 140–5; and the assaults on Šolta, 149–60; increased help for, 174–5; build Vis airstrip, 176; uniforms, 178–9; Mljet operation, 179–83; meetings in London, 187; Germans attack Tito's headquarters, 188–90; Germans hunt for Tito,

190–1, 232; Brač raid, 193–4, 195, 197–9, 202, 204, 206–12, 218–9, 230–1; and the LRDG, 242–3; hostility towards Allies, 245–7; on Vis, 248; Churchill's talks with Tito, 249–50; and German withdrawal, 255–6, 273; air support for, 266–71; Operation Ratweek, 268–70; Floydforce and, 273–92, 295–311; deteriorating relations with British, 274, 296–7, 310–11, 315–16; want control of Trieste, 245, 315; British objectives in helping, 319–21; post-war relations with Britain, 322–3; Fourth Army, 316; Boka Brigade, 306; Bokajl Brigade, 283; II Corps, 271, 299, 301, 303; IX Corps, 246–7; 1st Dalmatian Brigade, 120n., 135, 163, 257; 2nd Dalmatian Brigade, 281, 283; 3rd Division, 68; XXVI Division, 193; 29th Division, 303; 5th Montenegrin Brigade, 46; 10th Montenegrin Brigade, 306, 307; Primorska Group, 275–6, 302, 306; 1st Proletarian Division, 80–1, 89–90; 4th Sector, 153
Paul, Prince, 11, 12, 13–14
Pavelić, Ante, 11, 20–1, 23, 76
Peak, Lance-Corporal, 215, 216
Pearl Harbor, 43
Pearson, Colonel, 193–4
Pečanac, Kosta, 23–4, 26, 42
Pelješac peninsula, 103, 104, 108, 253–5, 266
Perast, 285, 286, 300, 304
Pero, 153
Persia, 83
Peter, King of Yugoslavia, 11, 14, 77, 97, 137, 250, 310
Petrovac, 2, 32, 34, 39
Petrovo Polje, 71
Philby, Kim, 320
Pioneer Corps, 124
Pirie, 223
Pitt, Captain, 295, 308
Pitt, Lieutenant, 246–7
Pius XII, Pope, 20
Piva, river, 66
Planica, 197, 198, 211
Ploesti oilfields, 176
Plotsville, 88
Podgorica (Titograd), 40, 297, 299, 303, 305–8
Podhan, 277–80, 285, 300
Podvlake, 258–60
Point 542, 206, 207–8, 212
Point 622, 192, 196, 206, 207, 212, 217–18, 221, 227, 229
Point 648, 206, 212
Popović, Koča, 90–1, 269
Popular Front, 29, 35
Poreč, 55
Portishead, 1, 3, 23